Errata

p. 3, line 4, should read:

"nia and Japan; its emphasis on the simultaneity
of the installation on two"

Contemporary Film Directors

Edited by James Naremore

The Contemporary Film Directors series provides concise, well-written introductions to directors from around the world and from every level of the film industry. Its chief aims are to broaden our awareness of important artists, to give serious critical attention to their work, and to illustrate the variety and vitality of contemporary cinema. Contributors to the series include an array of internationally respected critics and academics. Each volume contains an incisive critical commentary, an informative interview with the director, and a detailed filmography.

A list of books in the series appears at the end of this book.

Albert Maysles |

Joe McElhancy

UNIVERSITY OF ILLINOIS PRESS
URBANA AND CHICAGO

Manufactured in the United States of America
1 2 3 4 5 C P 5 4 3 2 1
∞ This book is printed on acid-free paper.

Library of Congress Cataloging-in-Publication Data
McElhaney, Joe, 1957–
Albert Maysles / Joe McElhaney.
    p.   cm. — (Contemporary film directors)
Includes bibliographical references and index.
ISBN 978-0-252-03429-9 (cloth : alk. paper) —
ISBN 978-0-252-07621-3 (pbk. : alk. paper)
1. Maysles, Albert—Criticism and interpretation.
I. Title.
PN1998.3.M39752M34   2009
791.4302'33092—dc22   2008037212

This book is dedicated to my parents,
Joseph and Louise McElhaney

Contents |

Acknowledgments |

While not exactly a collaborative project on the scale of an Albert Maysles film, this book would not exist without the strong help and contribution of several individuals. My thanks to James Narcmore for inviting
me to contribute a volume to this series and for supporting my choice
of Albert Maysles. At Hunter College, Sam Di Iorio supplied me with
a wealth of material and shared with me his keen insights into Maysles's
films. Also at Hunter, Ivone Margulies continues to be a model friend
and colleague. Special thanks to Catherine Russell for some necessary
research material. Many of my arguments about *Grey Gardens* were
initially presented at the Graduate Center of the City University of New
York and the Department of Art and Art History at Stanford University.
My thanks to David Gerstner and Paula Massood of CUNY and to Scott
Bukatman of Stanford for inviting me to present this material. A PSC-
CUNY grant provided the necessary financial support. Steve Barnes,
as always, provided support, both financial and otherwise. At Maysles
Films, Inc., Laura Coxson was responsible for supplying me with copies
of many rare Maysles films, and Sara Maysles patiently took me through
the company's photographs, many of which are reproduced in this book.
But most of all I must thank Albert Maysles himself. His generosity in
relation to the research and production of this book was exemplary, and
I only hope that the finished product does his work justice.

Albert Maysles |

Works of Art and Factual Material |

I try to stay neutral somehow.
Meet Marlon Brando

Within the history of documentary cinema, the name Albert Maysles has assumed near-mythical status. Maysles, usually in collaboration with his brother David, was a central figure in some of the most important documentaries of the 1960s and 1970s, culminating with three feature-length films that continue to generate intense debate about the ethics and aesthetics of documentary form: *Salesman* (1969), *Gimme Shelter* (1970), and *Grey Gardens* (1975). The series of Maysles films dealing with Christo and Jeanne-Claude's large-scale art projects, including the Academy Award–nominated *Christo's Valley Curtain* (1973), have been described as among the greatest documentaries ever made about the process of creating art. And in his unfinished *The Other Side of the Wind* (1972), Orson Welles used the Maysles brothers as the inspiration for a parody of documentary filmmakers. Since David's death in 1987, Albert Maysles (mainly in collaboration with others) has continued to shoot an enormous amount of footage in both film and video, including two additional Christo and Jeanne-Claude films. Nevertheless, there has been little sustained attempt to examine this body of work in any detail. The first book-length examination of their films, Jonathan B. Vogels's *The Direct Cinema of David and Albert Maysles*, was published in 2005. In looking at the ways in which their films engage in a complex and sometimes contradictory search for authenticity, Vogels places the Maysles brothers within various modernist traditions. I have no particular quarrel with this reading, but my own concerns will be of a somewhat different nature.

Before proceeding further, an explanation of the title of this book is in order. *Albert Maysles* is a volume in a series of books on contemporary filmmakers. Maysles's reputation rests almost entirely on the films he did with his brother, even though he worked on films before David began collaborating with him, and he has continued to work long after David's death. Maysles Films, Inc., initially begun with his brother, is a company in which Albert plays a central role, although the day-to-day management has been handled by others. Maysles Films produces many nonfiction works, from television commercials to promotional films to various documentary commissions for theatrical, television, and video release. Albert Maysles is involved in many of these projects, sometimes credited as codirector, sometimes only credited as cinematographer. Even during the years in which he worked with his brother, Albert Maysles typically assigned codirector credit to his editor, a testament to the editor's enormous input in determining the final shape and meaning of the films, as well as to the importance the brothers placed on collaboration. In no way do I wish to diminish this collaborative input, especially given Albert Maysles's frequently stated admission that he does not edit his own footage. The title of this book, then, might appear to be misleading, as though it is attempting to assign full authorship to one person on films that were, at every level of production and postproduction, collaborative.

On the Maysles brothers' films, David was officially responsible for sound (as well as for much of the interviewing of subjects, and he had a great deal of input into the editing), while Albert was the cameraman. Even here, though, Albert Maysles's claim to total authorship of the images on some of his most famous films is complicated. On a number of these (including *Gimme Shelter* and the Christo and Jeanne-Claude films), he was a primary but not sole cameraman, and assigning precise authorship to every image would be laborious if not impossible. A late

Maysles film such as *Umbrellas* (1995), for example, not only required an enormous camera crew to capture the simultaneous installation of Christo and Jeanne-Claude's fabric and aluminum umbrellas in Califor-

continents precludes any romantic possibilities of a single "man with a movie camera" magically being everywhere at once.

In spite of this, as I will argue throughout the book, Maysles's cinema is repeatedly drawn toward particular kinds of images, and these images, in turn, strongly determine much of the meaning and impact of the films, regardless of whether Albert Maysles himself was in fact behind the camera. While the nature of these images is undoubtedly recognizable as belonging to a particular school of documentary filmmaking (that of direct cinema), and without losing sight of the paradoxes and complexities of authorship, there is a certain inflection to the images that cannot be solely ascribed to a group style and may be isolated as a Maysles style. Moreover, through Maysles Films, Albert Maysles remains a very public figure, giving interviews, making frequent appearances, and generally representing and embodying the goals of the filmmaking practice he and his brother established more than forty years ago. If he cannot lay total claim to the authorship of these films, he is certainly the living figure whose name is most indelibly and symbolically linked with them.

| | |

Albert Maysles was born in Dorchester, Massachusetts, on November 26, 1926. David was born on January 10, 1932. When Albert was thirteen, the family moved to nearby Brookline, where his mother was able to find work in the public school system. In a coincidence that would determine the individual roles they would each assume as filmmaking partners, Albert was born during the late period of the American cinema's silent era, while David was born five years after Hollywood had begun to convert to sound. Albert Maysles has characterized himself as an emotionally withdrawn child, barely speaking at all. As Jews, the Maysles family were something of an anomaly in their predominantly working-class Irish Catholic neighborhood. Maysles has said that his father often felt Irish as much as Jewish, although he has also stated that his family were frequent victims of anti-Semitic verbal and physical abuse. Maysles's father was a postal clerk and, according to Maysles, not terribly ambitious, while his mother was a teacher (reportedly the first Jewish teacher hired by the Brookline public school system) and an extremely active and dynamic presence within her family and community. (She was a member of the American Jewish Congress.)

After serving in the tank corps during World War II, Maysles received a bachelor's degree from Syracuse University and a master's from Boston University, both in psychology, and he taught psychology for three years at Boston University. (David later received a B.A. in the same discipline, also from Boston University.) In spite of the fact that he had never made a film before (although he had an amateur fascination with still photography), in the mid-1950s Maysles became interested in filming mental hospitals in the Soviet Union, an outgrowth of his work as a research assistant in a mental hospital and as the head of a research project at Massachusetts General. This interest eventually led to him being hired by CBS to go to the Soviet Union with a "'wind-up 16mm Keystone camera'" (qtd. in Cunningham 208). The film that resulted, *Psychiatry in Russia* (1955), while not shown by CBS, was televised on *The Dave Garroway Show* on NBC, on public television at WGBH-TV in Boston, and on network television in Canada. Two years later, he would return behind the Iron Curtain, this time with his brother, and shoot two other films, *Russian Close-Up* (1957) and a film on the student revolution, *Youth in Poland* (1957). The latter was also broadcast on NBC. A visit to Moscow in 1959 brought Maysles in contact with two other young documentary filmmakers, Richard Leacock and D. A. Pennebaker. Pennebaker was impressed by *Psychiatry in Russia*, which he recommended to Robert Drew, a former photojournalist who was interested in applying the techniques of photojournalism to documentary filmmaking. Drew and Leacock had already worked together several years prior to this, as Drew Associates, with the sponsorship of the Time-Life Broadcast Division.

None of the work Drew and Leacock did for television had satisfied them up to this point, and it was not until they made *Primary* in 1960 that the breakthrough they were hoping for was finally achieved. On this film, which captures the Wisconsin primary battle for the 1960 presidency between John F. Kennedy and Hubert Humphrey, Drew and Leacock made use of a new lightweight 16mm camera, the Auricon Cine-Voice, sometimes synchronized with lightweight tape recorders, allowing for the recording of direct sound. While much of the film was shot silent with traditional Arriflex cameras and with the sound added in postproduction, enough of the film drew upon the possibilities of the Auricon to create a strong perception of a breakthrough in documentary cinema. "'For the first time,'" Leacock later said, "'we were able to walk in and out of buildings, up and down stairs, film in taxi cabs, all over the place, and get synchronous sound'" (qtd. in Mamber 30). The film's most famous shot, though, was done with an Arriflex, conceived by one of Drew's recent associates, Pennebaker, and executed by his newest associate, Albert Maysles: the shot following Kennedy into a building, down a hallway, up a flight of stairs, and then out onto a stage where he greets hundreds of his followers at a Polish American hall.

For the remainder of this sequence, which mainly concerns itself with the speeches of JFK and Jacqueline Kennedy, Maysles was responsible for filming Jacqueline. Here he captured one particular shot of her that is often strongly criticized. As she is giving her speech, there is a cut to her white-gloved hands, folded behind her back, nervously fidgeting. Criticism of the shot has largely to do with how the meaning of this detail is aggressively forced on the spectator when it should (according to the shot's detractors) be more seamlessly integrated into the sequence, allowing for spectators to discover the meaning of the shots on their own. The nature of this type of criticism is almost entirely bound up with a set of discourses emerging in the aftermath of *Primary*, simultaneously generated by the artists responsible for the film and by critics who wrote about it, either positively or negatively.

Although regarded at the time by its makers and its admirers as a revolutionary development in documentary form, *Primary* is also part of much larger movements within the documentary field, particularly in the United States, France, and Canada, and practiced by filmmakers as diverse as Jean Rouch, Pierre Perrault, Michel Brault, Jacques Rozier, François Reichenbach, and, slightly later, Frederick Wiseman. These movements have been given various names, preeminently cinéma vérité (particularly in its French and French Canadian practices) and direct cinema (particularly in its American practices). The two terms, however, have been frequently used interchangeably. Stephen Mamber's seminal critical study of the American practice is entitled *Cinema Verite in America*, while Jeanne Hall's important essay on *Primary*—written in 1991, long after the intensity of the debates surrounding these films had died down—continues to use the term.

Throughout this book I will employ the term *direct cinema* rather than *cinéma vérité* to discuss Maysles's work. My reasons for this are twofold. First, the French origin of the term *cinéma vérité* more usefully designates the French and French Canadian practices of this type of documentary cinema, while the American origins of the term *direct cinema* perform the same function for the American practices. However, the distinctions between these two practices, while important, are not absolute, and there is a certain amount of overlap in their concerns. The second reason I prefer *direct cinema* in relation to Maysles is that Maysles himself prefers this term, likewise distinguishing between the work of his American colleagues from that of their approximate French counterparts.

As Louis Marcorelles has noted, direct cinema "has as many styles as it has filmmakers" (*Living Cinema* 96). And indeed its history, like that of cinéma vérité, has been caught up in a number of highly charged polemics. At the time that Maysles was working with Drew and Leacock, Drew had put into practice his own version of this new type of documentary filmmaking. As with cinéma vérité, the development of lightweight 16mm sound cameras in direct cinema led to another kind of role for the cameraman, one more fully integrated into the physical space and social world of the subjects, even while the filmmaker strove to remain detached enough from these subjects and their worlds to depict them with a certain measure of objectivity. Unlike Rouch, who would often actively intervene in and provoke situations that he was filming, Drew explicitly refused this kind of intervention.

In contrast to much of the overtly aesthetic and political documentary filmmaking style of the 1920s, 1930s, and 1940s (including Dziga Vertov, Alberto Cavalcanti, Humphrey Jennings, and Joris Ivens), with its emphasis on montage and a symphonic organization of sounds and images, editing in Drew's films often aspired to transparency, since the goal was to allow the spectator to observe the reality of the situation being filmed in as neutral and unobtrusive a way as possible. Brian Winston has written: "Direct cinema is the exact opposite of *cinéma vérité*. It seeks more completely than any previous mode of documentary production to hide the processes of filmmaking—to pretend to an unblinking objectivity supposedly similar to that possessed by a fly on the wall" (Winston 518).[1] Voiceover narration, that staple of so much sound documentary cinema prior to this—particularly in newsreels—was generally eliminated or used sparingly, as was musical underscoring. The standard "talking heads" interview format, by then predominant on television, was likewise prohibited or downplayed in these films, which focused instead on behavior and social interaction.

Central to Drew's approach was the "crisis" structure, in which major public figures (mainly political ones) are shown in situations of great emotional and personal difficulty. Upheaval is at the center of these films, as we observe the subjects responding to and eventually overcoming a crisis. *Crisis: Behind a Presidential Commitment* (1963), shot for ABC largely by Leacock and Pennebaker, shows this structure in its purest state as we observe John F. Kennedy, Attorney General Robert Kennedy, and their associates responding to Alabama governor George Wallace's refusal to observe a federal desegregation law at the University of Alabama. While the crisis structure was thought by Drew to be fundamentally a tool for character revelation, in which the film records how various public figures react under extreme pressure, in its blending of character and action it became a convenient way to structure a film along classical narrative lines, particularly melodrama. But in Drew's work, the melodrama is veiled by the manner in which it seems to spring directly out of real situations.

While Maysles would work with Drew on seven other films after *Primary,* by 1962 he had begun to tire of certain elements of Drew's approach—in particular, his insistence on life-and-death situations being at the center of his films. By this point, David Maysles had joined Drew Associates and was researching other possibilities for making films that could retain elements of Drew's direct cinema while diverging from it in crucial ways. In 1962, David and Albert officially left Drew Associates to form Maysles Films. After making a short commissioned work together for NBC, *Anastasia* (1962), they shot their first film together in 1963, *Showman,* a portrait of the film producer Joseph E. Levine. *Showman* follows the day-to-day activities of Levine as he meets with his staff, participates in a reunion with his old Boston friends, appears on David Susskind's radio show, attends the Cannes Film Festival, and presents Sophia Loren with her Oscar for *Two Women* (produced by

Levine). Rather than using the crisis structure of the Drew films, the Maysles brothers allowed for a looser form to predominate, one ostensibly predicated upon a duplication of the structure of daily life. Mamber would later write of the film that it "is an almost pure form of revelation through situation; each scene looks as though it was selected for nothing more than insight into the film's main character" (Mamber 142).[2] While Levine was not entirely happy with the film and would only allow it to be shown on television (a difficult sell for the Maysles brothers, as television networks at the time rarely bought independent documentary films), *Showman* was screened at the Marché International des Programmes et Equipments de Télévision in Lyon, France. There, Marcorelles saw *Showman* and acclaimed it as one of the "'ten or fifteen great films that I have had occasion to see since the war.'" But Roberto Rossellini was unimpressed, dismissing the film as formless and the antithesis of art (qtd. in Wakeman 656).

Such sharply divided responses would mark the release of most subsequent Maysles films, up through *Grey Gardens*. Their next two films, *What's Happening: The Beatles in the USA* (1964), detailing the Beatles' arrival in the United States, and *Meet Marlon Brando* (1965), which captures a round of press interviews Brando gave in New York to promote his new film *Morituri* (1965), likewise generated extreme responses. Antony Jay, the head of features for BBC-TV, found *What's Happening* to be "'hardly a film at all,'" and Brando was apparently so displeased with *Meet Marlon Brando* that he refused to allow it to be commercially screened (qtd. in Mamber 146). It was precisely this looseness of form, the sense that nothing of particular urgency seemed to be happening in the films, that was thought by others to be the sign of the emergence of something distinctive in documentary form. Not surprisingly, Jonas Mekas was a strong early supporter of Maysles. In a January 22, 1962, column for the *Village Voice*, "The Changing Language of Cinema," Mekas writes of a new type of filmmaking that he sees as "no longer embarrassed by its own stammerings, hesitations, side steps," a cinema that "is beginning to move freely, by itself, according to its own wishes and whims, tracing its own steps" (Mekas 49). While he only mentions the Maysles brothers in passing as being part of this trend, Mekas would increasingly write about and defend them over the next few years, culminating with a 1966 interview.

But it was the Maysles brothers' encounter with Truman Capote, through a film they otherwise regarded as an assignment for television, *A Visit with Truman Capote* (1966), that pointed them in a direction they began to increasingly follow. Capote's self-proclaimed "nonfiction novel" *In Cold Blood* (1965) became a touchstone for them. Capote's novel allowed the Maysles brothers to imagine a documentary-cinema equivalent of what Capote was achieving in prose. In the film, Capote speaks of his desire to "create a work of art out of factual material," something that would be "a synthesis of journalism and nonfiction technique."

In the aftermath of this confrontation with Capote and *In Cold Blood*, the Maysles brothers began to speak of their desire to create a new type of nonfiction cinema, feature-length and as compelling as a fiction film but comprised entirely of documentary material. When they spoke of this to Mekas, he astutely pointed out that their "cold-blooded direct cinema style" was already close to Capote's even before the publication of *In Cold Blood* (Mekas 225). Capote's book, then, did not so much directly inspire a transformation in the way that the

Truman Capote with Albert and David Maysles during the shooting of *A Visit with Truman Capote*. Photo by Bruce Davidson. Courtesy of Maysles Films, Inc.

Maysles brothers thought about their own work as it created, through its enormous critical and financial success, a legitimate cultural space within which the implications of their cinema could be more extensively pursued. Three years later, the release of *Salesman,* a film that focuses on the lives of four "ordinary" Bible salesmen rather than the celebrities or political figures of their earlier films, allowed Albert and David Maysles to realize this dream of the nonfiction feature. While acclaimed in certain quarters, many adherents of a pure direct-cinema approach (presupposing that such a thing exists) were critical of *Salesman,* finding it overreliant on conventional Hollywood dramatic structure.

Other controversies arose in relation to their two subsequent films, *Gimme Shelter* and *Grey Gardens.* While *Gimme Shelter* was originally intended to be little more than a commissioned project to film the Rolling Stones on tour, the sudden eruption of violence and murder in the midst of the culminating concert of this tour at Altamont Speedway in California inevitably resulted in a very different kind of film. *Gimme Shelter* was criticized for being everything from a reactionary, anti-youth film to a self-aggrandizing, self-mythologizing work. *Grey Gardens,* a film about Edith and Edie Beale, respectively the aunt and cousin of Jacqueline Kennedy, only intensified the anti-Maysles discourse. It was felt by many that the Maysles brothers had exploited the two women, living in poverty in a run-down, once-glorious home on Long Island.

Grey Gardens was the last Maysles film to generate such an intense response. Since then, Albert Maysles—up through his brother's sudden death in 1987 and then afterward with such collaborators as Susan Froemke, Deborah Dickson, Muffie Meyer, Ellen Hovde, and Antonio Ferrara—has shot largely commissioned work, primarily films about artists and classical-music celebrities as well as television commercials, all of which help to generate revenue for Maysles Films, Inc. While many of these later films have been critically acclaimed and received numerous awards, the excitement and controversy that once surrounded the appearance of a new Maysles film has died down. Nevertheless, the Maysles brothers' early work continues to be vital, and Albert Maysles maintains a strong, if not iconic, and very public presence within the documentary field, still firmly committed to the goals of the documentary cinema that he helped to establish with his brother.

This overview of Maysles's life and career contains certain threads that will be central to the arguments I will be making about the films. The first is the specificity of Maysles's origins: Jewish working-class in a predominantly Irish Catholic neighborhood in the Boston area, with an extremely close relationship to a younger (and, by all reports, more charismatic and colorful) brother, and with an interest in psychology that eventually translated into a larger fascination with the moving image. Boston is a primary setting or reference point for several Maysles films: *Showman, Salesman,* and *Ozawa* (1985). The city's identity was historically rooted in an English Puritan tradition, but the influx of Irish Catholics in the mid-nineteenth century gradually moved its politics away from conservative Republican to liberal Democratic, a political makeup that the city maintains to the present day and of whom the Kennedys (the subject of *Primary* and major unseen figures in *Grey Gardens*) remain its most notable examples.

Boston is strongly marked by the presence of such major figures in progressive American literary and philosophical history as Ralph Waldo Emerson, Henry David Thoreau, and Louisa May Alcott. It is also a region historically shaped by its immigrant population, not only the Irish but also Italians, Russian Jews (from which the Maysles family descended), and later, African Americans. Albert Maysles has described the Boston of the period of his adolescence as "a highly contentious city, full of ethnic conflicts. Then, it was every race, every ethnic group: the Irish, the Italians, the Jews, and so forth" (Trojan 27). During the period when Maysles was growing up, a local radio show (broadcast to 435 stations around the country) hosted by a Catholic priest, Father Charles Coughlin, a supporter of Hitler and Mussolini, regularly engaged in anti-Semitic diatribes. This experience of Boston partly explains Maysles's later attraction to filming human subjects who are outsiders within their own culture.

Taking this basic historical, cultural, and family situation a step further, we may see how a number of Maysles's most important films rework elements of this early period in the lives of both brothers, even though the films themselves do not directly address this history.[3] In many ways, Maysles's cinema is attracted not only to outsiders but to the idea of family and community as a source of refuge as well as oppression, something that can both nurture and destroy. These are very general themes, of course, and David and Albert Maysles can scarcely lay claim to inventing them. Nevertheless, there is a certain articulation of them in the films that bears attention.

For a start, the Maysles brothers' insistence upon collaboration (while doubtless having some of its genesis in the experience of working with Drew) is of a different nature from most direct-cinema and cinéma-vérité practitioners. At one extreme within these schools of documentary cinema is Wiseman, whose films often feel like one-man operations, their form and final shape strongly controlled by Wiseman himself. At the other extreme is Rouch, the form of whose later films would often be determined by the input of his subjects, who would offer feedback on the editing or, in the case of *Jaguar* (1967), write and speak the voiceover commentary. All of this emerges out of Rouch's notion of anthropological dialogue, ostensibly a refusal to go into a culture and film it in such a manner that the anthropologist—the white, powerful outsider—has the last word.

While Maysles has often spoken of the importance of developing a close relationship with his subjects—one that may, at times, be equivalent to that of a conversational partner—he and his brother did not encourage their subjects to become actively involved with the shooting or editing of the films. In only two instances, *Gimme Shelter* and *The Burk Family of Georgia* (1978), did they ever invite and include within the film itself commentary by their subjects—in the former, the idea was not their own but that of their editor and codirector, Charlotte Zwerin; and in the latter it was imposed on them by the film's producers. In both instances, this Rouch-like structure is used in a hesitant manner, as though the brothers did not completely believe in it or, at least, know what to do with it. It is not through these methods that a collective atmosphere in Maysles brothers' work emerges. Instead, a Maysles film frequently and directly depicts collectives working on projects in which, the films imply, the value of the final result would not have been possible without collaboration, with the collectives serving as analogues to the manner in which the films themselves are produced.

In looking at the list of codirectors credited on Maysles films, one is struck by how often these are women. Almost invariably, their initial input on the films was as film editors. Even though David would reportedly supervise or at least have important input into the editing on the earlier Maysles films, the decision to hand over the footage to editors in the way that the Maysles brothers did works against the standard methods by which direct-cinema and cinéma-vérité filmmakers operated. Mamber stresses the importance of the direct-cinema filmmaker functioning as his or her own editor: "When editing is viewed as an independent function, left to people who did not participate in the filming, a whole new set of priorities and biases, based solely on the footage, can conflict with the commitment not to distort the event itself" (Mamber 3). But Albert Maysles has frequently spoken of the enormous trust he and his brother placed in their editors. He has also stated that he is simply incapable of the sustained attention required for editing (he suffers from attention deficit disorder) and is therefore dependent on others to edit his footage. Hovde has said, "'Al never comes in on structure; he has never, to my knowledge, been in on the structuring of a film'" (qtd. in Rosenthal, *Documentary* 374).

Doubtless a research project could more precisely sort out the authorship on Maysles films. In interviews, the women who worked with Maysles articulate an extremely cogent understanding of these films, more than Maysles himself often does, particularly in relation to *Grey Gardens*. Froemke has stated the case for these women when she declares that Zwerin and Hovde were the "geniuses" and the "foundation" for Maysles (Stubbs 24). Certainly the editing of these films is central to their meaning, and this will be addressed throughout the book. Nevertheless, Zwerin, Hovde, and all the other collaborators on these films have done so (however creatively) within the direct-cinema style and the parameters established by David and Albert Maysles. *Showman* and *What's Happening*, two of the greatest Maysles works, were edited by individuals who did not later become part of the "foundation" for Maysles Films. And as early as *Psychiatry in Russia*, a number of the elements that would later become central to the Maysles approach to filmmaking are evident. The individual voices of these collaborators are difficult to trace and muffled within the larger Maysles mythology. The

Charlotte Zwerin (with Albert and David Maysles)
editing *Gimme Shelter*. Photo by Amelie R.
Rothschild. Courtesy of Maysles Films, Inc.

documentary work I have seen by Zwerin, Hovde, and Meyer apart from
Maysles, while interesting, does not bear a strong relationship to the
work they did with Maysles. (It may also have been a deliberate decision
on the part of these collaborators to break with the Maysles style once
they began working on their own.)

More significant than a precise sorting out of authorship is how the
Maysles brothers so often surrounded themselves with female collaborators upon whose input into the final shape of the films they extensively
relied. Rather than isolate the individual authorship of these women,
I would prefer to draw attention to this fundamental *need* for the input and presence of women, as though the Maysles brothers believed
that the films would be incomplete without it. This reliance on women
is often manifested in the films themselves. In the families in Maysles films, husbands, fathers, and other male figures are often absent,
weak, or dead, while marriages and creative partnerships (Christo and
Jeanne-Claude, for example, or Vladimir Horowitz and Wanda Toscanini

Horowitz) are presented in such a way that we are led to believe the husband's creative life would be virtually nonexistent without the presence or collaboration of his wife. If collectives and collaborations are a touchstone for Maysles, they are also unimaginable without this strong female presence, even if this presence is simultaneously subordinated to that of the more dominant male figures. At the end of *Islands* (1986), after the triumphant completion of their latest project, Jeanne-Claude asks Christo, "Is it like you wanted? Did we do a good job for you?"

Finally, the importance given to families (extended or otherwise) and to enclave-like communities in Maysles relates to the question of work. Labor is vital to much of the first fifty years of documentary cinema (if not to the history of cinema itself during this period), in the midst of major political and economic upheavals and two world wars: work as something desirable and necessary, dignified labor tied to the soil and to community (as in Robert Flaherty); work as an extension of a culturally and politically unified nation state, and even as a form of collective ecstasy (as in Dziga Vertov). Rather than fulfilling the utopian fantasies of the prewar period and allowing for greater freedom and flexibility in work, the developments in industrialization after the war frustrated and limited economic satisfaction for the worker who, most often laboring within politically conservative or repressive regimes, felt trapped. "I think the tragedy of our times is that hardly anyone chooses his job," says one of the subjects of Jean Rouch and Edgar Morin's *Chronicle of a Summer* (1961). "You don't select—you fall into it."

Within the school of direct cinema, Wiseman has treated the subject of work the most extensively, situating it within corporations and institutions in which workers find themselves absorbed into a structure where resistance is presented as a virtual impossibility. In his great film *The Store* (1983), Wiseman films the employees of a Neiman-Marcus department store in Dallas. While none of them protest or seem markedly unhappy in their jobs, Wiseman repeatedly employs rhetorical cuts to mannequins or to the objects, at once luxurious and lifeless, being sold; or he films employees and customers from high-angled shots; or draws attention to the rigorous process of the training and presentation of the workers. The cumulative effect is to place the workers within an atmosphere of mechanization, immobility, and control, epitomized by the sequence in which the workers file out of an exit door while having their bags examined by a security guard. Wiseman's methods are the obverse of Maysles's. Wiseman's camera, x-ray like, concerns itself with uncovering the surface of the worlds being depicted, hence the emphasis on grotesquerie, caricature, ugliness, and on movements predicated on their relationship to stillness, embalming, or death: the mannequins in *The Store* or the statuary in *La Comédie- Française* (1996). While mindful of the dehumanizing aspects of work in contemporary American culture, Maysles never goes to the extremes of Wiseman. Instead, however dehumanizing work may become (particularly in a film such as *Salesman*), it is usually bound up with notions of the performative, the aesthetic, and the transformative power of the individual who finds fulfillment working within a larger collective.

| | |

Central to the ways that Albert and David Maysles understood their own position as filmmakers is that, rather than making their social or political views explicit, the film is shot and structured in such a way that the viewer is given a choice in their interpretation. This concept of the viewer completing the film in an "open" manner is the antithesis of the political documentary cinema of Vertov or Emile de Antonio, for whom the forces of montage are used in the service of a more or less clear political thesis. Even in comparison with the American liberal tradition of Barbara Kopple (who originally worked for the Maysles brothers and often cites them as primary sources of inspiration), Maysles films are less overtly political. Kopple's most representative films, such as *Harlan County USA* (1976) and *American Dream* (1991), have clearer political aims than virtually anything in Maysles. The Maysles approach more or less follows Drew's insistence on the film not putting forward a clear or didactic political viewpoint. Instead, the film is intended to raise questions more than it is meant to supply answers. Mamber supports this thesis when he writes that "Maysles films do not attempt to 'hide' a message in a surface of uninterpreted observation; they simply refuse to spoon-feed interpretation when the material itself is open to consideration from a number of points of view. . . . [N]one of the thinking is done for you in the form of narration or an easily followed plot" (Mamber 147).

Be that as it may, it is true that several Maysles films have engendered highly contradictory and even violent responses, suggesting that these films (especially *Salesman, Gimme Shelter,* and *Grey Gardens*) are relatively "open" texts. While their meaning is not infinite, the diverse range of responses highlights the need for careful attention to the formal structure of the films and to the nature of their reception over the years, especially as the reception of some of them has shifted over time. Maysles films, like virtually all films that emerge out of the direct-cinema tradition, partake of what one may loosely term a liberal humanist viewpoint: a belief in the ultimate solidarity of cultures, races, and classes; an investment in the notion of spontaneity and freedom; and a skepticism toward the value of overly organized and systematic belief systems, including those of politics, labor, and organized religion. But unlike the films of Wiseman (another Boston native), Maysles films rarely examine the social and institutional underpinnings of the worlds they depict. The closest Maysles has come to doing this is *Concert of Wills: The Making of the Getty Center* (1997, in collaboration with Susan Froemke and Bob Eisenhardt), an atypical film in its form (with its heavy reliance on the talking-heads interview) and subject matter (its focus on the clash of egos within an institutional framework). More typically, Maysles's liberal humanism focuses on behavior, gesture, spoken language, personality, and interactions among people.

Abortion: Desperate Choices (1992, in collaboration with Froemke and Dickson) almost entirely concerns itself with the personalities of its primarily female subjects inside and outside of an abortion clinic in Pittsburgh: the agony of the women who decide to undergo abortions, and the anti-abortion protestors outside the clinic attempting to dissuade them from going inside. But the film pays very little attention to the specifics (including the economic) of running the clinic itself. Everything is focused on the emotional turmoil engendered by the decision to have an abortion, while the fathers, boyfriends, or husbands are often absent from the film or presented as weak figures. The film is fairly balanced in its view, turning neither the pro- nor anti-abortion subjects into objects of ridicule, although its emotional weight is arguably aligned with those who believe in women having access to legal abortion.

This position is especially clear given the emphasis on a series of harrowing interviews that interrupt the film's presentation of the day-to-day activities at the clinic: footage shot in black and white of women from the 1920s up through the 1960s who had abortions under illegal circumstances. Such testimony emotionally (and, one might argue, ethically) outweighs the reasons given for the anti-abortion crusade. One of these anti-abortionists, for example, delivers a monologue about her mother telling her that she had seriously considered an abortion before she ultimately decided to give birth to her—a conversation that shocked her and influenced her views on abortion. While doubtless sincere, her motivations for joining the anti-abortion movement are fuzzy and self-involved in comparison with the confessional material of the other women that surrounds her testimony. But the film never lapses into simple didacticism or becomes something that Maysles has consistently denigrated since the 1960s: propaganda.

There is certainly a great tradition of didactic and political documentary film that need not be swept aside in favor of the approach taken by Maysles, even if Maysles's contempt for this approach allows him to create the kinds of films that he has. Rather than completely aligning myself with Maysles in terms of his own statements, I want to concern myself with the specifics of his work and attempt to understand its value as fully as possible, without engaging in polemics. The tendency among documentary critics and scholars to wholeheartedly agree with the opinions of the filmmakers on whom they are writing has flawed some otherwise first-rate work.

Vogels has argued that the sensibility behind Maysles (and direct cinema in general) is related to the search for authenticity typical among the New Left of the 1960s and its investment in a more open and participatory form of democracy (Vogels 4). While this is undoubtedly true, Maysles's films are equally informed by the universal humanism of the previous decade. During the immediate postwar period, the cinema was thought to play a particularly vital role in the concept of universal humanism. Such a concept was central in the aftermath of the rise of fascism in the 1920s and 1930s and its tremendous (and ultimately violent and totalitarian) investment in the purity of national identity. Numerous fiction and nonfiction films of travel and exile were made after World War II, centering on the meeting or clash between two cultures, often resulting in a sense that national boundaries were becoming more fluid and less distinct. Maysles has never completely abandoned this ideology.

The desire to connect with other cultures in Maysles's work often plays itself out through language. The portability of not only lightweight cameras but also of sound equipment has been regarded as a hallmark of direct cinema and cinéma vérité. At the time of their initial release, the films had a distinctive look and sound, capturing accents, vernacular, and dialect. As Marcorelles writes, "For the first time in history speech can move, breathe, be seen, take up space" (*Living Cinema* 15). In referring to early Maysles films, he describes how "[l]anguage becomes an exciting mixture of expressions, flung out spontaneously; and it confirms the fact that there has been a revolution in sound" (63). It is not simply spontaneity through language, though, that is achieved in Maysles; there is also an enormous desire to engage with other cultures, using language as a fundamental way in which two seemingly different cultures can communicate with one another even if, as some of the films demonstrate, this desired connection is extremely difficult if not impossible to achieve. Hence the importance in Maysles of characters speaking (however haltingly at times) second languages, of at least attempting to communicate with another culture rather than simply imposing one's language of origin on it. This central element of Maysles's work is already in place in *Primary*, when Jacqueline Kennedy speaks at the Polish Meeting Hall to a group of Polish Americans in their native tongue. While she clearly learned this speech phonetically, the gesture itself is what matters: the acknowledgment and embrace of cultural difference expressed through language.

While these attitudes have their basis in postwar humanism, Maysles also traces them back to his family situation. He has spoken of "the way my parents had trained us, we always saw the good in people" (Trojan 27). He has drawn particular attention to his mother, whose curiosity and lack of prejudice made its mark on her sons: "When she went on tour with [the American Jewish Congress] to Israel, my mother spent all of her time meeting and talking with Arabs" (Trojan 28). In one of the Maysles brothers' most neglected films, *A Journey to Jerusalem* (1968, direction credited to Michael Midlin Jr.), this anecdote is given an indirect enactment. The film chronicles Leonard Bernstein's visit to Jerusalem after the Six Day War in 1967, a visit that culminated with his conducting of Mahler's *Resurrection* symphony. As Bernstein drives through Israel, he remembers his first trip to the country in 1948, singing Arab songs in an armored car while armed Arabs hid out in the hills. He insists on singing these songs again, wanting to make a connection to Arab culture rather than rejecting it: "It's just thrilling to see Jews and

Arabs mingling." For Bernstein, the Mahler symphony is not only the Israeli national anthem but also speaks to "the deep belief that good must triumph."

It is significant that Maysles's first three films, made during a period when cold-war anxieties were at their height, took life behind the Iron Curtain as their subject. *Psychiatry in Russia* clearly attempts to avoid an overt political ideology. There is no significant effort to analyze or critique the Soviet government. Instead, in a fashion that would become typical of all of his later work, Maysles emphasizes the basic humanity of the people he is filming. There is a clear desire to resist stereotype and instead focus on the humor and naturalness of the Russian people. In the first-person voiceover narration (written but not spoken by Maysles), we hear, "I found myself caught up in an aura of naturalness." *Psychiatry in Russia* offers some criticism of the anti-Freudianism of the Soviet methods of psychotherapy, with its emphasis on Pavlovian theory—getting patients up on their feet and functioning again rather than attacking the root of the psychological problem. But the film does not overemphasize this critique. Instead, it sees this limitation as also having value in its need to restore patients to the society of which they are a part.

We also see in embryonic form in this film the basic Maysles fascination with the function of women in relation to the collective through its presentation of the largely female Soviet doctors as maternal and caring toward their patients. These women bring to their patients what the narrator calls "a woman's touch." The implication and example of the film is that American and Soviet cultures are not diametrically opposed but instead may profit by a more open dialogue and mutual understanding. The film ends with the narrator explaining, "Russian doctors have one thing in common with doctors around the world: they want their patients to get well." However, most of the Maysles films from the 1960s and after are set in America, and while embracing a pluralistic vision they nevertheless imply that whatever its flaws, America remains the ultimate space for humanistic and democratic principles. *Ozawa* brings this point home with a clarity verging on the didactic, as the conductor of the Boston Symphony, the Japanese-born Seiji Ozawa, extensively discusses his difficulties as a conductor within an emotionally rigid Japan that has no place for him. Only in America, the film implies, can someone as spontaneous and youthful as Ozawa find his true home.

Albert Maysles surrounded by (mainly female) Soviet doctors and hospital workers during the shooting of *Psychiatry in Russia*. Courtesy of Maysles Films, Inc.

The film ends on a freeze frame with an ecstatic Ozawa conducting . . . Mahler's *Resurrection* symphony.

Almost every major Maysles film takes as its starting point a meeting or confrontation between two worlds, played out directly within the films themselves and subjected to various permutations. This confrontation usually involves a breakdown of the previously held distinction between these worlds, as the subjects of one world enter into or invade the spaces of another: the Christo and Jeanne-Claude films play this conflict out on a gargantuan scale, and its structuring presence throughout Maysles is no doubt a heritage of the crisis structure of early direct cinema and its need for dramatic conflict. One can find such a structure even in a comparatively minor Maysles film such as *Accent on the Offbeat* (1994, in collaboration with Froemke and Dickson), detailing the production of a ballet staged by Peter Martins to a score by Wynton Marsalis. The film is shaped by a set of schematic conflicts and oppositions: between the jazz world of Marsalis and the ballet world of Martins; between the world of popular culture and the world of "elite" culture; between music and dance; between black culture and white culture. Such a structure is indicative of larger American concepts, their dualistic drives and desires to reconcile seemingly irreconcilable opposites. How Maysles specifically enacts these dualistic drives is a complex matter, as individual films articulate this in different ways with not all of them geared toward an unambiguous resolution of the conflicts they initially establish. But the films continually return to this dualism, as though wanting to reinvest in this notion even while attempting to acknowledge its fundamental limitations.

| | |

The discourses surrounding documentary cinema, whatever their differences, have returned time and again to questions of ethics, addressing not only the choices a documentarian makes in relation to such formal matters as editing and sound but also in terms of how the subjects of a particular film have been treated: Has the film fictionalized or otherwise distorted the day-to-day reality of its subjects? Or has the camera been turned into an instrument of abuse, invading the privacy of its subjects and making them objects of ridicule? Within such discourses, the documentary image can never reveal an undistorted and unmediated reality. Not surprisingly, filmmakers who foreground their processes of production (Vertov or de Antonio, Rouch or Errol Morris) often assume exemplary status within the literature on documentary cinema—although such practices mask as much as they reveal.

The films of direct cinema are particularly vulnerable to criticism in this respect. Their apparent investment in the camera's capacity to directly reproduce and reveal reality, their reliance on continuity editing in a kind of mimicry of classical narrative cinema, and their frequent lack of interest in directly implicating the work's source of enunciation have drawn sharp criticism ever since the form's emergence over four decades ago. The statements that most direct-cinema filmmakers have made about their own work only confirm such criticism. Over and over again, these filmmakers state their commitment to a documentary cinema in which truth and reality are simply out there in the world, waiting to be captured on film—perhaps no one more so than Albert Maysles. A typical quote: "'The contemplation of things as they are, without error or confusion, without substitution or imposture, is in itself a nobler thing than a whole harvest of invention'" (qtd. in Marcorelles, *Living*

Cinema 63). Filmmakers such as de Antonio and Morris have famously taken direct cinema to task for the kinds of sentiments Maysles invokes here. Morris has declared that the claims of direct cinema are "'spurious'" and that "'style does not guarantee truth'" (qtd. in Cunningham 57), while de Antonio more bombastically dismisses direct cinema as a "joke" and a "lie" based upon a "childish assumption about the nature of film" (Rosenthal, "Emile de Antonio" 7).

Documentary critics and scholars have traditionally held documentary filmmakers accountable for what they say about their own work in a way that would be unimaginable for scholars of Hollywood cinema to hold accountable the (often questionable) statements made by, say, John Ford or Howard Hawks about their own work. I essentially agree with Stella Bruzzi, who argues that direct cinema has been misdefined and has misdefined itself (72). The implied continuity between the statements made by direct-cinema filmmakers and the works themselves has too often closed off other possibilities for reading these films. This does not mean that the statements Albert Maysles makes about his own films should be ignored or regarded as absurd as we focus solely on the final product. On the contrary, these statements provide an extremely useful understanding of what motivates Maysles to create the kinds of images he does, even if they are clearly insufficient when measured against the final results.

The first issue worth addressing in this regard is the notion, seemingly so central to direct cinema, of the filmmaker's nonintervention in the filmmaking process. Theoretically, in the purest type of direct cinema, as in so-called classical narrative cinema, the traces of authorial inscription are least apparent—films that appear to present unmediated access to the world and in which the filmmaker does not overtly intervene in the filming process. Maysles has expressed discomfort with the very word *director* "because I don't feel that the way I shoot that I'm directing anything" (Haleff 21). He thus refuses (at least officially) the conventional role of the controlling *metteur-en-scène* while insisting on the ability of the camera and microphone to record spontaneous events. The problem with this position is that, however sincerely it is intended by Maysles, the films themselves do *not* consistently unfold as directly transmuted reality. Whatever their publicly expressed devotion to humility before their camera's subjects, the Maysles brothers often make themselves physically present in their films, arguably more so than any other American direct-cinema practitioners. For one thing, the Maysles were sometimes faced with people who did not behave like proper direct-cinema subjects and instead acknowledged not only the camera but the flesh-and-blood presence of the filmmakers themselves, most notably the Beatles in *What's Happening* and especially the Beales in *Grey Gardens*. Beyond these extreme examples, though, the Maysles brothers often play a game of presence and absence in their films, with images of them filming sometimes being briefly reflected in mirrors or other reflective surfaces; or we may hear their voices (mainly David's) off camera speaking to their subjects. (In the 1990 film *Christo in Paris*, Christo and Jeanne-Claude introduce the brothers on camera, still standing behind their equipment, to Michel Boutinard-Rouelle, the Paris director of cultural affairs.) Albert Maysles's description of his relationship with his subjects as akin to that of a conversational partner suggests that he sees himself as considerably more than a passive or neutral observer of spontaneous, unfolding action.

The ideals of transparency in direct cinema, then, have been impossible to achieve. This has been argued on numerous occasions but most often from a position that seeks to either discredit or at least to seriously call into question some of the assumptions behind direct cinema. An example of the latter is Jeanne Hall's important essay on *Primary*. While conceding the film's historical centrality, Hall draws attention to a number of elements in the film that contradict the stated intentions of its makers to offer an unmediated access to the real. Hall notes that the film (like some of Drew's other films of this period) violates a number of the explicit terms of direct cinema in its use of voiceover narration and musical underscoring, its fairly obvious rhetorical elements, its use of interviews and even partially fictionalized moments (such as the voices of hypothetical voters being played on the soundtrack over a montage of the feet of various Wisconsinites standing in voting booths), and the sometimes clear physical presence of the filmmakers. "To see the early films of Drew Associates for the first time today," she writes, "is to be amazed at how remotely they resemble their descriptions" (Hall 29). While Hall's attention to detail is admirable, her conclusion effectively leaves to others the possibilities for looking at direct cinema in new ways. Conceding that Drew and his collaborators failed to achieve their goals, she writes that "the very way in which these filmmakers 'failed'—the remarkable means by which they refracted the light passing through cinéma vérité's 'window on the world'—is something about which we have yet much to discover" (46).

The act of discovering something more than the explicitly stated goals of direct cinema—and of Maysles—will be one of my major concerns here. At almost every turn, it is true that Albert and David Maysles and their collaborators violate the ethical codes of direct cinema: *Showman* makes use of voiceover narration; there is musical underscoring in many of their later films; in almost all of the films the subjects address the camera directly in various ways; and the films are sometimes edited in a blatantly nonchronological manner. (*A Visit with Truman Capote* even contains a flashback.) But what makes these films such fascinating and often brilliant documents is not their purity and perfection of form. The ideals of direct cinema are, at best, loose ideals. What is so compelling in Maysles is this struggle, sometimes anguished but more often ecstatic, to seize moments of revelation through human interaction and through the human form itself.

For the Polish Legion Hall sequence of *Primary*, for example, the shots that are used in the final version of this sequence emphasize Jacqueline Kennedy's hands folded behind her, fiddling nervously as she waits to speak. If these frequently criticized shots assume a fiction-like isolation of detail, it has largely to do with how they fit into a larger structure of how the body is filmed and edited in *Primary*. As the film shows, much of the process of politics involves continuous handshaking, from the opening of the film, with Hubert Humphrey shaking the hand of a farmer, to the decision made as to how to fold one hand of John F. Kennedy's over another for a photo session, to the close-ups of Kennedy's hands during his own speech that follows Jacqueline's and the orgy of handshakes that follow these speeches in the meeting hall. The shots of Jacqueline's hands undoubtedly force attention on a detail. But that detail, in turn, arises out of a larger pattern of abstracting elements out of the "reality" of what is being filmed. If these Maysles films consistently fail to capture reality in the "pure" manner its own practitioners and early defenders claimed they did, this is only a starting point from which to find other ways to understand these films. As Bruzzi has argued, "[T]he documentary text is predicated upon and created by

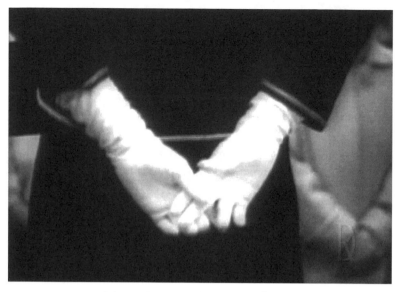

Primary: The nervous hands of
Jacqueline Kennedy.

the central dialectical relationship between an unadulterated truth and representation, not destroyed by it" (72).

In an interview on WCBS-TV promoting *Salesman,* Maysles stated that he has "a religious feeling" about the ability to capture reality: "It has to be a camera with love, with empathy. You're filming people's vulnerabilities" (*Salesman* DVD). The choice of words here is revealing. The "religious" feeling about reality and the camera's ability to record it and the use of the word "love" to describe his empathetic response to his subjects suggests a tie to Bazinian discourses on realism. Even Maysles's belief in "the contemplation of things as they are" evokes a famous statement made by Rossellini, that exemplary filmmaker for André Bazin: "'Things are there. Why manipulate them?'" (qtd. in Gallagher 485). At the same time, as the history of cinema and indeed the history of realism in general have shown, an investment in the real invariably entails a fascination with its apparent polar opposite: the false, the artificial, the constructed, the *un*real.

Is the first projected motion picture, the Lumières brothers' *Workers Exiting the Factory* (1895), also the first documentary film, vividly capturing the reality of the end of a workday for a group of French factory employees? Or is it a carefully staged and re-created event, the first major instance of filmmakers discovering the power of mise-en-scène and choreographed action? The film works on both of these levels at once, and the tension between them gives it its mesmerizing presence. The film is abundantly, magically real, a supreme testament to the power of the indexical image, and perhaps because of this the film also seems artificial—a work of enchantment, or "an hallucination which is also a fact," to borrow Bazin's phrase for the experience of the photographic imprint (16). In writing on Jean Eustache's documentary *La Rosière de Pessac* (1968), Jean-Louis Comolli notes that in this film, "little by little, the extreme reality effect changes into a dream impression." The human subjects, while taken from the "real world," begin to fuse with and resemble figures out of myth and fairy tale. "Fiction triumphs over the real, or rather it gives it its true dimension, relating it back to archetypes and constantly recalling the moral of the fable" (Comolli 228). Such a paradoxical experience of a documentary film is hardly surprising. It taps into one of the most persistent myths about the cinematic image as it attempts to capture the reality in front of its lens: namely, that the camera's powers of indexicality are so strong and immediate that they transform their subjects into something extraordinary and unreal. Consequently, I want to retain this sense of wonder, of discovery before the documentary image, to treat the Maysles films not exactly as though they were works of fiction but neither as though they were "pure" documentaries. Instead, I want to focus on what underpins and structures these images that the Maysles present to us, what obsessions and fantasies, what fetishes and desires drive this cinema forward, giving it its particular force.

In 1963, Maysles served as a cameraman for Jean-Luc Godard on an episode for the omnibus film *Paris vu par . . . .* The episode is not a major work for either of them, but the idea of pairing these two talents (apparently that of the film's producer, Barbet Schroeder) is interesting in and of itself. While prior to this, Godard had written negatively of the direct-cinema school of filmmaking (focusing his attack primarily on the work of Leacock),[4] Godard praised Maysles for being "a painter in his way of seeing" (213).[5] The episode Maysles shot for Godard, "Les plus belles Escroqueries du monde Montparnasse-Levallois," features a character who is an "action sculptor"—he throws bits of metal into the air and arranges them according to how they fall. "It means that chance enters into the creation of the sculpture," the sculptor says of his process. The film itself is billed as "un action-film organize pars Jean-Luc Godard et filme par Albert Maysles." Maysles is clearly being used by Godard for his documentary abilities to think quickly on his feet, with none of the meticulousness of a conventional cinematographer. But in a typically paradoxical move, Godard praises Maysles not for his skills as a documentarian but as an aesthete, someone capable of producing beautiful images.

Nevertheless, the beauty of a Maysles image most often arises through its startling immediacy, capturing, framing, and seizing the spontaneity of a moment in all of its dynamic motion rather than freezing the image into one of overly aestheticized beauty. Moreover, this image will often encapsulate the entire dynamic of a particular film. One example: In *Grey Gardens*, as Edie Beale asks her mother to pass a hand mirror to her, Maysles zooms in to a shot of the mirror being passed. The framing focuses almost entirely on the gestures of the two women. We see Mrs. Beale's hand pass the mirror over, but not quite far enough for her daughter to easily grab it. Instead, Edie holds her hand and wiggles her fingers toward the mirror without firmly taking hold of it. Neither mother nor daughter will make the final gesture that brings this request to a close. The history of the complex dynamic between these two women, at once loving and destructive, nurturing and withholding, is contained within a single gesture and a single image.

Maysles's explicitly stated desire to get close to his human subjects has several implications in terms of how these images may be understood and experienced. The "conversational partner" closeness Maysles speaks of is, on one level, psychological and predicated on his ability to gain the trust of his subjects so that they "open up" for the camera and reveal themselves to it. The accusation that Maysles sometimes exploits this relationship, though, suggests that his methods are more insidious than he would admit. As part of his training in psychology, Maysles studied hypnosis. Within film theory, hypnosis has sometimes been used as a metaphor to account for not only the mesmerizing power of the cinematic image but also for the behavior of the controlling auteur who dominates his actors and crew members through the sheer force of his creative will

Grey Gardens: Edie Beale reaches for the mirror,
held by her mother

and personality (Fritz Lang, Josef von Sternberg, Federico Fellini). This image runs completely counter to Maysles's stated methods for filming in an atmosphere of happy collaboration in which he does not dominate his human subjects but instead relaxes them and gains their confidence.

If his interview statements are any indication, gaining the confidence of the person being filmed is not simply a matter of the filmmaker having a winning personality that seduces his subjects into accepting his presence. A certain manipulation is also involved, even if it is not as overt as it is might be in the work of a dominating auteur in narrative cinema. Maysles has said that he keeps his camera on his shoulder continuously while filming so that his subjects lose any sense of when it is running and when it is not. This can be seen clearly in *Horowitz Plays Mozart* (1987, in collaboration with Zwerin and Froemke) when at one point Horowitz walks toward the camera, looks into it and uncertainly asks, "This is off?" Froemke has described David Maysles's strategy of deliberately looking away from his subjects even as he talked to and recorded them; this staged bit of distraction got the subjects to lose their awareness of the camera and to "get them right back into their own real life" (Stubbs 31). The documentary filmmaker in such instances, while not working with a screenplay that predetermines action, still functions as a type of psychologist—gauging, controlling, and responding to behavior as it develops in front of the camera.

But Maysles's background in psychology allows for another method of understanding how the camera functions in his films. Objections to Maysles films often involve outrage over the ways in which the films violate the privacy of the individuals being filmed and thereby subject them to embarrassment or ridicule. Calvin Pryluck's essay "Ultimately We Are All Outsiders: The Ethics of Documentary Filmmaking" is the clearest example of this attitude, even though he addresses larger ethical issues within documentary cinema rather than the work of the Maysles alone. Pryluck sees the relationship between "actuality-filmmakers" and physicians, sociologists, and psychologists as being closely related in one respect: "[S]cientists and direct cinema depend for their success on subjects who have little or nothing to gain from participation" (260). Maysles later indirectly responded to this position in an interview with Pryluck himself. Pryluck asked Maysles if a hypothetical drunk, vomiting in the street, did not have the right to his privacy rather than being stared at or, implicitly, filmed. Maysles responded by saying, "He's got a right to his privacy but, at the same time, the reason that he may be an alcoholic is that no one's paying attention to him. He doesn't need people passing him by; let the camera take part in the recognition" (Pryluck, "Seeking" 13). For Maysles, the act of being filmed is, for the subject, not an invasion of privacy but an act of psychological healing. "'The camera's like a non-directive therapist'" (qtd. in Haleff 23).

Far from gaining nothing in being a camera subject, for Maysles being filmed is a type of therapy in which one feels better about oneself afterward, since being filmed is recognition. "I'm all for filming incompetent people," Maysles told Pryluck. "They're the ones who need it the most" (Pryluck, "Seeking" 12). In Shirley Clarke's film *Portrait of Jason* (1967), Clarke's subject, Jason Holliday, states this position from the point of view of the subject rather than the filmmaker: "You know, it's a funny feelin' having a picture made about you. . . . I feel sort of grand sitting here. . . . People are going to be diggin' ya, ya know? I'm gonna be criticized. I'll be loved or hated or whatever. What difference does it make? I am doing what I want to do, and it's a nice feeling that somebody's taking a picture of it. This is a picture I can save forever." The camera validates the subject (he feels "sort of grand") and stokes his narcissism ("it's a nice feeling") but also gives him a form of immortality, a picture he "can save forever."

The intimacy with which some of Maysles's films were made, with the camera crew sometimes consisting of two, only reinforces the therapeutic atmosphere of a camera and of filmmakers who look at you carefully— "with love," as Maysles has so often phrased it—and listen. While Maysles's attitude is undoubtedly limited by its idealism, it is no more limited than the attitude one finds in Pryluck, which is built on a belief about the inherent innocence of human subjects prior to being filmed, an innocence forever tarnished by the merciless exposure of the camera. I question whether such a neat distinction between private and public exists in the schematic way that Pryluck situates it. When Pryluck exempts "staged performances" from his belief in the right to privacy, since such performances are "the right of self-expression," one wonders how he can always confidently identify behavior in a film as a staged performance or not ("Ultimately" 261). I write these words in the midst of the phenomenon of reality television, where validation and meaning for the individual is wholly a matter of living life in front of the camera, a camera that the subject alternately ignores and directly addresses and in which divisions between private and public have become irrelevant. Reality television, of course, is merely one instance of the larger blurring of the divisions in the "society of the spectacle" between private and public space and behavior. Whether the cinema of figures such as Maysles prepared for this society or whether it is up to something fundamentally different is a topic too complex to address here. But certainly the theatrical and performative strain running throughout much of direct cinema has, for better or worse, blurred the boundaries between private and public, between the natural and the theatrical. My aim here is not to denounce this blurring as a violation of documentary ethics but instead to treat it as one of a number of structuring elements at work in these films.

| | |

Finally, to get extremely close to his subjects Maysles creates a particular atmosphere. Maysles's cinema is extremely physical, the camera highly alert to the faces and bodies it films, to the slightest gesture or shift in facial expression. What is perhaps most memorable about *Letting Go: A Hospice Journey* (1996, in collaboration with Froemke and Dickson) is not the often painful spectacle of death and mourning, or of doctors, hospice workers, and clergymen offering inadequate words of hope to the dying and their loved ones, with all of this family drama played out for the benefit of the camera. What is most memorable about the film is something "smaller"—the frequent images of the hands of the dying being touched by those who have to visit with or console them.

Such images are typical of how Maysles's camera is remarkably alert to the dynamics within a situation, to noting multiple activities and responses within an environment or even within a single shot. A typical camera move in Maysles will often involve a sustained look at a person or object before noticing another detail to which it responds by a pan or tilt, recasting our initial impression of the meaning or expressive power of the shot. A minor example: At the beginning of *Ozawa*, the camera holds on Seiji Ozawa for a fairly extended period of time, observing his sweating face in close-up as he conducts his orchestra. The framing is such that his hands only periodically enter the bottom of the frame. Otherwise, the shot allows for a "study" of Ozawa's facial expression as he conducts, sometimes slightly panning to follow his movements. But after about a minute and a half of this, the camera pans to the left, away from Ozawa, and turns its gaze on the audience. The camera then racks focus to find two men sitting together, effusively responding to Ozawa's conducting. These two men could not possibly see what the camera sees on Ozawa's face, thereby placing the film viewer (and the filmmaker) in the most privileged of positions for observing this moment. At the same time, the filmmaker, film viewer, and film subjects are all linked with one another in this moment of musical ecstasy, so strongly articulated through facial and bodily expression. Such a desire to apprehend the physical world with a camera and to regard that physical world as concrete, tangible, and innately expressive gives the images in a Maysles film so much of their weight and seductive force. It is the aim of this book to do justice to those images.

Hard-Working People:
Salesman, Showman, and *Meet Marlon Brando*

It sounds like I'm selling, but I'm not.
I'm giving you factual information.

—*Showman*

At the beginning of *Meet Marlon Brando,* Brando talks to a group of journalists about the various jobs he might have had if he had not become an actor. He also discusses his brief stint at manual labor, declaring, "I hated that." Becoming an actor allows Brando to avoid the drudgery of manual labor. But acting still involves work, in particular the selling of oneself and of the finished product in which one has acted through the machinery of publicity and advertising. "Every time we get in front of the television," he says, "everybody starts hustling."

This section will focus on three Maysles films in which work assumes a central role. Although these are not the only Maysles films to address this topic, they collectively present the most interesting range of possibilities for understanding how the subject of work functions within Maysles. Moreover, each of these films shows how different forms of work lead to different forms of direct cinema. In all three, work is public, social, and interactive, and whatever their differences, the types of work we see are fundamentally related to selling products in an aggressive manner. But in different ways this selling is also strongly tied to issues of performance in which selling becomes a form of theater.

Of these three films about "hustling," *Salesman* occupies an especially significant position. Released in 1969, it was not only officially the Maysles brothers' first feature-length theatrical film; it was also an attempt to break into commercial channels of exhibition through their new brand of nonfiction cinema. But these ambitions would pose particular problems for the brothers in terms of the film's reception. With *Salesman,* the tone, if not the content, of the discourses surrounding their filmmaking began to change. The film opened at a first-run theater on Manhattan's Upper East Side, the Sixty-eighth Street Playhouse, and was screened for mainstream critics. While it received some favorable notices, other critics were not only unimpressed but offended, the most common complaint being that it condescends to its subjects and that it lacks a clear point of view. (The film was not a financial success.)

Surprisingly, one of the harshest reviews came from Jonas Mekas. Clearly feeling betrayed at the desire of the Maysles brothers to make a film that could speak to a wide audience, he wrote that *Salesman* was "a big pancake, without any sense of structure" (Mekas 349). Mekas uses the word "boring" six times in his short review. Louis Marcorelles likewise expressed disappointment, although he was much less harsh. Finding it "a remarkable exercise in style," he nevertheless thought that the film lacked a "critical dimension" in its attitude to reality (*Living Cinema* 65). Stephen Mamber, while claiming that the film is "in many ways the most important product of American cinema verite" (161), also felt that it carried "the Maysles approach several steps forward and perhaps a step back" (169). For Mamber (as for Marcorelles), this step back is the result of the filmmakers' refusal to directly interrogate and question their own investment in reproducing reality, a by-now standard criticism of much of direct cinema. And where Mekas sees a film without any structure, Mamber (more accurately) sees a film "as neatly constructed as if it were largely prescripted, full of devices heretofore more the province of fiction film" (161). Mamber objects to the editing structure, the crosscutting among the four salesmen, the decision to foreground Paul Brennan as the "star" of the film, and the attempt at a dramatic climax in the final shot: Brennan standing alone in a hotel room, looking desolate after he is repeatedly shown to fail at being a Bible salesman. Mamber writes: "The film is wholly discussable in terms of the view of American life it portrays, the metaphoric possibilities in the situation, the contradictions between religion and hawking Bibles, pervading sense of *angst,* etc. This kind of explication, while certainly fruitful, sidesteps major questions. The crux of this argument seems to be that a cinema-verite approach can lead to superior fiction, when the real question should be why we need fiction at all" (163).

Mamber's objection to *Salesman* sidesteps a major issue: the extremely close theoretical and practical ties between fiction and documentary cinema that long precede the appearance of *Salesman* but that reached one of their most complex manifestations during the late 1960s and early 1970s, as direct cinema and cinéma vérité began to undertake new directions. *Salesman* was released during a period when films such as Jacques Rivette's *L'amour fou* (1968) and Haskell Wexler's *Medium Cool* (1969) were self-consciously mixing documentary and fiction modes in such a manner that the divisions between them were simultaneously foregrounded (calling attention to the process of documentary production within the films themselves) and blurred (the difficulty of always precisely identifying the fiction and documentary elements within the pro-filmic).

These experiments were merely coming at the end of a decade in which fiction and direct cinema were increasingly interacting. In American filmmaking alone in the 1960s, there is the direct-cinema style of John Cassavetes in the otherwise fictional films *Shadows* (1961) and *Faces* (1968), Shirley Clarke in *The Connection* (1960) and *The Cool World* (1964), and Robert Kramer in *Ice* (1968) and *The Edge* (1968). Norman Mailer directed two fiction films during this period, *Beyond the Law* (1968) and *Maidstone* (1970), but they were shot in an improvisational manner with D. A. Pennebaker operating as cinematographer. When the Maysles brothers filmed Orson Welles for *Orson Welles in Spain* (1963), Welles explained his idea for a new film: while a work of fiction, it would be "shot like a documentary, without a script." The film Welles was discussing eventually became the unfinished *The Other Side of the Wind,* yet another instance in this period of the overlapping of documentary and fiction modes.

Alongside these films, *Salesman,* in its desire to use documentary form to create an experience more generally associated with the world of fiction filmmaking, may seem rather old-fashioned. The same year in which *Salesman* was released, Jim McBride made his hilarious documentary pastiche, *David Holzman's Diary* (1969), in which first-person documentary images are unable to reveal or express anything outside of the failure and mediocrity of their own fictional filmmaker. McBride's film is distributed by (so the tongue-in-cheek credits tell us) "Direct Cinema Limited."

The Maysles brothers remained undeterred by criticism of *Salesman.* Seven years after it was released, Albert Maysles stated that "*Salesman* is the closest to what we always wanted to do—and still want to do" (Pryluck, "Seeking" 15). To this day, *Salesman* is the film Maysles invariably shows if given the choice of a single film to screen in order to discuss his work.

The film's editor and codirector, Charlotte Zwerin, has described *Salesman* as "a big step forward that wasn't followed" (DVD commentary track). While Zwerin does not go into detail, her comment may be read in two related ways: the example of *Salesman* was not followed by the Maysles brothers themselves, which is largely true in that there is no other Maysles film quite like it; and the film stands alone as an experiment within the documentary field. This later argument is more difficult to sustain, as a number of documentaries loosely follow *Salesman*'s form of a camera "invisibly" capturing the day-to-day lives of nonpublic figures. But *Salesman* still has its own particular weight and richness that deserves close attention, not only within the body of work of the Maysles brothers but also within the history of documentary cinema and its ongoing dialogue with fiction filmmaking. The result is not "superior fiction" but something else entirely. *Salesman* is at once linked with and the polar opposite of the films being made during this period by Rivette and Kramer, Cassavetes and Clarke. If these other filmmakers have stories to tell, characters to present, and actors (professional and otherwise) to put into an arena in which the realms of documentary and fiction ambiguously commingle, the Maysles brothers take the raw material of their documentary subjects and shape it into a structured form. This form at times evokes fiction—literary, theatrical, and cinematic—but it is no less geared toward what it perceives to be the truth.

For Mekas, though, the Maysles brothers in *Salesman* merely follow in "the good old naturalistic tradition." It is a film in which "they abstain from (or are not capable of) any interpretations, commentaries." Moreover, the film "has no sense of humor" (349). Every one of these observations is off the mark, but Mekas's objections make useful starting points for discussing the film. The reference to "the good old naturalistic tradition," like Mamber's objections to the film's strong sense of structure, suggests that the film attempts to shape its material into something that approaches the realist novel in psychological observation if not in form. This likely was a fundamental problem for those who had previously embraced the work of the Maysles brothers. *Showman* and *Meet Marlon Brando* were films that, to their admirers, owed little to preexistent art forms but instead forged a wholly new type of film language, one created in relation to (as Mekas puts it) "new times, new content, new language" (49). These earlier films were not without structure, however.

Showman has a clearly announced beginning with the first words of the voiceover narrator: "It starts here." While this line refers to a meeting with Levine and other businessmen in which "here" the process of selling a film "starts," the line also effectively raises the curtain on the film. A series of events link the various sequences: Levine's campaign to get Sophia Loren her Oscar dominates much of the first half of the film, culminating with her win; the second half uses the Oscar statuette as a kind of talisman that Levine carries from place to place, with the ultimate goal being to present the statuette to Loren in Rome, an event that occurs near the end of the film. Other smaller events and situations also give the film a sense of cohesion: Levine's search for Kim Novak, a meeting that never directly takes place, although Novak herself is shown at a press conference; and the tensions between Levine and one of his employees, Mort Nathanson, which culminate in Levine firing Nathanson near the film's conclusion. Nevertheless, the film does communicate, if not randomness, at least a looseness of form.

Meet Marlon Brando, in contrast, has a much more unified sense of time and place. The film is entirely set inside and just outside of a New York hotel along Central Park, where Brando is giving a round of press interviews to promote his latest film, *Morituri.* But *Meet Marlon Brando* is more elliptical than *Showman.* It begins in mid-action, with Brando already giving interviews, and the effect is as though the filmmakers have suddenly walked into the room and turned their camera on to catch something that has already begun. And while the film ends with one of the press interviews likewise coming to an end, we are not led to believe the last interview in the film is necessarily the last interview Brando gave that day.

Rossellini's objection to *Showman* as being shapeless and the antithesis of art, while on one level patently ludicrous, has a certain logic to it if we place these early Maysles films in relation to Rossellini's type of realism. I suspect that what disturbed Rossellini about *Showman* was not its form (Rossellini was not an obsessive formalist) but rather the absence of a precisely articulated revelation within the film itself: We are taken to a world, the subjects are filmed, we observe the minutiae of existence within the recognizable language of documentary realism, but there is no epiphany. In *Showman,* a fascination with a phenomenonology of the real remains at ground level, so to speak, and makes no connection with the invisible or spiritual real central to Rossellini. "I find it very odd," he said of the films of Rouch and Maysles, "that one should give such importance to something that is not even an experience" (Aprà 139). Throughout *Showman*, reminders of the end of the neorealism that Rossellini had been so central in pioneering are caught by Maysles's camera. We see the beach at Cannes dotted with posters for such films as Michelangelo Antonioni's *Eclipse* (1962) and *Boccaccio '70* (1962), an omnibus film with sequences directed by Federico Fellini, Luchino Visconti, and Vittorio De Sica, while the film that Loren wins her Oscar for is another directed by De Sica, *Two Women* (1961). Whatever their qualities (some of them substantial, in the case of *Eclipse* and parts of *Boccaccio '70*), all of these films move away from the immediate postwar style of Italian neorealism toward a more glamorous art-cinema and movie-star-dominated Italian filmmaking of the 1960s in which realism (if present at all) is overlaid with elements of chic and glamor (although these elements were never entirely absent from earlier Antonioni and Visconti films).

Much more than either *Showman* or *Meet Marlon Brando, Salesman* is structured in a manner that evokes classical narrative cinema. It begins with a shot of a Bible being opened. The famous and frequently debated final shot of the film is of Paul Brennan standing in the middle of two doorways in a motel room, one door that opens onto the world outside (although we cannot see through it) and another door behind him that opens onto something that we also cannot see. Classical cinema often depends upon a perpetual opening up and closing down of spaces and worlds: The opening of a book as a visual metaphor for the opening of a film is a cliché of Hollywood, particularly if the film is adapted from a well-known literary source. Furthermore, what Brennan is describing as he opens the Bible is a passage from the New Testament describing the birth of Jesus Christ, within Christianity the moment where "it starts here." And the door is one of the most persistent tropes of classical cinema, portentously marking the passage from one space to another. Paul has, by the end of the film, undergone a major crisis in his life, realizing that he is a failure as a Bible salesman, and the placement of the doors in this shot allows them to assume a symbolic function in terms of his (closed or open?) future.

But there is no attempt at character development or metaphoric use of space in *Showman* or *Meet Marlon Brando*. Levine and Brando do not learn anything new about themselves by the end of their films, nor does either film pretend to know anything about these two men other than what occurs directly in front of the camera. This is not true of *Salesman*. With *Salesman,* the Maysles brothers undergo a passage not simply from documentary short film to nonfiction feature but from anecdote to something approaching, within the compact space of ninety-one minutes, epic form with a self-consciously American dimension, simultaneously literary and theatrical.

The controversy over *Salesman*'s obvious links with theater and literature is part of an ongoing debate over cinematic specificity and is unique to neither *Salesman* nor the 1960s. It has manifested itself in numerous ways within the history of film theory and criticism, particularly at moments when theater and literature are taken to be threats to the uniqueness of film form—as in the debates over the future of cinema in relation to the coming of sound. Once the myth of cinematic specificity is dispelled, the ambitions and importance of *Salesman* become clearer. There is, for example, the film's larger relationship to the history of realism. The shift in subject matter alone, from celebrities to "ordinary" people, is part of the move toward a style that is close to nineteenth-century European and American realism and its concern for the reproduction of the factual details of daily life, particularly that of the working class. Few films of the period (documentary or fiction) capture working-class or lower middle-class domestic environments as acutely as *Salesman,* not so much through the décor alone (Maysles has little interest in filming interior spaces apart from the physical presence of their inhabitants) as through the faces, bodies, clothing, gestures, and accents of the salesmen and their clients.

While this attempt to reproduce realistic details is also apparent in the Maysles brothers' earlier films, the earlier films were less obviously tied to traditional narrative and character development and were almost wholly preoccupied with the world of the rich and famous. *Showman* and *Meet Marlon Brando* are shot in a handheld direct-cinema style, but they have an aura of glamor to them, partly due to the presence of movie stars (in addition to Loren and Novak in *Showman,* we see Deborah Kerr, Tony Randall, Burt Lancaster, and Stanley Baker—and footage of Natalie Wood and Warren Beatty was shot but not used in the final cut) but also due to the ways in which they are filmed. Loren is no less stunning and beautiful in *Showman* than she is in any Hollywood film (she's certainly more glamorous here than she is in the strenuously "realistic" *Two Women*). Maysles's camera seems enraptured by her, as in the memorable shot that pans from her foot, encased in a white high-heeled shoe, up her leg and the rest of her body to her face, as she speaks in Italian on the telephone. Documentary cinema here does not strip away fiction filmmaking to expose the "reality" of the human subject but instead uses documentary film language to confirm the experience of fictional filmmaking. When Levine's wife looks directly into Maysles's camera and says of Loren, as the movie star narcissistically sails by, "She's just fabulous, isn't she?" it is difficult to know whether to laugh at this comment or nod our heads in agreement. Perhaps a bit of both.

Likewise, Brando is at his most attractive and appealing in *Meet Marlon Brando*, a film in which he is ostensibly deconstructing his own status as a film star. "Physically and mentally," a flirtatious female reporter tells Brando early in the film, "you're not an ugly American. You're anything *but.*" "When was the last time you saw me nude?" is Brando's response, one which, while self-deprecating, also pushes the content of the exchange even further in the direction of the erotic. Virtually every encounter with a reporter in the film, whether the reporter is male or female, revolves around Brando foregrounding some element of the reporter's physical nature. Most attempts to "seriously" interview Brando are thrown off course as he draws the reporters' attention to their own bodies. "You've got the longest fingernails of anybody I've seen," he tells one male reporter; he asks another if he bites his nails. With women reporters, this fixation on the body has an element of seduction, particularly with the last and most attractive of the reporters, a former Miss USA. As she tries to ask questions, he interrupts by drawing attention to the way her hair hangs down over one eye, or he imitates the way she talks out of the side of her mouth: "It's charming. It's a physical idiosyncrasy but a charming one." As another female reporter attempts to talk to him, Brando bypasses the content of what she is saying and instead responds by telling her, "I'd like to analyze the quality of your voice."

No one is fabulous or seductive or beautiful in *Salesman*. But Maysles's camera, if it does not glamorize its subjects, is compelled to present them in an extremely vivid and physical manner. After viewing *Salesman,* which he largely admired, Arthur Miller felt that the great limitation

Meet Marlon Brando: Brando and the reporter with the longest fingernails that Brando has ever seen. Courtesy of Maysles Films, Inc.

of the Maysles brothers' approach was the relentless present-tenseness of the situations due to the spectator's lack of access to the past lives of the characters: "'You are stopped at the wall of skin'" (qtd. in Canby 10). Miller refers to our psychological distance from the characters, but his choice of words, "wall of skin," also points to the literal flesh on display. *Salesman,* like much of Maysles, is very much a film about the human figure, albeit human figures encased within raincoats and inexpensive suits, or housewives whose heads are weighed down by enormous hair rollers. Landscapes and other exteriors and interior spaces (domestic or otherwise) are important only insofar as they contain and surround the subjects who move through or live within them.

As in much of direct cinema, with its emphasis on filming its subjects speaking in close-up or medium close-up, *Salesman* places particular emphasis on the face and hands as markers of expressivity. The opening shot is not only a close-up of a Bible but of Paul Brennan's hand opening it. The hand itself, as we see in a shot later in the sequence, has long and arthritic fingers that stroke the leather cover of the enormous book. These hands are part of Brennan's gestural repertoire for selling. ("He's going to wear that hand out," says one customer later in the film.) Within the larger context of the film, his gnarled fingers embody Brennan's struggle to sell and contrast with the hands of another salesman, James Baker. Baker appears to be missing a finger but uses this "disability" as a form of gestural dexterity, repeatedly pointing with a raised index and pinky finger at the Bible, as he turns the pages and draws attention to things of interest. Like Brennan, the young and skeletal Baker is often shown to fail at selling, but unlike Brennan he maintains a fundamental optimism, a desire to override the limitations of his hands. (In *The Store,* Frederick Wiseman uses the hand as an extension of selling as well, although for different effects than Maysles. The employees of Neiman-Marcus are trained to have a "positive attitude" toward their job, conveyed through proper facial expression and gesture. The women workers in the film do hand exercises prior to their workday to limber up for this process of utilizing gesture as part of their selling process.)

In their struggle to sell, Paul's hands come to represent his suffering, his agony over his failure. In the last shot of the opening sequence,

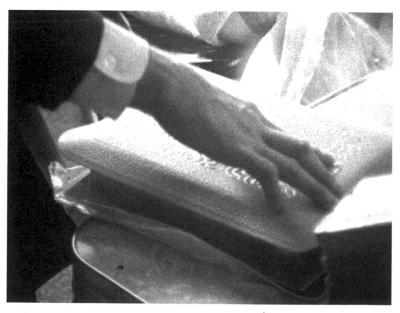

Salesman: The arthritic hands of Paul Brennan.

Zwerin cuts to a close-up of Paul, his face registering his attempt to suppress his misery at another failed sales pitch. But Maysles frames the image in such a way that we can see behind Paul: to his right, hanging on a wall, is a painting of Christ, hands folded on his lap in front of him, a funny but also poignant bit of exhausted Christian symbolism. To sell becomes a way of marshalling the forces of the body, especially the hand that gestures and the foot that allows one to move from place to place, into a space or, sometimes, to just keep moving. "A showman must keep moving," the narrator of *Showman* tells us. In some ways, this is a development out of *Primary*, which repeatedly emphasizes the degree to which Kennedy and Hubert Humphrey keep on the move, the camera time and again filming their feet as they walk. This is especially true of Humphrey who, in contrast to the movie star–like and autograph-signing Kennedy, is linked with the farmers, with soil and the land, and to a form of politics based more directly on one-to-one interactions (like those of a salesman).

| | |

In an interview with the critic Jack Kroll on WCBS-TV to promote *Salesman*, Albert Maysles states his belief that all works of art are essentially autobiographical. In this category, he includes *Salesman*. While in no direct sense does *Salesman* tell the life story of David and Albert Maysles, the origins of the film, the attractions of the subject matter, and, in particular, the decision to foreground Paul Brennan as the protagonist have their basis in the Maysles brothers' backgrounds as Boston Jews who suffered from anti-Semitic violence within their predominantly Irish Catholic neighborhood. If *Salesman* emerges as autobiography, though, it does so in a highly roundabout manner, engaging in a number of displacements and reversals of the life story of the two filmmakers. The strongest element in this regard is the decision to focus on salesmen who are Irish American. Albert has said, "We chose four Irishmen doing the job of what Jews normally do—which is being a salesman—not with the idea of getting even with the Irish or putting down Catholicism, but really with the intention of making a bond between ourselves and these people" (Trojan 27).

Paul Brennan reminds the Maysles brothers of their father, who, whatever Irish anti-Semitism he was a victim of, also identified strongly with the Irish. "My father," states Albert, "was a postal clerk who should have been a musician. Paul Brennan should have been more than a door-to-door salesman. [*Salesman* is] a lot about my sadness for my father" (Chaw). The Irish backgrounds of the salesmen are emphasized by the men themselves as they make their rounds or do their sales pitches, as though this foregrounding of their ethnic roots will create a bond with their clients. (Baker: "Your mother's got an Irish personality. I'm Irish myself. And Scotch. That's a good combination.") Several of the salesmen (especially Brennan) sometimes self-consciously and playfully adopt an Irish brogue, and as Brennan drives through the streets of Miami Beach he sings, "Too-Ra-Loo-Ra-Loo-Ra," an Irish lullaby. Irishness pervades the film, coincidentally and miraculously arising at certain moments, as when an Irish maid in Florida sings an Irish song while making a bed in the motel room that the salesmen are staying in ("Tell me where did you get that Irish brogue / And before you left Killarney / Did your mother kiss the Blarney Stone / And that little touch of brogue you can't deny"). If Brennan is isolated as the film's star and principal protagonist, he stands out not only for his "loser" status in contrast to his successful colleagues but also through his Jewish connection. Maysles has described Brennan as someone who was strongly Jewish-identified (DVD commentary track). And while this is never explicitly treated in the film, *Salesman* spends much of its early section in Boston showing Brennan dashing from one house to another singing "If I Were a Rich Man," the Russian Jewish Tevye's dream of economic success from the Broadway musical *Fiddler on the Roof.*

The salesmen leave Boston early in the film, first for Chicago and then for Florida. But by the end, after Brennan's defeat, it is clear that they are about to return. Levine returns to Boston in *Showman* and attends a dinner in his honor. This dinner is comprised of friends from his childhood (at one point we see one who has become a Catholic priest), but Levine appears completely unimpressed with the (presumably hypocritical) tributes being paid to him. Boston becomes an ambivalent site of nostalgia and bitterness, defining Levine but also shaping his drive to move away. The ultimate value of Boston for Levine is as a space in which to make money and another place to open his films, as when *Showman* films Levine going over grosses with an assistant who refers to "the fine performance in Boston," followed by a dissolve to Levine walking down a Boston street. *Meet Marlon Brando,* while set entirely in New York, concludes its round of interviews with a reporter from a Boston radio station, the former Miss USA. Boston is a touchstone that all three films use as a structuring element, perpetually leaving and returning to the city. The three films each end, literally or figuratively, by returning to Boston.

Beyond providing the strongest Irish/Jewish/Boston connection, *Salesman* presents its own variation on the myth of the American melting pot. The salesmen come across customers from a variety of ethnic backgrounds, and the encounters frequently revolve around the salesmen calling attention to ethnic differences. When James Baker visits Mr. and Mrs. McDonald and Mrs. Wadja, he begins to tell a joke about a Scotchman loaning an Irishman a half dollar. But he is interrupted by Mrs. Wadja, who begins to tell her own joke about a Scotchman, an Irishman, and a Jew who were going to get a beating (although she never finishes the joke itself). Brennan, by contrast, often fails to make these kinds of ethnic connections. He misjudges Mrs. O'Connor as being Irish when, in fact, she is Polish and then hastily attempts to recover from his error. And his bitterness over failing to make any sales to Italians one day in Florida causes him to refuse to have dinner with Martos in an Italian restaurant: "No more fuckin' Italian food for me after these Guineas." As he is driving through Opa Laka, Florida, he is confronted with a neighborhood in which the architecture and street names all have an Oriental (or Orientalist) basis: Sinbad Avenue, Ahmad Street, and so on—a neighborhood he later refers to as "the Muslim district." Lost in this maze-like environment, a world of fabricated ethnicity and racial difference ("like an Arab community without any Arabs" is how Maysles describes it on the DVD commentary track), Brennan tells his colleagues that "all I could think of were fairly tales." And like the protagonist of a fairy tale, Brennan undergoes a figurative descent in which the world around him gradually becomes unreal and threatening.

The film's fascination with Brennan over the other three men is a symptom of its simultaneous attraction to and distance from the possibilities of the melting-pot myth. If the other men ever responded negatively to the ethnicity of their difficult customers in the same way that Brennan does, the film never shows this. (We do see a painfully funny and extended sequence of Baker trying—and failing—to communicate with a disinterested Cuban housewife. But we are never shown his response to this woman after the failed sale.) Brennan at once reconciles the divide between the Jews and the Irish and repeatedly gives voice to and lives out the extreme difficulty of a successful fusion of larger ethnic and racial differences. An orchestral version of "This Land Is Your Land" is heard on Brennan's radio as he drives through the snow to a series of appointments with clients who are not at home. The irony could not be clearer, not only in terms of the bitter counterpoint between Brennan's failure at achieving the American Dream and the optimism of the song, but also in the source of the song and what happens to it here: a patriotic song emerging from the American Left of the 1930s (via its composer, Woody Guthrie) about the desire for unanimity among the vast strata of American society is given a Lawrence Welk–like arrangement as it accompanies a desperate, middle-aged salesman on his failed attempts to sell products to people who have no real use for them.

In *Showman* and *Meet Marlon Brando*, the notion of the melting pot is given over to a form of internationalism. In the case of Levine, this is primarily a question of selling films, since he is a central figure in the producing and marketing of international coproductions: films in which the economic resources of two or more national cinemas are marshaled to lighten the economic burden while broadening the marketing potential of the film. Typically, such productions rely on international casts who are then dubbed into a single language for various markets. These coproductions can effectively erase national differences and language barriers through dubbing, although such a gesture hardly constitutes an elevated form of humanism, since one culture usually overtakes another in these films. In *Two Women*, for example, the French star Jean-Paul Belmondo plays an Italian, and his voice is dubbed in the Italian prints. In the French prints, Belmondo is heard in his own voice and language, while Loren and everyone else is dubbed, speaking French in a film with an Italian setting. Another of Levine's coproductions of this period is Godard's *Contempt* (1963), in which Godard foregrounds the film's status as a coproduction by having his cast speak in their native tongues with a crucial role given to the character of Miss Vanini, a translator who mediates among the characters and their respective languages. "The stakes are high. The market is the world," the voiceover narrator states at the beginning of *Showman*. The concept of the international here is entirely related to global selling through motion pictures. At no point does the film show that Levine is interested in the art of cinema as such. He could be selling vacuum cleaners. It is all product, all connected to the business hustle.

Brando's internationalism plays itself out strongly through language. Brando the "corn husker" (as he describes himself to one reporter) from Nebraska is also multilingual, speaking in English, French, and German. By contrast, Levine cannot even get Sophia Loren's first name quite right, pronouncing it as "Sophie." When a reporter makes a reference to Brando playing a German officer in *Morituri*, Brando jokingly responds in German. While Brando most likely thought that this tactic would surprise and confuse the reporter, the reporter quickly responds, and a playful dialogue in German takes place. In a sequence outside the hotel, Brando meets with French reporters and responds to their questions in French. It is the most serious moment in the film, as he is asked about the value (if any) of an actor's involvement with political issues. He gives a somewhat modified existentialist response about the total responsibility of everyone in terms of politics and commitment to social issues: "We are all responsible." Even here, however, Brando quickly turns the exchange into an erotic encounter. Noticing a beautiful young black woman walking by with a child, he invites her over to discuss the "Negro situation" in the United States. The star-struck woman ("Are you Marlon Brando?") gives a serious response to Brando's question as to whether the government is adequately addressing the problems facing African Americans. (She does not believe that they are.) But an atmosphere of a possible sexual pickup is nevertheless created. Language for Brando becomes another tool for moving through and manipulating worlds and the individuals with whom he comes into contact: everything is selling and seduction.

| | |

During the CBS interview with Jack Kroll, Albert and David Maysles do not speak of Truman Capote and *In Cold Blood* but instead of their admiration for Herman Melville's *Moby Dick* and for Eugene O'Neill, while also situating *Salesman* in relation to the tradition of the American Dream of the rugged individualist. Albert calls these Bible salesmen "Irish poets," while David compares Paul to Hickey from O'Neill's play *The Iceman Cometh.* But what strategies do the Maysles brothers and Zwerin specifically employ that cause this sense of the literary and theatrical to arise? One of the most persistent charges against the film is that the filmmakers deliberately staged or fictionalized certain elements of what they were shooting. The most notorious of these charges is Pauline Kael's. In the midst of a negative review of *Gimme Shelter* in the *New Yorker,* she claims that the Maysles brothers staged much of *Salesman* and that Paul Brennan was not an actual Bible salesman but a professional actor. This review prompted the Maysles to threaten legal action against the *New Yorker.* While Kael's claims of fictionalization are absurd, the charge of deliberate manipulation and staging of events in the film still sometimes arises.

Stella Bruzzi, for example, has referred to elements in the film that complicate the notion that *Salesman* simply presents the viewer with "undirected situations." She refers to sequences in which the salesmen or potential customers enter certain spaces to find the camera already running when they arrive. No one registers surprise at this or at the sight of the Maysles brothers themselves, suggesting that the sequences were set up (71). Even more recently, Haskell Wexler, who at one point operated a second camera on the film, has claimed that he convinced David Maysles to set up a scene with one of the salesmen in a hotel room, coaching the salesman to call his wife and tell her that he was in Las Vegas (Cunningham 88). But the sequence Wexler refers to is not in the finished film. Why it was eliminated is unclear, but one possibility is that the filmmakers had second thoughts about using this kind of manipulated material. As for the suspect status of some of the moments Bruzzi isolates, the salesmen most likely did not act surprised to see a camera in their hotel room because the Maysles brothers were regularly in those rooms, filming. And the sequence in Boston (referred to by Bruzzi) in which Mrs. Wadja enters the home of her friends, the McDonalds, to find the Maysles brothers there filming clearly has two cuts at the moment of her arrival, suggesting that some of her surprise at seeing them was eliminated in the editing room. (Interestingly, in watching this sequence again for the *Salesman* DVD, Maysles expresses surprise at the woman's lack of self-consciousness at having a camera in the room. He does not seem to notice the cuts in his own film.) Moreover, the camera does not follow Mr. McDonald around the corner from the kitchen to the unseen door through which Mrs. Wadja enters. It is entirely possible that he quickly briefed her on the situation before she came around the corner. As she makes her entrance into the kitchen, Mr. McDonald can be heard making a reference to "the candid camera." In refuting (or at least complicating) these claims about sequences in the film being staged, I am not suggesting that what we have is a pure, unadulterated work of observation. Instead, the strong sense of structure as well as the novelistic, theatrical, and psychological density of the film emerges in ways other than the Maysles brothers "cheating" by covertly behaving like traditional *metteurs en scène*.

The most obvious element of imposed structure and meaning in the film occurs through the editing. But *Salesman* is scarcely the first Maysles film to have an editing style that is forceful and in which one strongly feels the weight of the individual cuts. *Showman* (primarily edited by Daniel Williams) does anything but unfold in a fluid manner: The cuts are often jarring, and the film relies heavily on sound editing as well as manipulations within the soundtrack to cover up obvious limitations that arise through the assemblage of the images. But this "rawness" is also part of the film's overall attempted looseness of form and spontaneity. *Meet Marlon Brando*, edited by Zwerin, is even more extreme. The film disregards causality by returning to footage of one reporter several times over the course of the film. We develop no strong awareness that Brando spoke to any of the other individual reporters in the order in which the film presents them. Each encounter is cut in a fragmented manner, flagrantly displaying how manipulated the footage was in the editing room.

By contrast, *Salesman* is more polished and professional, more linear in its editing style but also more rhetorical. The two clearest instances of this rhetorical impulse are the frequently criticized sequence of Brennan looking out the window of a train, crosscut with a Chicago sales meeting he will be attending; and the final sequence that culminates with a desolate and defeated Brennan looking out of the door of his hotel room. Manipulation is evident in the later sequence through the "reaction" shots of the other salesmen as they listen to Paul while he affects an Irish brogue and speaks of "hard-working people" and their pensions. Some of these reaction shots look as though they were taken from other sequences and pasted in to give Brennan an audience. (One of the salesmen, Charles McDevitt, wears two different ties in two different shots.)

The sequence on the train is another matter. There is crosscutting from Brennan on the train to other salesmen in Chicago as these men stand up and declare their commitment to the goals of the Midwestern Bible Company. The voice of the supervisor in Chicago is used on the soundtrack over shots of Brennan on the train, declaring, "If a man is not a success, he's nothing." By crosscutting from the men who are (or desperately want to be) successful to Brennan looking pensive on the train, the film undercuts the forced dynamism and ambition of the men in Chicago: men like Paul Brennan, the editing implies, are the victims of this oppressive drive toward economic success. But the crosscutting has another function: in this manner, the film moves beyond a basic level of documentary observation and respect for the integrity of the moment being filmed and presumes to know what Paul is thinking. As he looks out the window, the voiceover and crosscutting imply that Paul is anticipating the Chicago meeting, that he is seeing and hearing it before it has even happened, that he has been through meetings like this on other occasions, and he has been unable to put their empty rhetoric into successful action.

While Albert Maysles quickly came to dislike the manipulation at work in this sequence, the crosscutting essentially puts into montage form an approach that is present throughout the film's shooting style: the sense of an extreme intimacy with these subjects (Kolker 184).[6] Because of this intimacy, the filmmakers presume knowledge of the men's thoughts and emotions. In this manner, they approach their subjects like fictional characters in a fictional scenario. We do not simply observe Brennan on the train but come to understand how he privately thinks and feels. He does not put his frustration and disappointment into words, nor does he gesture, but simply looks out the window. There is no one present with him except for the camera. To this camera he is either oblivious (lost in thought) or is soulfully performing, assuming his tragic role that the Kuleshov-like editing insists on. As Brennan looks out, there is even a quick cut to a view outside of a train window. Whether this was shot at the time or separately is unclear, but within this context it serves as Brennan's point-of-view shot.

There are other, equally skilled methods at work in the film that create an atmosphere of fictionalization or spectacle, such as the extended credit sequence introducing the four salesmen in which we get a brief introductory scene showing each of the men on their sales rounds. Every segment ends with a shot of the salesman alone, his first and last names printed in large type and, underneath these names in smaller type, his nickname: Paul Brennan, "The Badger"; Charles McDevitt, "The Gipper"; James Baker, "The Rabbit"; and Raymond Martos, "The Bull." The decision to open the film in this manner is undoubtedly an economical way to clearly identify each of the four salesmen.[7] But this identification also makes them seem larger than life, like fictional characters within a compelling narrative. The opening in some ways anticipates the opening of *Mean Streets* (dir. Martin Scorsese, 1973), in which each of the gangsters likewise receives a brief, individual sequence establishing their personalities, with the end of each sequence punctuated by the name of the character onscreen. This fictionlike atmosphere in the opening of *Salesman* culminates with the hyperbolic display of the film's title, emerging from the left rear of the frame, getting progressively larger until it fills the screen, a form of graphic presentation that evokes credit sequences from 1950s Hollywood melodramas like *The Bad and the Beautiful* (dir. Vincente Minnelli, 1952) and *Executive Suite* (dir. Robert Wise, 1954).

Furthermore, this style of presentation has a slightly heightened quality to it, in which the identification of the salesmen via their full names with their nicknames in quotation marks suggests actors playing roles: Paul Brennan "as" the Badger. This is not a mere flourish on the part of the filmmakers, since performers are fundamentally what the salesmen become in order to sell their Bibles. (In *Gimme Shelter,* the Rolling Stones are individually introduced in a similar manner.) The film's placement of Paul as the first of the salesmen turns out to be significant in terms of the film's overall structure, since he emerges as *Salesman*'s unofficial "star," here receiving top billing. In this regard, the shift in Maysles's early work from focusing on celebrities and performers to people from "real life" does not involve a forsaking of his earlier concern with the performative.

Much of the film occurs in spaces that, while largely domestic, effectively become spaces in which the subjects must put on a show. Each salesman enters the home of a potential customer and then turns that domestic space into a theatrical one, the success of the sales pitch determined by how well the salesman "performs." When they are not "onstage"—in their motel rooms or in coffee shops conversing with one another—they often seem uncomfortable and aware of the camera. In the motel rooms, the men furtively look at and then away from the camera, as though they are uncertain as to how to behave "naturally." Their silence in the sequence as they sit in the coffee shop, a sequence perhaps placed there to demonstrate the poignancy of these exhausted men who have little to say to one another, may also be read through a theatrical framework: The men say little to one another because, like performers, they are saving their energy for when they go onstage. The film draws attention to the theatricality of their sales pitches early in the film, during an extended sequence in Florida in which Kennie, the salesmen's supervisor, puts them through what is essentially a rehearsal. Kennie plays the role of the salesman, while Baker and McDevitt play the roles of husband and brother-in-law. The three men engage in a type of improvisational theater, working within a loose dramatic situation as Baker and McDevitt imagine and then play out various possibilities for clients to resist a sale, and the supervisor devises ways to overcome this resistance.

To sell something in this film is to act, to be a performer—one who casts a spell over his audience. The film could have been called *Showman* as much as *Salesman*. At the beginning of *Showman*, the voiceover narrator says of Levine, "He's out to sell you. And up to now, you've been buying." If Levine the showman is a success on an international scale through selling, the protagonists of *Salesman* represent the obverse: the Jewish Levine of Boston is figuratively split into four Irish Bible salesmen from the same city, three of them successful (within a limited economic and social sphere), and one of them memorably unsuccessful. The notion of the salesman as a performer ties in to larger American traditions of selling, not simply the door-to-door salesman but other types of traveling businessmen for whom the act of turning a fast buck involves an overt form of performance: carnival barkers, medicine men, auctioneers, preachers, politicians, card sharks, professional gamblers, and carpetbaggers (the last of these is the title of one of Levine's most successful films of the 1960s). Command of language is central to the act of selling: having a vocabulary of enormous breadth, negotiating one's way in a sales pitch through a combination of prepared text and improvisation, and being able to speak quickly and efficiently—all to seduce the listener, to render them so overwhelmed that they may not be able to process the content of what they are hearing. American literature, theater, and cinema are filled with examples of this character type. (If there is a Melville connection to *Salesman* it is not so much *Moby Dick* as *The Confidence Man*, in which the title character's profession involves numerous disguises as he hawks his phony medicine to the naïve and vulnerable over whom he exerts an almost hypnotic power.)

The salesmen of the Maysles film are never able to achieve this transformation of self through selling. Even the most successful of them (McDevitt and Martos) are devoid of magic or mesmerizing charms. In *Salesman*, it is not selling that allows one to become a successful performer. McDevitt, Martos, and, to a lesser extent, Baker are not confidence men but lower middle-class variations on the postwar idea of the organization man. To be good at selling in this film involves a certain erasure of personality, as one becomes a figure who is too closely tied to the ideology of the corporation. McDevitt and Martos are shown to have the greatest success, but they are also the two least quotable, least memorable of the salesmen. The opening of *Showman* presents a variation on this idea in which the men who surround Levine look surprisingly similar in face, hair, eyeglasses, and style of dress, almost indistinguishable from one another—all watered-down versions of Levine.

In an ironic reversal typical of *Salesman*'s basic impulses, the salesman who is the biggest failure is also the film's greatest performer, its "Irish poet," and the one to whom Maysles's camera is most strongly drawn. While the film is consistent with direct cinema's stated prohibition against talking-heads interviews, *Salesman* allots a fair amount of time to sequences in which Brennan does not so much talk to the camera in an interview format as perform directly for it. Brennan drives around Boston, Miami Beach, or Opa Laka, commenting on the scenery around him, singing songs, or discussing the personalities of the other salesmen. Even though he addresses the camera (and implicitly the Maysles brothers themselves), the effect is not of an interview. These sequences become monologues for Brennan, showcasing his skill at improvisation and performance. This Irish poet is also, as the film represents him, an Irish vaudevillian, able to sing songs, tell jokes, and adjust his monologues in relation to evolving circumstances.

Hence the Maysles brothers' insistence on connecting him to Hickey in *The Iceman Cometh* rather than the more obvious link of Willy Loman in Arthur Miller's *Death of a Salesman*. Loman is already defeated in

Miller's play, borderline suicidal. Death and exhaustion hover around Hickey as well, but, like Brennan, he also adopts a manic optimism as a mask. And like Hickey, an element of showbiz hovers around much of what Brennan does. In addition to singing "If I Were a Rich Man" during his Boston drives, Brennan cites John Ford's *The Informer* (1935), referring to Victor McLaglen's character of Gypo Nolan while adopting an Irish brogue and engaging in word play ("I'm infarmin' you that I'm here"). The lullaby he sings in Miami Beach is not a pure Irish folk song but one with show-business origins, originally performed in a 1914 Broadway musical called *Shameen Dhu* and widely popularized in 1944 by Bing Crosby in *Going My Way,* in which Crosby plays an Irish American Catholic priest.

In another instance of editing sleight-of-hand, there is a sequence in Florida in which Brennan drives his car and explains the origins of the nicknames of his fellow salesmen. As he begins describing the first of them, he nods his head to the right and there is a cut to McDevitt, as though McDevitt is in the car with him. But it a false eyeline match, since clearly neither McDevitt nor the other men, who are also discussed immediately after, are there with Brennan. The film artificially places the men in the car while just as clearly demonstrating the impossibility of these spatial links: both Brennan and McDevitt are shown in the driver's seat, for example. But the cutting has a more important logic. By following Brennan's train of thought in describing the men and their nicknames, the insertion of the shots of these other men as Brennan talks gives him the power of a master of ceremonies, the type of show-business figure who works within a predetermined format of the vaudeville presentation while improvising in relation to changing circumstances and making direct contact with the audience.

Brennan seems comparatively liberated in these driving sequences, no longer confined to domestic spaces in which he must sell and away from the stultifying command of language evidenced by a very different person in the film, Melbourne I. Feltman, the designer and theological consultant of the Mid-American Bible Company who delivers the film's memorable speech in Chicago to all of his salesmen. It is a deadly serious and pompous sermon, a conflation of selling and spirituality in which he instructs his salesmen to "hold your heads very high" and concludes with the words, "God grant you an abundant harvest. Thank you." (Coincidentally, Feltman looks a bit like Joseph E. Levine, although is unclear whether Feltman is Jewish. If the film had made this explicit, the Irish/Jewish connection would have been even stronger and more ironic.) The speech, delivered in a crowded and smoke-filled room with low ceilings, sounds agonizingly scripted and rehearsed and stands in marked contrast to the relative freedom Brennan enjoys in his car as he talks into the camera, neither forced to listen to the likes of Feltman nor forced to turn his performative nature into a sales pitch, into work. Here in the car, he evidences little more than a sheer love of playing to the camera.

Unlike Paul, though, Brando shows an awareness of the contradictions and complexities of this attempt to transform an environment into a space of performance. "We are all actors," Brando tells a reporter. "You conduct yourself differently here than if you were at a bar with some of your friends," he says. "One is able to adjust oneself to a situation." At one point, he even indirectly gives voice to one of the common objections to direct cinema's investment in the camera's capacity to elicit spontaneous and natural behavior from its subjects when he argues that "people change subconsciously when they're on camera." The voiceover narration at the beginning of the film isolates Brando's specialness: "The reporters asked many predictable questions. Mr. Brando gives few predictable answers. Marlon Brando has always reserved the right to think for himself, to answer for himself, and, if necessary, to go against the grain." Nevertheless, Brando's lucidity and iconoclastic nature is no guarantee of breaking out of the system of selling. He is repeatedly positioned by the film as someone who uses his skills as an actor (including his command of language) while also showing that he is still trapped within (and *understands* that he is trapped within) the cycle of selling and artifice.

In this regard, his relationship with the press throughout this film is different from the famous sequence in *Don't Look Back* (dir. D. A. Pennebaker, 1967) in which Bob Dylan interrogates a reporter from *Time* magazine. Dylan operates from a position of a total belief in his own ethical superiority over the reporter in a way that Brando (while ultimately perhaps no less hostile to the press than Dylan) avoids, at least overtly. The film shows Brando to be chronically incapable of getting any member of the press to seriously listen to his discourses on falseness and authenticity since, if they did listen and respond, they would be forced to question their relationship with Brando at this moment. "There's a merchandising aspect of the press that's not fully recognized," he notes. But it also seems clear that Brando uses his much-vaunted authenticity and talent in going "against the grain" as a subtle form of power over others. (By contrast, Welles's power over his audience in *Orson Welles in Spain* is a fait accompli, as he narrates his idea for his new film to a spellbound group of people as Maysles's camera circles around them, the movement reinforcing the sense of a closed, mesmerized world under Welles's control.) Brando draws attention to the artifice and mannerisms of the reporters but in ways that also embarrass or unnerve some of them, particularly the women. Brando the actor calls attention to the acting of those who are nonprofessional actors and to their "performance of self in everyday life," to borrow Erving Goffman's well-known phrase. At the same time, Brando remains an actor, putting on a show and rewriting the text of this theatrical piece he's performing, making him at once real and fully performative.

| | |

In publicizing *Salesman,* David and Albert Maysles discussed their own backgrounds as door-to-door salesmen prior to becoming filmmakers: Albert had sold vacuum cleaners and encyclopedias, and David had sold Avon products. But the connection between the Maysles brothers and the salesmen has broader and more allegorical implications. Albert Maysles told Kroll: "We all live in borderline areas in our own morals, where ideals converge with questions. . . . Well, we have to make money for our family, and every one of us making a dollar is willing, at some point, to make a compromise." This statement arose in relation to a discussion of a sequence in *Salesman* in which Brennan lies to a woman who is no longer interested in purchasing a Bible. Through his lies, Brennan manipulates her into buying something she obviously cannot afford. (We have already seen in a previous sequence that she and her husband don't even have a checking account and that they and their children live from paycheck to paycheck.) Brennan's behavior is clearly unethical, but Maysles cautions against becoming overly judgmental. His partial defense of Brennan suggests that the connection between Brennan (and, to a lesser extent, the other salesmen) and the Maysles brothers runs deeper than regional and ethnic contexts. As the Maysles brothers surely realized, being a documentary filmmaker (whatever ethical intentions one might possess) does not preclude one from also being a showman and a salesman.

Since 1963, the Maysles brothers have done television commercials as well as promotional shorts for major corporations. In this way, they have always maintained, the money from the commercial work can be put into more personal projects. The close ties between not only fiction and documentary but also between advertising and art have become virtual givens in the modern age. In the cinema alone, "art" filmmakers from Antonioni to Godard, whom one might fantasize as being utterly removed from the ugly world of commerce, have made television commercials. And the Maysles brothers are not alone within the world of documentary in doing so much advertising: Errol Morris, for example, has made commercials an unapologetic cornerstone to his work. One can hardly blame Maysles Films for relying on these commercials, especially given the vagaries of funding for documentary projects.[8]

While I shall leave extended analysis of these advertising films to others, one element is worth singling out: While often shot with 35mm cameras and equipment and on a production scale often absent from or denied to the Maysles brothers when making their own personal projects, these commercials are not anonymous hack work but often recognizable as Maysles films. Frequently they appropriate direct-cinema form, using nonprofessionals (people on the street, employees of a corporation, and so on) to discuss the product being sold (in one commercial from the 1980s, people on the street are invited to "take the Pepsi challenge") or to sell the image of the company. The Maysles commercials are even thematically relevant to their personal projects. Many of them deal in condensed form with topics of family and work, collaboration and team-work, aging and aesthetics. If *Salesman* is, in the words of Albert Maysles, a film that "questions the very core of capitalism, a belief in the individual" (DVD commentary track), their commercial and corporate work is an attempt to, in the words of David Maysles, "'humanize the corporation. To show that management is human and they care'" (qtd. in Loevy 18). Without being overly moralistic about the economic need of the Maysles brothers to continue producing work, the implications of David's comment are slightly ominous, as though the social and political values of direct cinema, and of a film like *Salesman,* are being hijacked by the corporate world. What possible long-term value is there in humanizing the corporation, except to even further strengthen the power of that corporation, which can now comfort itself on the myth of its own humanity? The limitations of the version of liberal humanism we find in Maysles, its lack of interest in examining the precise workings of institutions so that the films can focus on the human, are no clearer than in this advertising work in which the corporation is given a human face and all employees are shown to be happy. Effectively and symbolically, there is no corporation in these commercials—just a lot of contented "real" people making, selling, and buying products. Direct cinema becomes another effective advertising style, one that can happily coexist with a range of other styles for selling products.

At the same time, there is something extremely touching about a number of these commercials. Their highly selective use of the codes of realism and documentary to humanize the corporate world creates a strange universe of its own, a utopia of the present in which corporations treat their workers with the utmost respect and economic fairness while their products fulfill real needs for consumers. In some of these spots, the product is barely shown at all (sometimes appearing as a "tag" at the end), while the spot instead sells the value of human connections.

In terms of sheer volume, the commercial work of the Maysles brothers far exceeds their personal projects. In fact, after *Grey Gardens,* neither Albert Maysles alone nor Maysles Films has released a single film that was not commissioned. But as one examines their body of work and the circumstances surrounding its production, the line between the commercial and the personal is not always clear, even apart from their advertising work. Some of their best and most representative films, including *What's Happening, Meet Marlon Brando,* and *Gimme Shelter,* originated as assignments. (Even *Orson Welles in Spain* is essentially a "commercial" for Welles, who asked the Maysles brothers to make the film for him as an attempt to raise funds for *The Other Side of the Wind.*) In looking at Maysles's later work, one might be tempted to assume that the classical-music films and videos were commercial assignments, while the socially oriented films *Abortion: Desperate Choices, Letting Go: A Hospice Journey,* and *Lalee's Kin: The Legacy of Cotton* were personal. But in fact they were all assignments. The way that Maysles operates has certain analogies with the way that a studio contract director in Hollywood might have worked in the 1930s, 1940s, or 1950s, sometimes taking on projects that deeply concern him but otherwise filming on assignment and then attempting to transform the project into something personal.

In contrast to Paul Brennan, then, the Maysles brothers are extremely *good* at selling. Ironically, though, it is not their commercials or their work for Sony that needs to be aggressively sold: the markets for this work are already in place. Instead, it is films such as *Salesman* and *Grey Gardens* that must be taken door-to-door, as it were—sold to distributors and audiences who may be as skeptical of viewing them as the potential buyers for $49.95 Bibles. And here the Maysles were aggressive but in some ways unsuccessful; neither *Salesman* nor *Grey Gardens* made money, while much of their early work had only limited distribution.

The foregrounding of Paul Brennan and the comparative marginalizing of the more successful Bible salesmen is bound up with a network of ambivalent attitudes. The film sympathizes with Brennan, since this bonding allows the Maysles brothers to heal the wounds of the Irish/Jewish divide of their adolescence. But they foreground and embrace Brennan because he is a failure, rendered powerless by the film in terms of everything but an exhausted Irish showbiz charisma. He is an Irish double of the filmmakers' postal-clerk father (or so they have maintained) and a negative image of the act of selling in general. Brennan's failure gives the film its center and its structural counterpoint to the three successful men, while his performative qualities make him a natural star. Moreover, his failure allows the film to raise the possibility that capitalism and the culture of selling are destructive of the needs of the individual. (In this regard, it is the ideological flip side to the contented world of the Maysles commercials.) Typical of the "openness" of Maysles, though, *Salesman* does not relentlessly insist on this point, particularly since the other salesmen are successful and do not experience the self-doubt or express the melancholia that Paul so often does. Still, the overall tone of the film—its unsettling mixture of the comic and the melancholic, combined with its black-and-white visual style, at once beautiful and austere—creates a world that seems to be fading to neither black nor white but to perpetual grayness. ("Life is gray, neutral tints," is a statement from *Chronicle of a Summer,* "not black and white.")

In this film that ostensibly attacks the fundamental core of capitalism, the Maysles brothers choose to focus not on a multimillion-dollar corporation at the height of its powers but instead on a declining profession, the traveling salesman. While the film's focus on decline and melancholia might mask the very real, present-tense destructive elements of capitalism, there is another possible reading: its fascination with decline (a fascination that will become stronger in later Maysles films) has in it an allegorical impulse in which these salesmen and their customers epitomize a structure of desperate buying and selling endemic to capitalism in general, a structure that is finally connected to death. David's insistence on *The Iceman Cometh* rather than *Death of a Salesman* as a crucial point of reference for the film is again significant. O'Neill dramatizes a world dominated not simply by failure and destructive memory (as in Miller's play) but by ruin and dirt—a multiethnic, multiracial world of left-wing political disappointment in which language is marked by vernacular and dialect. *Salesman*'s visual style, its depiction of the almost interchangeably desolate environments of Massachusetts, Chicago, and Florida, keeps the film poised in some ambiguous realm of time and space, simultaneously evoking a past that is slowly fading away, a drab present tense, and a future that looks as dehumanizing as the black-and-white world of Godard's *Alphaville* (1965).

In speaking of the influence of Capote and *In Cold Blood* on the Maysles brothers, Zwerin cites Capote's gift for getting close to his subjects so that they open up to him as something that made a strong impact on them (*Salesman*, DVD commentary track). But the ways in which they put this influence to use are fundamentally different from Capote. Capote achieved an intimacy with Dick and Perry to get them to discuss their pasts more than their present: their backgrounds and childhood, the history of their friendship, and especially the night of the murder of the Cuttler family. This raw material (along with Capote's interviews with others) was transformed into a series of extended first-person narratives (essentially monologues) building up to the night of the murder.

In *Salesman*, the Maysles brothers largely work in the present tense, filming activities as they occur rather than relying on oral testimony of past events. The intimacy that they are after in *Salesman* has more to do with getting non-show-business personalities to relax in front of the camera, to "be themselves" for the film to accurately capture the daily lives of these men and their customers. Two activities of selling must take place for this film to exist: those that take place in front of the camera, in which it is irrelevant whether a sale occurs or not, provided a sequence of interest transpires; and the others we don't see, either because they were never filmed or because they were eliminated in the editing room. The Maysles brothers must "sell" their own presence as filmmakers to the customers so that they can walk inside the doors of these homes along with the Bible salesmen. In either case, it is especially ironic and symptomatic of the strategies of this film that the Maysles brothers chose to largely erase themselves physically from *Salesman*—the film to which, in terms of subject matter, they are the closest.

Salesman offers the viewer little information about the personal lives of its protagonists. Much of the material about the families of the salesmen was eliminated. At one moment in the film, when Paul briefly discusses his childhood, happily growing up in a cold-water flat ("I never laughed so much in my life"), the effect is startling since the salesmen otherwise talk so little about their past. By largely stripping the men of their relationship to their own families and of any life outside of selling, the film allows them to seem even more like outsiders than they already do as they step into these homes. They become shadowy, parasitic, and slightly undefined figures—likeable vampires in inexpensive business suits.

To sell, to perform in this film, the salesmen must first get inside the door of a home. In this regard, selling here is distinct from selling in *Showman* and *Meet Marlon Brando*; in these earlier films, selling is public and social. In *Salesman,* the selling takes place entirely in domestic spaces. Doors become one of the film's primary motifs—the salesmen must pass through a door as one passes through a magic portal, the space that marks the passage from the outside world to the inside. Hence their enormous frustration when they are kept on the other side of a door by uninterested customers. Paul's frustrations at being a salesman often revolve around these doors through which he cannot pass.

But the film does not simply contrast the salesmen with the families they visit. When the men cross the threshold from the outside world to the inside, they enter into spaces that are dominated by women. The only instance we see in the entire film of the salesmen confronting male customers is a hypothetical one: the rehearsal. Otherwise, the sales are directed either to women alone or to male/female couples and families in which the sales pitch is more strongly directed toward the wife than the husband. This undoubtedly has its basis in historical reality, as traveling

Salesman: Paul Brennan attempts to get to the other side of the door.

salesmen typically went door to door during the daytime and preyed on housewives while they were alone. But the intensification of the opposition between male and female in *Salesman* allows for the basic Maysles structure of the clash between two worlds to take place—male/female, outdoors/indoors, selling/buying—with the door marking the passage between these worlds. In one sequence, the camera tilts down to show two of the salesmen wiping their feet on a welcome mat just prior to passing through the door, the shot giving this entrance the feeling of a portentous ritual. The men enter what are, effectively, female spaces, so the passage from the outside to the inside reflects an element of transgression.

However, the film's emphasis on failure mutes the degree to which the salesmen's movement into these domestic spaces could be seen as a form of male aggression. Even those who succeed in selling are presented as somewhat overwhelmed by the domestic worlds into which they enter. In one of the film's strongest and funniest sequences, Martos makes a successful sale to a woman whose hair is unapologetically in curlers for the encounter. But the woman's husband is also home, indifferent to the sales exchange. He indirectly expresses what one can only take to be his aggression toward Martos by loudly playing a record while Martos and the wife talk: a dreadful orchestral version of the Beatles song "Yesterday" on a defective turntable that distorts the playback.

The film's fascination with failure creates a strange type of suspense that builds as the film unfolds. The spectator becomes increasingly uncertain as to whom to root for in these encounters: the salesmen who fail, or the customers who resist buying something they do not want. Our response to each of these encounters hinges on an outcome about which we are ambivalent· we do not want these men to fail, but we do not want these customers to buy something they cannot afford.

Salesman is the first Maysles film to extensively build upon this notion of not only the subjects of the film but also of the camera itself as going somewhere it ordinarily does not go, filming something ordinarily not seen. In spite of Albert Maysles's persistent declarations that he films his subjects "with love," the responses to his films over the years suggest that this love may also be driven by its need to transgress, to uncover. The Maysles brothers' love for their subjects is marked by a network of complicating factors that push their films away from unmediated adoration toward more ambivalent associations and obsessions that implicate their own filmmaking practice. This element becomes even stronger in their later work.

"It's a Funny Place, This America": *What's Happening: The Beatles in the USA* and *Gimme Shelter*

> You should take his picture. He is a good-looking man.
> —*Horowitz Plays Mozart*

Although Maysles's cinema is often structured upon a confrontation between worlds, it is equally drawn to representing large social collectives, since collectives allow for the possibility of a resolution to the problems posed by this initial confrontation. One can see this realized in a particularly complex manner in two films that are at once closely linked and markedly different from one another, *What's Happening: The Beatles in the USA* and *Gimme Shelter.* Both films involve British rock bands, respectively the Beatles and the Rolling Stones, coming to America and facing a new world that turns out to be stranger and, in the case of *Gimme Shelter*, more chaotic and violent than they had imagined.

Gimme Shelter's reputation, today and at the time of its release, is that it is the film that symbolically announced the end of the dream of 1960s youth culture. (Although the extensive coverage of the concert in *Rolling Stone* magazine in January 1970, several months before the release of the film, had already begun to color the ways in which the event was interpreted.) *Gimme Shelter* is often contrasted with Michael Wadleigh's grandiose, epic-length *Woodstock* (1970), a widescreen/split-screen celebration of 1960s youth culture and rock music. *Gimme Shelter* reveals the decadent underside of the culture *Woodstock* celebrates, culminating with the stabbing death of a concertgoer, Meredith Hunter, at Altamont Speedway near San Francisco. The stabbing was done by Marty Passaro, a member of the Hell's Angels motorcycle group enlisted by the Rolling Stones as bodyguards for the event. Unfortunately, *Rolling Stone*'s largely negative coverage of the filming of *Gimme Shelter* significantly misrepresented the work of the Maysles brothers and their collaborators. The magazine claimed that hasty planning for the event and the desire on the part of the Rolling Stones and the Maysles brothers to outdo Woodstock in scale and spectacle had led to the violence. According to the magazine, the concert was essentially created to be filmed. While these claims have since been disputed, *Rolling Stone*'s coverage undoubtedly colored some of the contemporary reviews of the film, most famously the extremely negative notices from Vincent Canby in the *New York Times* and Pauline Kael in the *New Yorker*. Even critics favorably disposed toward the film often read it in moralistic terms. For example, Michael Sragow's long, sympathetic essay refers to *Gimme Shelter* as a "cautionary tale for the counterculture."

What's Happening, in contrast, seems to optimistically usher in the sixties, or at least a version of that decade that would posit the period after 1963 as officially marking its mythical beginning. Compared to *Gimme Shelter*, *What's Happening* is innocent in a number of ways. We see no drug taking, no sex, no violence—just an atmosphere of adolescent vitality and energy, created by the Beatles themselves and by their legions of fans, mainly teenage girls. It is also a smaller film in every way than *Gimme Shelter*, less obviously ambitious, much lighter in tone and simpler in its production means, all of the footage apparently shot by David and Albert Maysles alone. *Gimme Shelter* (like a number of other rock documentary/concert films of this period, including *Woodstock*) is a comparative superproduction, relying on a large camera crew (George Lucas and Walter Murch among them) in which Albert Maysles's camera becomes one of many, particularly in the filming of the Altamont concert. Even Zwerin's job as editor was shared by a large group, in contrast to her earlier work with the Maysles brothers, turning the film into, as Zwerin put it, "a collaboration on a grand scale" (DVD commentary track).

Both films began as commercial assignments. *What's Happening* came about when Granada Television in England asked the Maysles brothers (after Richard Leacock had turned it down) to film the Beatles' arrival in New York City for a program to be broadcast in England. *Gimme Shelter* was intended to be a more or less straightforward filming of a Rolling Stones tour of the United States that would end with a free concert in San Francisco. The Rolling Stones probably imagined something along the lines of D. A. Pennebaker's 1968 concert film *Monterey Pop* (on which Albert Maysles served as a cameraman). While loosely following the crisis form of early direct cinema, the murder at Altamont transformed *Gimme Shelter* into something else: a kind of documentary murder thriller with a detective story–like framing device involving the band members Charlie Watts and Mick Jagger viewing assembled footage and commenting on it as part of the film's search for an answer as to how such a murder could have taken place. In a far less anguished manner, *What's Happening* was likewise transformed from an assignment into one of the Maysles brothers' great films, a thrilling example of their pre-*Salesman* approach in which the revelation of personality takes precedence over any attempt to create a fictional structure and tone out of raw documentary material. Even so, *What's Happening* (more than *Showman*) anticipates elements of later Maysles films.

In writing about *What's Happening*, however, a historical problem presents itself: since 1964, there have been at least five different versions of the film. The first was a forty-minute version that aired on Granada Television in England on February 12 and February 13, 1964, entitled *Yeah, Yeah, Yeah! The Beatles in New York,* an "instant documentary" quickly edited before the American tour had even finished. This was followed by a fifty-minute version broadcast by CBS on November 13,

1964, *The Beatles in America,* hosted by Carol Burnett (as part of a short-lived television series called *The Entertainers*), that included footage from the Washington and Miami sections of the tour as well as the Beatles' return to England, none of which appeared in the Granada version. There is a cut that the Maysles brothers prepared, running for about seventy-four minutes, that was screened occasionally in the mid-1960s as *What's Happening: The Beatles in the USA.* There is a 1991 theatrical reissue, financed by the Apple corporation after it purchased the rights to the film from the Maysles brothers, *The Beatles: The First U.S. Visit,* running for fifty-two minutes; and there is a DVD version of *The First U.S. Visit,* running for eighty-one minutes.

I will refer to the version that Albert Maysles himself prefers, the seventy-four-minute version, which is, among other things, the first feature made by the Maysles brothers, albeit a feature in a somewhat "underground" manner, given its restricted exhibition history. My reasons for emphasizing this version over the others are twofold: it is far and away the best of the versions I have seen, and Maysles is correct in preferring it. Moreover, the Maysles cut is of historical significance, as certain spectators at the time of the film's early screenings felt that it was part of an important new development in cinema. Of *What's Happening,* Jones Mekas wrote in 1964: "You have to see the Maysles film to realize what really good photography is, or what cinema is, or what really the Beatles are" (158). With a similar fervor during this period, Susan Sontag wrote that "there is more vitality and art in the Maysles brothers' film on the Beatles in America, *What's Happening,* than in all American story films made this year" (159).

Such claims cannot be made for the later versions. Two Maysles collaborators, Susan Froemke and Kathy Dougherty, worked in producing and editing capacities with Apple on *The First U.S. Visit*—although, as Maysles indicates in my interview with him in this book, Froemke and Dougherty were compelled to work within strict limitations set down by Apple. While this version is not without interest, as it does include some bits and pieces of Maysles footage not shown in the original cut (and the DVD version also contains some interesting outtakes), it is not only markedly inferior to the first *What's Happening,* it is another type of product entirely. Much of Maysles's original footage was either eliminated or significantly recut, mainly to allow for the inclusion of some long excerpts from the Beatles' *Ed Sullivan Show* appearances. For a Beatles fan, these clips are probably a treat—although the *Ed Sullivan* material is available elsewhere. But if one is interested in the original film, these excerpts are a persistent intrusion, completely interrupting the structure, visual style, and atmosphere built up in the surrounding Maysles footage.

Today, screenings of *What's Happening* are rare. (The rights to the film are controlled by Apple.) Its status as a work commissioned for television, combined with its release in the same year as the Beatles' official debut film, Richard Lester's *A Hard Day's Night,* has made *What's Happening* seem like something of a poor cousin in the Beatles filmography. (Many books on the Beatles do not even mention the Maysles film.) Reportedly, Beatles management attempted to, if not suppress the film, certainly marginalize it in favor of the more marketable and attractive *A Hard Day's Night.* In its original form, *What's Happening* shows little interest in showcasing the Beatles's musical talents, as Lester's film so abundantly and charmingly does. There are no extended musical numbers in *What's Happening.* The film is more interested in capturing the excitement and atmosphere of the encounter between the Beatles and American culture. *The First U.S. Visit,* by contrast, is largely a performance film in which Maysles's footage assumes a supplementary function. Lester's film has a documentary-like flavor at times, one probably influenced by *What's Happening,* although in comparison with the Maysles film it is a polished work. (Shooting began on March 2, 1964, less than a month after *Yeah, Yeah, Yeah!* aired on Granada.) *The First U.S. Visit* is an imitation of an imitation, a shadow of Lester's film and of the original *What's Happening.* I shall not extensively engage in comparisons of the different versions of *What's Happening/The First U.S. Visit;* I refer the reader to the appendix detailing the differences between the seventy-four-minute cut with the most widely available DVD version of the film.

| | |

In *What's Happening,* as the Beatles are in their suite at the Plaza Hotel in New York, they listen to their transistor radios as the disc jockey Murray the K plays their records and talks to his listeners. Murray's vocabulary is pervaded by a final gasp of 1950s be-bop-influenced lingo.

A typical example, heard later in the film, spoken by Murray in virtually one breath: "They're loose like a goose, they're hangin' in there, they put some ice cubes in their pockets, they're stayin' cool, man." As Paul McCartney listens with his transistor up to his ear, he finally turns to his bandmates and asks, "Does anybody understand him? I can't understand a word he says." None of them do, which eventually prompts McCartney to declare, "It's a funny place, this America." The American version of the English language heard here becomes something close to dialect in need of translation. In *Chronicle of a Summer,* Jean Rouch famously turned his anthropological eye away from Africa and directed it toward France, he and Edgar Morin examining their own country as though it were a foreign subject. In *What's Happening,* the Maysles brothers do not film the Beatles as though they are outsiders (thereby turning them into oddities) but instead allow their camera to so strongly inhabit the world of the Beatles that the film often shares their view of America as a "funny place." (The film's origin as a commission from British rather than American television may have also been a factor in its take on America.)

Language is one of the areas in which a cultural divide occurs. Most insistently, there is the language of advertising that the Beatles listen to in amazement, often through their transistor radios, which are in themselves a type of portable advertisement: they assume the form of a Pepsi-Cola machine. The pervasive and virtually nonstop language of radio commercials interspersed with the playing of Beatles records, and the seamless transitions that the Beatles directly experience through the radio announcers, creates an environment in which there is no break between selling and performance: George Harrison finds himself trapped by this type of language when, in the midst of what he thinks will be a telephone interview with a radio announcer, the interviewer suddenly barrages him with an unexpected segue into an ad for Castro convertible sofas.

The arrival of the Beatles in America is covered by the radio and television media in language that repeatedly invokes battle or conquest. Walter Cronkite's television news broadcast states that their arrival constitutes an "invasion," another "D-Day." Murray the K declares that the Beatles are "taking over" while also opining that "a little fish and chips never killed anybody." Throughout the film, the Beatles behave in a comically anarchic fashion, closer to the Marx Brothers (to whom they were often compared by American journalists at the time) than to, say, Bob Dylan in his visit to England in *Don't Look Back* a year later. Dylan's name arises in *What's Happening*. As Murray the K sits in his radio station conducting a telephone interview with the Beatles from their hotel room, various members of the group choose records for him to play. When Dylan's name comes up, one of the band members says, "Mr. Robert Dylan. Fantastic. Very good indeed." But the track of choice, Dylan's version of "Corinna, Corinna," cannot be located on the album, leading to a sequence of comic befuddlement, and the track is never played.

In *Don't Look Back*, Dylan is discussed as someone who represents a break with contemporaneous rock and pop performers. Instead of fans who scream throughout the performance (as Beatles fans do, although the Beatles are not mentioned by name in *Don't Look Back*), Dylan's audience sits quietly and listens to the lyrics, thereby allowing him to assume his mystical role as poet/prophet. Dylan also has his camp followers, waiting outside of stage doors. But they are smaller in number and less maniacal than those who pursue the Beatles. David Hajdu has argued that in *Don't Look Back*, Dylan and Pennebaker were essentially attempting to reproduce the impact of *A Hard Day's Night*, including the depiction of fans following Dylan. Prior to this, Dylan had never experienced these kinds of camp followers (250–51). Nevertheless, while Dylan may technically be a 1960s version of a folk singer, the Beatles engender a more immediate, folklike response on the part of their audiences. Their fans scream through the songs because they already know and have absorbed the simple lyrics and melodies. At the beginning of *What's Happening*, Murray the K plays "She Loves You." After a few bars are heard, there is a cut to fans standing outside of the Plaza Hotel who continue the song a cappella. With this cut, the song is symbolically passed from the Beatles to their fans, circulating through the culture in the manner of a traditional folk song.

Dylan is self-contained and chilly throughout Pennebaker's film, barely affected by England. In one sequence, the management of the hotel he is staying in confronts Albert Grossman, Dylan's manager, with complaints from other guests regarding the noise coming from Dylan's suite. Rather than apologize, Grossman aggressively insults the manager and his staff, throwing them out of the room. Dylan and his entourage bring a privileged sense of entitlement, his dark glasses becoming emblems of his disinterest in looking at or directly confronting anyone or anything around him. He could be in Iowa as much as England.

The Beatles, in contrast, joyfully dominate any space they enter, from their hotel room to Central Park and from the Peppermint Lounge to the train that takes them to Washington, D.C. Watching the film today, it is astonishing to see the directness and immediacy of the Beatles in relation to their surroundings and the people with whom they come into contact. The film shows no evidence of the band attempting to construct barriers between themselves and the outside world. The narcissistic aloofness Dylan exhibits is nowhere to be found. Instead, like great farcical comics, the Beatles transform their surroundings and use them to their own ends. On the train to Washington, for example, rather than conveying irritation at the retinue of photographers incessantly taking their pictures, Ringo, Harpo Marx–like, appropriates the camera bags and slings them around his shoulders, this equipment weighing down his small frame so that he has to stagger about; or George Harrison suddenly emerges from behind a door on the train in a waiter's uniform and hat, carrying a tray of drinks.

Much of this spontaneity is undoubtedly constructed by the film as it carefully omits certain details to convey a restricted impression of the Beatles. The group was, in fact, surrounded by bodyguards and police throughout their visit, something the film only slightly acknowledges, as in the shot of the police cars following them in their drive through Central Park. Moreover, the emphasis on comic celebration results in the most melancholy figure of the group, John Lennon, being marginalized in favor of the more outgoing and performative Ringo Starr and Paul McCartney. (One could well imagine a very different film emerging had the Maysles brothers chosen to foreground Lennon instead.) George Harrison's illness upon his arrival (he was suffering from strep throat and is consequently absent from a number of their early activities) is only touched on, in a slightly puzzling reference (if one is unfamiliar with the circumstances) made by a radio announcer who asks Harrison about the status of his throat. In *What's Happening*, all four Beatles are happy and healthy.

Their sexual "innocence" is also carefully constructed. Their visit to the Playboy Club, for example, on the same night in which they went to the Peppermint Lounge, was either never filmed or deleted from the released versions. (The Playboy Club is briefly discussed by the band members as one of a number of possibilities for their nightclub adventures, but the film's editing implies that the Peppermint Lounge was their ultimate destination that evening.) And although Lennon's first wife, Cynthia, was with the group in New York, she is glimpsed only fleetingly, usually wearing sunglasses, and is never specifically identified, thereby allowing the Beatles to remain youthful bachelors.

Stephen Mamber is attentive to the manner in which the film presents the Beatles as "a commodity, a marketable product" within an "atmosphere of excessive commercialism" (147). Nevertheless, the tone of the film, its sense of comic exhilaration and the degree to which the Beatles are constantly aware of this atmosphere of commercialism surrounding them, gives the film a very different quality from a later Maysles film such as *Salesman*. Like *Salesman*, *What's Happening* follows four men in business suits (and, to the eyes of some at the time, the Beatles were physically interchangeable) as they peddle their wares to a primarily female clientele while spending much of their free time sitting around in hotel rooms.[9] But the four men of *What's Happening* are not exhausted and middle-aged, and what they are selling is not only desired by their public but puts sexual desire itself into play, as we see the ravenous teenage girls stalking the Beatles. This desire is entirely different from what is displayed in *Gimme Shelter*. The fans in *What's Happening* are female and teenage (as they also are in *A Hard Day's Night*), and the screams and collective chanting evoke a sexual longing that is intense but not yet available to be consummated.

The degree to which the film constructs this desire for the Beatles as a fundamentally innocent one is clear in a memorable sequence shot in a New York apartment. Here we observe pre-teenage girls sitting around their kitchen table watching the Beatles on the *Ed Sullivan Show,* and Maysles primarily focuses on the faces of the two older sisters as they watch. Instead of screaming and chanting like most of the girls elsewhere in the film, these girls are spellbound by the sight of the Beatles, their enraptured faces showing evidence of an awakening of which they are perhaps not yet completely aware. All of this takes place in the presence of a man whom we presume to be their father, as he silently witnesses his daughters being absorbed by this all-male spectacle on television.

(Their mother, while present at the moment of filming, is not shown.) One of the few comments made by the girls as they watch is the younger daughter's: "I love their movements."

The Beatles tap into something repressed within American culture and release it, not so much through direct physical contact with Americans but through a spectacle that engenders adolescent sexual hysteria. While this type of hysteria in relation to male pop music figures has two major precedents, Frank Sinatra in the 1940s and Elvis Presley in the 1950s, both of these performers were American. The attraction of the Beatles is foreign, working-class (as were Sinatra and Presley, although not all of the Beatles were of working-class origin), and comically adolescent. But they dress like middle-class businessmen in suits and ties while singing songs of adolescent sexual desire, the song titles and lyrics of extreme and almost archetypal simplicity: "She Loves You," "I Want to Hold Your Hand," "Love Me Do." The film never sets this world of the Beatles in opposition to the American family or to mainstream values. Instead, it repeatedly underlines what it sees as a basic innocence about the Beatles themselves that finds a welcome home in America.

On the train to Washington, for example, an extensive amount of footage is given over to Ringo Starr's encounter with a little southern girl in a Girl Scout uniform who blithely sits next to him and engages in conversation before he takes her on a walk through the train as the camera follows them. (How she was able to get so close to the star is not shown.) On their journey, they pass a number of much older people who show no evidence of being shocked at the presence of the Beatles. One of the older women even asks Ringo for his autograph. At the same time, the film suggests that America is a more transparent and spontaneous society than England. In a sequence in the backseat of a limousine, the Beatles' manager, Brian Epstein, speaks with amazement that in America listeners can simply call in on a radio show and talk to the guests, something unimaginable in England. Throughout *What's Happening*, the space of America is there for the Beatles to interpenetrate and circulate through, while at the same time, America is able to "meet the Beatles" face to face—to sit next to them in trains and dance with them in nightclubs. Space here is fluid, continuous.

Amidst the comic exhilaration of the Beatles, two other figures stand out: Murray the K and Brian Epstein, pivotal men in the popularity of the band. Murray the K (born Murray Kaufman in 1922) and Epstein were of Jewish origin, although this is never directly acknowledged or discussed within the film. Their personalities could not be more different from one another. The child of a vaudeville family, Kaufman's background prior to becoming a disc jockey was steeped in the world of advertising and music promotion. Murray the disc jockey in *What's Happening* is an extremely verbal as well as outgoing figure, totally American showbiz in nature. Epstein, twelve years younger than Kaufman, was from Liverpool, as were the Beatles. But unlike the Beatles, Epstein was from a well-to-do family that owned a furniture store and, later, a North End Road Music Store. And while Kaufman's background brought him in touch with the hard-sell show-business world of vaudeville, Epstein briefly attempted to become a "serious" actor at the Royal Academy of Dramatic Art. However, like Kaufman, he also became (like so many Maysles subjects) a type of a salesman, working for a branch of North End Road Music where he sold records. It was through his contact with the world of popular music at the North End stores (as well as his writings for the magazine *Mersey Beat*) that he eventually came to represent the Beatles. *What's Happening* effectively sets up a contrast between these two male figures so fundamental to the success of the Beatles. (The film's title is derived from Kaufman's litany, "What's happenin', baby?")

The film opens with Kaufman in his radio-station booth announcing the arrival of the Beatles in America, which might initially lead one to believe that Murray the K will become a presiding presence over the film, a master of ceremonies, as does another famous disc jockey, Wolfman Jack, for George Lucas ten years later in the fictional *American Graffiti* (1973). This does not quite happen, though, and ironically Kaufman's presence in the film becomes both ubiquitous and marginal. He is often with the Beatles in their hotel room or out on the town. But the degree to which he is welcome is not clear. At one point, Lennon jokingly calls Kaufman "Whacker the K," causing the disc jockey to nervously laugh. The comment reflects the ambivalence with which the group saw Kaufman: a necessary figure in terms of breaking into the

American radio market but, at the same time, someone whose aggressive presence is often resented. Early in the film he calls the Beatles in their hotel room, but Starr quickly gets him off the line, claiming that they are waiting for "an important call from London." The film often emphasizes Kaufman's outsider status. His slightly archaic use of jive talk already renders him something of a relic, and the Beatles often parody his method of speaking. A generation older than the Beatles, he often looks physically tired or disheveled, as though he is desperately trying to maintain the energy level of the "boys," which he is not quite able to match. In the hotel room after his telephone interview with them, he sits in a chair as the camera zooms in to his face. He runs a finger along his teeth and rubs his nose. Staring off into space, he seems oblivious to the fact that he is being filmed, before slightly rousing himself to sing along with the record playing on the radio.

At the Peppermint Lounge, Murray the K joins Ringo on the dance floor, but he looks rather desperate, his thinning hair parting in several directions and soaking with perspiration. After he sits down at the edge of the stage, the slightly blank, worn-out expression from the hotel room returns to his face as he stares off, again apparently unaware of the camera filming him. Behind him a woman frantically dances, visible from the waist down, her rear end twisting away as though inadvertently mocking the tired, middle-aged figure who does not seem to fully belong to this world. As in the hotel room, though, Kaufman rouses himself and begins to sing along and snap his fingers to the music, but he never quite erases the impression of emotional and physical exhaustion. At such moments, Maysles's camera brilliantly zeroes in on a detail just outside of the main flow of action. Such images give us access to painfully private moments occurring within very public spaces, finding a melancholic emotional core, an overwhelming sense of inevitable decline in the midst of all of this youthful energy.

While Kaufman's interaction with the Beatles frequently isolates him from the group's internal dynamic, Epstein is positioned by the film as literally, physically outside of the group's central actions. At no point does the film show Epstein and the Beatles in the same space. Our first (and only extended) view of him does not come until a sequence over halfway through the film, the morning after the visit to the Peppermint Lounge, where we see Epstein at work with his staff. In contrast to Kaufman, he

What's Happening: A sweating and exhausted
Murray the K at the Peppermint Lounge.

is reserved, formal, elegant, his physical attractiveness far more striking
than any of the Beatles themselves. While the Beatles play to the camera
or to the fans, Epstein behaves as though the camera isn't there. There is
a fascinating shot in this sequence in which Epstein, sitting on a couch,
leans back to listen to his secretary read something he has dictated. As he
leans back, he rests a closed fist against his cheek while he listens, as though
(consciously or not) posing for a photograph, not looking at the camera
but still aware of its presence. Like the Beatles, he wears a suit and tie.
And as he gets up to leave, putting on his coat, he wraps a decorative scarf
around his neck, giving him the appearance of a modified English dandy.
Epstein's homosexuality is not made explicit by the film. But his slightly
feminine gestures, physicality, and demeanor are so clearly different from
everyone else's that a subtle undercurrent of "otherness" is created.

In the concert sequence in Washington, D.C., Epstein is in the
audience watching the Beatles perform. Still wearing this scarf tucked
into a dress jacket, he is alone and smiles as he watches the group, some
of the young audience members occasionally turning around to look at
him. He stands out markedly here, in his dress and physical demeanor, a

What's Happening: Brian Epstein listens to his secretary read back dictation.

spectator to the pop-music phenomenon he has been central in creating, never permitted by the film to share the frame with them. It is difficult not to read these images of Epstein and Kaufman retroactively in light of the larger histories of these two men, both soon to be literally expelled from the world we are seeing: One year after *What's Happening* was filmed, Kaufman's radio station, WINS, switched to an all-news format, effectively stripping him of his central pop-music position; Epstein died of a drug overdose in 1967.

| | |

At a press conference early in *Gimme Shelter* announcing the Altamont concert (footage not shot by Maysles), Mick Jagger describes his dream of Altamont as one capable of "creating a sort of microcosmic society which sets an example to the rest of America as to how one can behave in large gatherings." The result was, of course, anything but exemplary. The structure of the film allows for the possibility of reading the murder as a culmination of a network of factors. Poor planning on the part of the Rolling Stones and the concert managers is one thread that runs through the film; the aggression of the Hell's Angels is another. But even stronger and more powerful than individual or collective blame is the suggestion that what took place was an eruption of forces that had been smoldering within the world of the film itself. In short, the knife that kills Meredith Hunter symbolically becomes the knife that kills the counterculture of the 1960s.

Gimme Shelter is marked by a tenuousness in terms of meaning. It is a documentary thriller in search of not the culprit for the murder (which is obvious) but of the circumstances that led to the murder. But the film is put together by filmmakers for whom the language of condemnation and the search for blame are antithetical to their sensibilities. (In this regard, the film is nowhere near as unflattering a depiction of the Stones as Robert Frank's *Cocksucker Blues,* made two years later.)

The diametrically opposed readings that *Gimme Shelter* has sustained over the years are the surest indication of this ambiguity. *Gimme Shelter* has become, if not a blank slate, at least a grayish one onto which spectators have projected their own readings, some of them so off the mark and inaccurate as to be grotesque. I shall not directly engage with these published debates, as my interest here is in examining the structure of ambiguity and tenuousness rather than putting forth a single reading. While Richard Porton has argued that *Gimme Shelter* "represents the decomposition of an ethos within American direct cinema which assumed that unscripted documentaries suffused with an aura of spontaneity could unveil a reality that was relatively conclusive, if not aboriginal" (83), the film could also be seen as a primary example of an ideal that Albert Maysles stated in his 1969 television interview with Jack Kroll: to create a documentary filmmaking practice that centers on a moral subject about which the viewer must make choices. *Gimme Shelter* is fundamentally uninterested in finding a clear meaning in relation to the murder but instead uses its images to address matters of more immediate interest to the Maysles brothers and Zwerin: the charisma and physicality of the Stones (especially Jagger) and the kind of spectacle that this engenders—a spectacle about which the film has mixed feelings, at once attracted to it, but also slightly distanced from it.

There is a fascinating shot when we see Jagger performing onstage for the first time. As he begins the song "Jumping Jack Flash," the camera holds on him for approximately a minute and forty-five seconds without a cut, slowly zooming in to and away from him as he performs, the action around him minimized. This is a "star" moment for Jagger, showcasing his dandyish and androgynous charisma as a performer. There is little to distract the viewer in this sustained shot, so that one can carefully observe certain devices Jagger draws upon: the famous strutting and snapping of fingers, the bobbing of the head and tossing back of the hair while periodically punching at the air with his fists for emphasis. The long pink silk scarf he repeatedly flings back during his performance seems to pick up on the more conservative scarf that Epstein kept tucked inside in *What's Happening*, as he attempted to maintain the pose of an English businessman. Jagger explodes Epstein's repressed femininity, brandishing this type of androgyny and using it in a bold, theatrical manner. And where the Beatles exhibit a boundless curiosity about America in *What's Happening*, Jagger appropriates Americanness as a camp stage prop through the stars-and-stripes Uncle Sam hat he wears at the beginning of the song before tossing it away. At one moment, Jagger points at something on the stage that distracts him. He looks at someone, either offstage or somewhere out of frame, this gesture of pointing presumably meant to convey his irritation and his desire for whatever it is that is distracting him to be removed or altered. He does not stop singing and incorporates these gestures into his performance, rolling his eyes and tossing his hair back in a feminine show of pique. Because we do not see the cause for Jagger's irritation, we focus solely on gesture, facial expression, and bodily movements detached from their cause. This sustained look carries with it an element of almost microcosmic revelation or an uncovering of Jagger's performance techniques, at once celebrating and unmasking them. It is as though we are observing him in an anthropological manner, perhaps even seeing the *process* of performance at work at the same moment in which we see the finished result.

The device of having Jagger and Watts look at and comment on the footage, while undoubtedly giving the film a conventional narrative "hook," allows for the specter of death to hover over *Gimme Shelter*, a sense of inevitability about the events and the clash of personalities involved. The film's unresolved question, however, is: Out of this network of forces that led to the death of Hunter, was there something about the Rolling Stones as a rock group, about their music and projection of self while onstage, that engendered this atmosphere of violence and death, even if the Stones are not directly culpable? The film's images are seemingly called upon to "speak," to at least raise questions if not to supply evidence or answers. How these images are to be interpreted, though, is not always clear, caught up as the film is (like *Salesman*, although for very different reasons) in a network of ambivalent associations. While for ninety minutes the film intercuts shots of Jagger and Watts looking at the footage (why Keith Richards, Bill Wyman, and Mick Taylor were not with them is not clear), they have little of real substance to offer in terms of commentary. They mainly appear to be dazed by the footage, making only slight and parenthetical comments. This could be read as either a sign of their inability to convincingly comment on what took place (hence a silent acknowledgment of their complicity) or as a sign of their simply being so overwhelmed by the visual evidence of Altamont that they are stupefied.

Maysles has compared the film to Michelangelo Antonioni's *Blow-Up* (1966) on the commentary track of the *Gimme Shelter* DVD. Certainly the sequence in which footage is constantly rewound to search for the knife that stabbed Hunter evokes the famous sequence in Antonioni's film in which the photographer Thomas (David Hemmings) repeatedly blows up his photographs of a mysterious incident in a London park until he is finally able to spot a man with a gun in his hand, hiding in the bushes. But the ultimate meaning of this search within images for a clue is very different in the two films. From square one, there is no question in *Gimme Shelter* that a stabbing by a member of the Hell's Angels has taken place. The larger question is, Who bears the ultimate responsibility for the murder? In *Blow-Up*, the discovery of the gun in the photograph, while a startling moment of revelation, does not lead to the identification of any single culprit or to any suggestion of pervasive guilt or culpability; the clue remains too vague. Whereas both films end ambiguously, *Gimme Shelter* resolves itself on a note of possible collective or shared responsibility for the murder; *Blow-Up* simply trails off at the end, as though it has lost interest in the entire question of culpability or resolution.

Gimme Shelter is self-consciously structured as a film of beginnings and endings. After a brief prologue showing the Stones having their photos taken on a highway in England for an album cover, the film switches to the band performing at Madison Square Garden. If the opening sequence of *Showman* underlines its status as an opening sequence by having the voiceover narrator intone, "It all starts here," *Gimme Shelter* performs a similar gesture by having the band's announcer declare on the soundtrack, "Everyone seems to be ready. Are you ready?" While this announcement itself is taken from the Madison Square Garden show and is directed toward the New York audience waiting for the band, its placement over a black screen allows it to be directed towards the film audience as well. When Jagger enters the stage in New York, he ironically calls this performance "the breakfast show," presumably a reference to the band's late entrance but also serving to reinforce the sense of early morning hours. "We're just gonna wake up," Jagger tells his audience. The penultimate sequence of the film shows the Altamont concertgoers packing up and leaving Altamont as the sun rises. In effect, this film seemingly so concerned with finality, with endings, begins and ends as the sun is rising. While Jagger's opening remark about the breakfast show is ironic and said indoors, in which the only visible light is artificial, the images of dawn at Altamont show an actual sunrise. The bedraggled concertgoers trudging home connote an image of defeat but also one of cleansing and of new beginnings. They have survived. On the soundtrack early in the film, during the editing-room sequence, a radio announcer is heard describing the situation at Altamont as one in which "there were four births, four deaths, and an awful lot of scuffles reported."

| | |

The most obvious differences between *What's Happening* and *Gimme Shelter* are not only historical (the difference between the early sixties and late sixties in terms of rock 'n' roll and youth culture) but also between the nature of these two rock 'n' roll bands: in the Stones, their self-consciously decadent, overtly sexual, and even, at times, theatrically satanic nature (in terms of the content of their songs and their style of live presentation) contrasts markedly with the comparative innocence of the Beatles in *What's Happening*. This, in turn, gives rise to a very different kind of audience and a different relationship *with* that audience. Although the Beatles freely and comically move through the space of America in *What's Happening*, the Stones move within an essentially closed world, briefly stepping out of limousines or helicopters into spaces of performance. Like Dylan in *Don't Look Back,* they show no curiosity about the world around them. Unlike the Beatles, the camera is never taken inside of the vehicles that transport them. There are no extended private glimpses of the band members, no real conversations among them, and no obvious moments of revelation for the viewer. We do follow the band into a motel room in Muscle Shoals, but the sequence is brief, and nothing of interest transpires.

What's Happening, in contrast, spends much of its time with the Beatles in their hotel rooms, where nothing of major significance happens: they listen to or call in to radio programs, smoke, play cards, talk to one another. In *Gimme Shelter,* shot after shot, sequence after sequence feels geared toward offering up some meaning or significance, however ambiguously articulated, in relation to the events at Altamont. But there is a looseness of form in the hotel-room sequences of *What's Happening,* a notable lack of concern with offering up stunning revelations or moments of crisis. The views presented in *What's Happening,* though, are not private, and there is not an overwhelming atmosphere of voyeurism created. (McCartney, for example, reads the newspaper coverage of the group's press conference while a photographer is directly up in his face snapping photos.) As the Beale women do in *Grey Gardens,* the Beatles constantly perform for and interact with the camera even when "alone," thereby overturning the Maysles brothers' desire (if any) to film the Beatles in "pure" direct-cinema style.

But the Stones often seem disinterested and even, at times, hostile to the presence of the camera. Maysles has said that early in the shoot Jagger told the filmmakers he was not going to act for their film, adding that he also didn't want "any of that Pennebaker shit" (DVD commentary). Jagger was possibly referring to Dylan's "performance" in *Don't Look Back,* in which his aloofness and apparent indifference to the presence of the camera constitutes a type of acting. In an outtake from *Gimme Shelter,* Jagger and Richards become belligerent during a recording session when Maysles's camera gets too close to them, breaking their concentration in listening to a playback. In the band's offstage lethargy, one is reminded of the men of *Salesman* who, when gathered together for ordinary social activity unrelated to business, seem exhausted or have little to say to one another. One performs for the purpose of business, of making money; otherwise, one closes down, saving energy for the next show.

Unlike *What's Happening* or more immediately contemporaneous films such as *Monterey Pop* and *Woodstock,* the audience in *Gimme Shelter* is a problem, at times even a monstrous other to be kept at bay. When Jagger gets out of a helicopter at Altamont, he is promptly assaulted by a concertgoer; and an out-of-control woman at Altamont has to be taken away by security men when she belligerently insists on seeing Jagger. By contrast, the Beatles fans in 1964 all appear to be of high-school age, the girls wearing dresses and the boys, like the Beatles themselves, in suits and ties, their hysteria connoting less collective madness than a type of youthful bourgeois anarchy. The Stones fans in 1970, while not much older than the Beatles fans in 1964, are presented by *Gimme Shelter* in very different terms. The overt and decadent eroticism of the Stones creates a collective atmosphere that inevitably reflects or duplicates this eroticism. While the Beatles create an atmosphere that leads to nothing but sustained, high-pitched screaming and hysteria, the Stones slow everything down. In one of the film's most powerful sequences, a red tinted frame plays over slow-motion images of fans as they listen to the band perform "Love in Vain." The camera is positioned low as it pans across the fans at the edge of the stage, emphasizing the degree to which these fans must look *up,* some of them reaching out to Jagger, who does not reach back. The faces and bodies of the fans register their spellbound but also (by implication) drug-induced responses. At the close of the sequence, a cut takes us to a close-up of a very sleepy Jagger in a recording studio, the red tint spilling over from the Madison Square Garden sequence into this shot. As the red tint quickly fades from the image, Jagger suddenly pops awake, as though the red itself has induced this drugged-out state.

The power of the Rolling Stones as performers depends on their maintaining a physical distance from their audience, a distance seemingly slight but ultimately inflexible. In a fascinating paradox, the Beatles are in fact much more physically remote from their audience when they perform, the stage (or the television set) keeping a safe distance even while their onstage buoyancy creates the illusion of collective ecstasy and direct contact. (In their final film together, Michael Lindsay-Hogg's documentary *Let It Be* [1970], this simultaneous distance and separation from the audience is played out once again when they deliver a concert on the roof of the Apple office in London to an audience on the street below, the audience hearing them but largely unable to see them.) In a performance at Madison Square Garden in *Gimme Shelter*, the fans are permitted to stand extremely close to the stage. As Jagger sings "Honky Tonk Women," first a woman and then a man attempt to run across the stage toward Jagger before they are grabbed by bodyguards. During the same song, other women attempt to sit on the edge of the stage while the band performs, but this likewise results in their being expelled. At the end of this performance, Jagger says to his audience, "We're going to kiss you goodbye. And we leave you to kiss each other goodbye." The Stones undoubtedly create an atmosphere of intense collective eroticism, one designed to be passed from the stage over to the audience. But it is a suspended eroticism, based on teasing, flirtation, and orgiastically singing about how they "can't get no satisfaction." "You don't want my trousers to fall down now, do you?" Jagger asks his New York audience, knowing that this is exactly what they wish to see but likely never will. But all of this teasing is repeatedly pushed to the breaking point, threatening to build to a moment of crisis whenever fans violate this implicit contractual distance.

This precariousness in terms of their representation of themselves is beautifully encapsulated in a shot of Jagger exiting the Muscle Shoals recording studio in Memphis. He is wearing a white suit, red hat, and long red scarf. As he gets into his limousine, the car door begins to be closed for him. But his red scarf is still dangling outside the door. Maysles zooms in to this detail, as though his camera is about to catch the door violently slamming into the scarf. At the last moment, Jagger quickly pulls the scarf inside as the door is slammed shut. Similarly, at Altamont fans attempt to climb the scaffolding to get a better view of the stage, but they are ordered to come down since the scaffolding cannot withstand their weight. Later in the film, once the music has begun, we see one lone man who has not climbed down, dancing away at the top of the scaffold, indifferent to (or most likely aroused by) the precariousness of the situation.

The difference between the fans in *What's Happening* and those in *Gimme Shelter* cannot simply be accounted for in terms of the shift from the cultural atmosphere in America from the early sixties to the cultural atmosphere in the late sixties. If one examines how audiences and the idea of the collective are treated in *Monterey Pop* and *Woodstock*, for example, we see something quite different from what we find in *Gimme Shelter*. As in *Gimme Shelter*, these films largely portray outdoor rock concerts. But *Monterey Pop* and *Woodstock* present their audiences and their performers in essentially positive terms. The outdoors in Pennebaker's and Wadleigh's films serve to reinforce the essential naturalness of the event, of rock music and youth culture. The construction of the stage at the beginning of *Woodstock* amidst the vast outdoor setting creates a sense that the three-day rock concert is part of the natural world that surrounds it rather than an intrusion—like the building of log cabins in *Drums along the Mohawk* (dir. John Ford, 1939). And while the film does give voice to some of the objections of the locals to the behavior of the youthful concertgoers, the overwhelming majority of the responses shown are strongly positive toward the version of America's youth we see in the film. The politeness of "the kids" is often stressed, as though in the midst of all of this youthful freedom social decorum and civilized behavior remain. One long sequence is devoted to showing the kids lined up at pay phones to call their parents, reassuring them of their safety in the aftermath of a violent thunderstorm.

The new culture coming to fruition in the film does not exist in opposition to dominant values but coexists within them. The U.S. army is described as being "with us, not against us" when they bring in medical supplies after the storm. Michael Lang, the concert's coproducer and promoter (who was also involved in Altamont and can be seen in *Gimme Shelter*) makes the ideology of the event and of the film clear when he states in an early sequence, "Everybody pulls together, and everybody helps one another, and it works." In *Monterey Pop*, the police and the flower children are shown standing together, laughing. "There's talk of the Hell's Angels coming down," a policeman says at one point. But in *Monterey Pop*, the Hell's Angels are a completely benign presence, another part of the diverse fabric of the crowd. And where the Stones create an atmosphere of intense but ultimately imaginary proximity with their audiences in *Gimme Shelter*, in *Monterey Pop* there is continuous fluidity between performers and audience. Performers sometimes sit in the crowd and observe the other performers, culminating with the film's spectacular finale, a performance by Ravi Shankar in which a number of the musicians are shown listening to Shankar in rapt amazement. Like a sixties "happening," there is no effective barrier in *Monterey Pop* between the space of performance and the space of reality. Each world spills over into and invigorates the other.

In *Gimme Shelter,* though, the youth/rock culture is significantly stripped of many of these utopian connotations. While *Woodstock* devotes an extended sequence to the concertgoers swimming nude, emphasizing the degree to which the Woodstock event is a "natural" state, Edenic in its implications, the nudity during the Altamont section of *Gimme Shelter* suggests bodies out of control: One overweight nude woman, filmed from behind, is taken away by security. In general, nudity and overt expressions of sexual desire in the film never completely escape a strong sense of disorder. While *Woodstock* devotes an entire sequence to a man whose duty it is to clean up the portable toilets, as though the film wants to underline the hygienic nature of youth, in *Gimme Shelter* we see men lined up urinating against a wall. Sexuality at Altamont is often linked up with animal-like states, as in the cut from a shot of a couple "making out" to a shot of one dog sniffing another. During the Stones's performance at Altamont, a German shepherd blithely walks across the stage as Jagger sings, indifferent to the magnetism of the hardworking rock star. When the crowd begins to dance during the Flying Burrito Brothers song, many of the individual shots of the dancers appear to be shot using variable camera speeds, giving the dances a strange, unnatural rhythm and movement, more mechanical than human.

The entire concert's passage from dusk into evening, from light into dark, suggests an eventual passage into the world of the gothic and the fantastic in which humans and animals exist side by side and in which elements and shapes that appear normal in daylight are transformed into something sinister and terrifying. The benign Hell's Angels referred to in *Monterey Pop* become angels of death. They lurk in the darkness and on the edges of this environment, ready to pounce, as in the extraordinary shot (taken by Stephen Lighthill) of Jagger in the left foreground, out of focus as he sings "Sympathy for the Devil," while a Hell's Angel in the right rear of the shot, in focus, carefully eyes him. It is as though this man whom the Hell's Angel has ostensibly been hired to protect could just as easily become his enemy—he could turn on him in a minute. But this look toward Jagger also threatens to become a look directed toward the camera and the viewer, as though it is a dangerous and life-threatening act to simply look at this man or attempt to capture his image.

In the midst of all of this chaos, though, one moment stands out. This occurs before the sun has set. Here we see a completely stoned man, in white t-shirt and button-fly jeans, the buttons open as though he has forgotten to tidy himself up after urinating, playfully attacking a sound man. He rolls around on the ground laughing, saying something incoherent about wanting to be smart but is only able to utter "you're just so far out." He pulls off the nervous sound man's glasses and examines them while continuing to roll around and laugh. But as he stands up, he takes the sound man's face in his hands for a moment, then briefly places his head against the man's shoulders before coming back up, the two men facing each other. The sound man places his hand on the other man's shoulder and for several seconds the two men look at one another, a pained smile on the face of the sound man, the other man's mouth slightly open as he looks a bit wide-eyed, staring back. It is a strange, moving little moment, as though against enormous odds and for only the briefest second in the midst of this disorder these two very different individuals, each coming to Altamont for different reasons, have managed to make some kind of connection.

| | |

What's Happening and *Gimme Shelter* each contain a sequence that, in condensed form, encapsulates the differences between these two rock bands and in the historical moment in which they are being filmed. In the case of *What's Happening*, it is the visit to the Peppermint Lounge; in *Gimme Shelter*, it is the recording of "Wild Horses" at Muscle Shoals. Both are dazzling sequences in which we witness Albert Maysles's extraordinary capacity for seizing the moment he is filming. The Peppermint Lounge sequence primarily concerns itself with Ringo and Murray the K jumping up from their table and hitting the dance floor, joining a group of mainly young and female dancers. The Muscle Shoals sequence simply consists of shots of various band members listening to a playback of "Wild Horses."

In *What's Happening*, Maysles literally joins Starr and Kaufman on the dance floor. The first sustained shot in this sequence lasts for over two minutes without a cut. The camera is in the midst of the action, with Maysles sometimes placing it above his shoulder, filming the dancers from slightly above; at other times the camera tilts down to the floor;

but most often it is at eye level with the dancers, who are almost on top of Maysles, passing back and forth in front of his camera as it moves slightly forward and back, panning from Starr to the woman with whom he is dancing, or from Kaufman to the woman with whom is he dancing. By not cutting for over two minutes, an enormous sense of mounting excitement is created: How long will the camera keep running here? When will a cut arrive? Where will we be taken next? Three cuts do occur, the first taking us to very close shots of Kaufman and his young dancing partner, Geri Miller, as the camera pans from one to the other for twenty seconds; this is followed by another closer shot of Kaufman dancing for ten seconds; and then another long take of over a minute, showing Starr, Kaufman, and the larger crowd again, followed by another shot lasting for approximately forty-five seconds of the same group. Even with these cuts, the sense of escalation, of propulsive intensity, is maintained. Near the end of the dance, pasted into the soundtrack, is Murray the K's "Hear what's happenin', baby," taken from earlier in the film. The camera's extreme proximity to the dancers does not allow us to get much of a specific sense of the dancing. Instead, we have an overwhelming sense of faces and bodies, the camera tilting down to catch jiggling breasts or a rear end, faces drenched in sweat but, except for Kaufman's tired presence, all of it connected to youthful energy and expressed through constant movement within a confined but nevertheless public and social space. (Frame grabs would not even begin to convey exhilaration of the sequence.)

With "Wild Horses," we move entirely to a space of work, a recording studio, with no one except the band and other necessary personnel in attendance. What we observe, though, is not the moment of recording but that of the playback, a moment devoted to neither work nor play but to a realm in between: in this instance, the Stones deriving pleasure from listening to the fruits of their labor. It is a sequence composed of four shots. The first three are of fairly brief duration: a close-up of Jagger followed by a close-up of Watts, eyes closed and then opened as he turns his head away from the camera, back to Jagger, who crinkles his nose and then rests his chin on a counter as the camera pans over to Mick Taylor. As in the Peppermint Lounge sequence, there is one rather long take, lasting for over two minutes, and this is the shot that immediately follows the close-up of Taylor. Keith Richards sits on a couch and listens to the playback, his eyes closed as he silently sings along with the recording. The camera zooms into his face, very close, as though examining the texture (slightly marked by acne) and the lips quietly moving in synchronization with the music. The camera then pans to the left, down to Richards's boots moving in rhythm to the song, and zooms in tightly to the tip of one of them. It is a snakeskin boot, and the tip is worn away. The camera pans back to the right—not, surprisingly, back to Richards but over to Jagger and then to Watts. Watts at first listens with his head down, his eyelids drooping and heavy, as though exhausted or stoned. He then lifts his head and looks into the camera for nearly ten seconds. Then the eyelids droop again as Maysles zooms further toward his face. After this, as the camera continues to hold on Watts, his eyes scan the room, twice very briefly meeting the camera's gaze, but quickly looking away from it before he finally turns his head entirely away from Maysles. The camera then pans left, not to Jagger's face but, in another surprising movement, to Jagger's hands before slightly zooming back to encompass part of his face. In a miraculous bit of timing, Maysles's

Gimme Shelter: The hands of Mick Jagger.

camera arrives at this moment during the song's conclusion, as Jagger's hands gesture outward at the song's final chord and then come together to quietly applaud.

The contrast with *What's Happening* and the Beatles is enormous. From a world of perpetual movement, of sweat and kinetic energy and hard work (even in the midst of play), we come to a world of infinitesimal movement, of people who have clearly worked hard to produce the recording we are listening to but who, in this sequence, convey a sense of lethargy, of decadence. It is a world that seems to be rotting from within, wearing away, like the tip of Richards's boot. Just prior to the moment in which they listen to the playback, Richards holds up a Minnie Pearl postcard and smiles. As he does so, the camera zooms towards his mouth, allowing us to see his rotting, brown teeth. While throughout the film, there is so much emphasis on eroticized bodies, either onstage or in the audience, in "Wild Horses" the film switches its concerns to the face. Jean-Luc Godard's description of Maysles as being like a painter in his method is reflected nowhere more clearly than in this sequence from *Gimme Shelter*. Panning from band member to band member, zooming in to their faces for details in skin texture or facial movements, the sequence is simultaneously structured upon a clearly demarcated experience of time (the duration of the song, which we hear from beginning to end) while also, in its lethargic rhythms and its exploratory movements, creating the effect of distended time. We have here a form of cinematic portraiture, at once still and mobile, the personalities of the four men (at least so far as the film is concerned) indelibly captured: Jagger, petulant and alert, ignoring the camera while also indirectly playing to it, the most physically, facially mobile of the four; Taylor, impassive and immobile, his long curled hair and angelic face giving his shot the quality of a Renaissance portrait; Richards, the only one whose entire body is filmed here, eyes closed but completely focused on listening to the music, body and face simultaneously youthful and decaying, his white, unlined skin marked by acne; and Watts, the only member who meets the camera's gaze.

Watts's look into the camera is not interrogative; it is not questioning or overtly confrontational. But Maysles and Watts also seem to want to outstare one another, and in this contest it is Watts who loses. He finally has to look away even while he is twice drawn back to return the look of

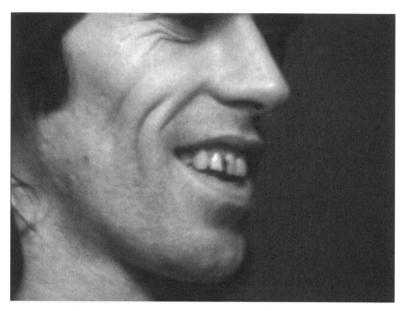

Gimme Shelter: The decaying teeth of
Keith Richards.

the camera, albeit briefly each time. Watts's extreme awareness of the
camera creates a problem for him, in that he does not know how to look
or where to look once he has decided to turn his eyes away. He attempts
to behave "naturally" by not looking back at the camera. But this only
makes him more self-conscious, and his only solution is to completely
turn his head away, leading to Maysles filming him in profile. Like the
film as a whole, the shot derives its force from its focused intensity, its
rapt fascination with the decadent spectacle of this world, capturing it
at the peak of its powers and at a pivotal moment of disintegration. The
subjects of *Gimme Shelter* simultaneously offer themselves up to the
camera and to their audiences even as they retreat from them, pulling
themselves back, looking away, and putting more needs and desires into
play than they are ultimately able to handle.

"I Feel Something Slipping":
Grey Gardens, The Burk Family of Georgia, and *Lalee's Kin: The Legacy of Cotton*

> When we find ourselves fading into shadows and unrealities, it seems hardly worth while to be sad, but rather to laugh as gaily as we may, and ask little reason wherefore.
>
> —Nathaniel Hawthorne, *The Marble Faun*

> I enjoyed being Miss USA. But I'd like to grow old gracefully.
>
> —*Meet Marlon Brando*

Virtually all of the Maysles brothers' films from *Showman* through *Gimme Shelter* center on male figures; the women in these films often assume subordinate roles to the central drives and desires of the men. Nevertheless, the women also threaten to unsettle these worlds dominated (however precariously) by the men. The destiny of the Bible salesmen, for example, often hinges on the acceptance or refusal of the women customers to buy their gilded, unnecessary religious products; and the teenage girls of *What's Happening* turn their Beatlemania into a spectacle that is more galvanizing than the Beatles themselves as the girls are driven to the point of collective hysteria, chasing the band down the street and frantically beating against the windows of their limousine. One of the most memorable moments in *Gimme Shelter* is Tina Turner's outrageously sexual performance of "I've Been Loving You Too Long," her tongue darting lizard-like in and out of her mouth while she uses the microphone and stand as ornate phallic props. As Mick Jagger watches this performance screened for him in *Gimme Shelter,* his jealousy toward Turner's charisma is obvious. "It's nice to have a chick occasionally," he sniffs. At this moment, Turner's blatantly female sexuality runs roughshod over the peek-a-boo androgyny of Jagger.

Grey Gardens, the fourth feature-length Maysles film (if we include the complete *What's Happening*), is the first of their major works to bring female subjects to the foreground. *Grey Gardens* depicts the close relationship between Edith Bouvier Beale, matriarch of her family, and her daughter "Little" Edie, unmarried and still living with her mother in her fifties. The Beales were first cousins of Jacqueline Kennedy Onassis (so memorably filmed by Albert Maysles in *Primary*), and

Grey Gardens began as a film about Lee Radziwell, Jacqueline's sister, before it ultimately changed its focus to the Beale women. At the time the Maysles brothers were filming them, the Beales were living together in their family mansion, Grey Gardens, on East Hampton, Long Island. Their wealth had largely evaporated by this point, reportedly due to a bad business investment on the part of Jacqueline's father, Jack Bouvier, resulting in the women living in nearly poverty-stricken circumstances, their home and the surrounding grounds decaying. The film shows the two women during one concentrated period, from late summer into early autumn, and depicts their close but often volatile relationship.

While *Grey Gardens* will be the primary concern of this section, the film will be discussed in relation to two later Maysles works, *The Burk Family of Georgia,* made for television in 1978, and *Lalee's Kin: The Legacy of Cotton,* a critically acclaimed, Oscar-nominated film shown on HBO in 1992. Neither of these later films is an achievement on the order of *Grey Gardens. The Burk Family of Georgia* is an hour-long episode for a PBS series focusing on American families from different areas of the country and from different socioeconomic levels. According to Albert Maysles, the Burk episode was an afterthought in the series. After the first five families were chosen, the producers realized that no lower-income family was among them. The Burks were eventually chosen to fill this void, and the Maysles brothers were asked to film them. The family came to the attention of the series producers thanks to a lawyer Albert Maysles knew from Dalton, Georgia, who had worked on legal-aid cases and was familiar with the Burks. (The Maysles brothers did no other episodes for the series.) While it contains many memorable moments, the Burk film has, especially in comparison with *Grey Gardens,* an anecdotal quality and lacks the strong sense of contrast and dialectic central to the best of Maysles.

Lalee's Kin is conceived on a much more ambitious scale. At the center of the film is a great subject, a former cotton worker, Lalee (real name: Laura Lee Wallace), and her relationship with her large family on the Mississippi Delta. The sequences focusing directly on Lalee are among the most memorable in all of later Maysles. But the film as a whole is assembled in an unusually emphatic manner, continually underlining its own effects. In contrast to *Grey Gardens* and *The Burk Family, Lalee's Kin* is given a conventional crisis structure involving the superintendent of the Tallahatchie school district, Reggie Barnes, and his need to raise the test scores of his students. If he fails in raising the scores, the state will take over the running of the schools. The film is replete with obvious crosscutting devices, the use of slow-motion, superfluous musical underscoring, and, most distracting of all, titles identifying places, times, characters, and their relationships to one another. It is as though the film, in its rush to be clear and economical, does not trust the spectator. At one moment, for example, a title announces "First day of school." But in the sequence immediately following it is perfectly obvious what day it is, as we see Lalee and her grandson sit down with a teacher to discuss the supplies the boy will need for the coming year. At such moments one may legitimately ask what the fundamental difference is between these kinds of explicit intertitles and the voiceover narration to which Maysles and other direct-cinema filmmakers have historically been so opposed. In spite of these weaknesses, both of these later films deserve extended attention, particularly when seen in relation to *Grey Gardens*.

All three films are linked in their emphasis on strongly matriarchal families in which male figures are either absent or marginalized and in which a great deal of attention is paid to the complex relationship these mothers have with their children. These are films filled with women, in front of the camera and behind it: *Grey Gardens* is edited by Ellen Hovde, Muffie Meyer, and Susan Froemke and codirected by Hovde and Meyer; *The Burk Family of Georgia* is edited and codirected by Hovde and Meyer; and *Lalee's Kin* is edited by Deborah Dickson and codirected by Froemke and Dickson—Albert Maysles's directing credit is not only listed third but is preceded by the word *with*, as though his contributions were of lesser stature than Froemke's or Dickson's. (Maysles takes issue with this credit in the interview at the end of this book.)

In early 1976, the Maysles brothers arranged a screening of *Grey Gardens* at the Paris theater in New York City. The brothers themselves did not attend (it was "for women only"); the screening was hosted by Hovde, Froemke, and Meyer. The film received a mixed response from the women in the audience, with many complaining about the treatment of the bodies of the two Beale women, the manner in which the Beales interact on camera with the Maysles brothers (felt to be unimaginable had the filmmakers been women), and the film's depiction of the Beales as eccentrics. One audience member compared the film with John Cas-

The filmmakers of *Grey Gardens.* Top row
(from left): David Maysles, Muffie Meyer, Albert
Maysles; front row: Ellen Hovde, Susan Froemke.
Photo by Marianne Barcellona. Courtesy of
Maysles Films, Inc.

savetes's *A Woman under the Influence* (1974): "I'm sick of seeing myself
trapped on the screen, sick of seeing myself lying around in a pile of
shit, with cats all around me. I wanted to go out of this theater feeling
strengthened, not weaker" (McIver 10). *Grey Gardens* opened at a time
when feminism was not only entering the mainstream of American culture but also when representations of women in American films were,
in terms of sheer volume, at their lowest historical point. The need for
"positive" images, inspiring and empowering to a burgeoning political movement, was of the utmost importance to many feminists. *Grey
Gardens* (like *A Woman under the Influence*) could scarcely be called
upon to fulfill this function, its concerns being of a different order.

Grey Gardens and *A Woman under the Influence* center on women
in domestic spaces (working-class women in the case of the Cassavetes,
decaying upper-class in the case of Maysles), whose eccentricity and desire to transform their homes into spaces of performance cause them to
be perceived as mentally unstable. The critic Molly Haskell, whose 1974
book *From Reverence to Rape: The Treatment of Women in the Movies*

quickly became a foundational feminist text, was horrified by *Grey Gardens* (as she was by *A Woman under the Influence*). She dismissed the Beales as "'travesties of women'" and found the film to be "'an ethical and aesthetic abomination'" (qtd. in Epstein, "*Grey Gardens*" 11). Ironically, this negative feminist response to the film was not significantly different from the kinds of responses the film received elsewhere. Although many of the early Maysles films provoked controversy when they were released, none did so as extensively as *Grey Gardens*. Time and again, critics registered their disgust or discomfort at viewing the often scantily dressed Beales, parading before the camera, exposing themselves not only physically but emotionally. As we shall see, though, the film is fully available to be read in relation to feminist discourses that, while not strong in the mid-1970s, have emerged in the years since its release.[10]

Even more than in *Gimme Shelter,* the methods employed by the Maysles brothers in *Grey Gardens* came under extensive attack for what were thought to be their invasive and exploitative nature. Once again, the *New York Times* was one of the most prominent sources of these attacks, the review this time coming from Walter Goodman rather than Vincent Canby. Goodman registered his disgust at virtually every level of the film but focused particular attention on the exposed bodies of the Beale women (Goodman 15). And again, the Maysles brothers defended their film in a long letter published in the *Times*. *Grey Gardens*, like *Salesman* and *Gimme Shelter,* emerged at a time when direct cinema was increasingly regarded as an exhausted, if not irrelevant, documentary practice. As Jonathan Vogels has noted, by 1975 direct cinema had become so absorbed into the mainstream that it no longer seemed like an alternative form. Moreover, by the late 1960s and early 1970s, direct cinema was attacked on various fronts, from other documentary filmmakers and film scholars to the media itself. In its concern with nonintervention, with the invisibility and objectivity of the filmmakers in relation to their subjects, direct-cinema practitioners were often seen as creating a cinema that, within the context of an increasingly politicized documentary and alternative filmmaking practice, was politically soft or evasive, inadequately confronting the major social concerns of the period and insufficiently interrogating the ethics of their own filmmaking.

For its makers, though, *Grey Gardens* was a film that, while not completely violating the ideals of direct cinema, pushed the form in new directions. As Hovde has said, "I guess it changed my feelings very much about *cinéma vérité*" (Rosenthal, *Documentary* 384). Albert Maysles stated at the time, "This film has everything a fiction film has. It's a drama, it takes place in one place, so it's almost a piece of theater; it has the depth of a human relationship, accurately explicated. And it has real people, which is an extra. . . . It may just be a turning point in moviemaking" (Sterritt 23). That these new directions were largely unrecognized at the time of the film's release is partly the result of some of the factors described above. The name Maysles had become synonymous with direct cinema, and the film was automatically connected to a type of documentary already under extensive scrutiny and attack. Michael Tolkin has argued that the film's reception was also affected by the Maysles brothers' failure to find a distributor after its New York Film Festival screening. They distributed the film themselves in what Tolkin writes "has become known as one of the clumsiest, most awkward sales campaigns ever," resulting in additional negative press: "They are dragging 'Little' Edie around like a trained seal with a half a lobotomy. She is coherent with some interviewers, off-the-wall with others. . . . Solicited testimonials from freelance writers are given the same weight in the ads as the quote from the *London Times*, 'One of the oddest, most beautiful films ever'" (140). Even so, this does not account for all of the vitriol directed at the film in 1975 and 1976. In its form and especially in the images it shows, *Grey Gardens* is an extreme film. The desire of the Maysles brothers and their collaborators to extend the possibilities of direct cinema resulted in a film that "got away" from them and began to take on a life of its own.

In contrast to much of the response the film engendered in 1975 and 1976, *Grey Gardens* is today the most passionately admired Maysles film. This admiration is based not so much within the field of documentary studies (which so far has devoted little sustained attention to the film) as outside of it, with scholarly essays focusing on such matters as its relationship to literary modernism or to nineteenth- and twentieth-century architecture. Beyond the academy, *Grey Gardens* has become a cult phenomenon. Like all cult films, it is ritualistically viewed by its admirers and cited and reworked in other cultural forms, from fashion to pop music. A documentary short, Liliana Greenfield-Sanders's *Ghosts of Grey Gardens* (2005), addresses this cult obsession—one shared by the filmmaker herself, who re-creates scenes and dialogue from the film. In 2006, Albert Maysles, in collaboration with the film editor Ian Markiewicz, released *The Beales of Grey Gardens,* a collection of Maysles footage of the Beales that did not make it into the original film. While certainly entertaining, this "sequel" is almost incoherent without an awareness of the original *Grey Gardens.* For fans of the original film, however, *The Beales of Grey Gardens* fulfills a desire to see some of the hours and hours of footage that did not make it into the original film. As of this writing, *Grey Gardens* has been turned into a stage musical (a very bad one, in my opinion, in spite of the expert performances by the two lead actresses who originated the roles, Christine Ebersole and Mary Louise Wilson). A feature-length nonmusical Hollywood film is to be released in 2008. In *The Beales of Grey Gardens,* a discussion ensues about a film that Edie claims Hollywood is interested in making about her, with Julie Christie playing Edie. While not pleased with the idea of anyone playing Edie Beale but Edie Beale herself, she nevertheless refers to Ethel Barrymore as the kind of actress who should be playing her mother (although Barrymore was long dead at the time). Ironically, however, Ethel Barrymore's granddaughter, Drew Barrymore, plays Edie in the Hollywood version of the Beale story, with Jessica Lange assuming the role of Mrs. Beale. The public fascination with the story and personalities of Edith Beale and her daughter, a fascination originally generated by the Maysles film, appears to be unstoppable.

If the stage musical version of *Grey Gardens* is any indication, however, admiration for the film and for the Beales does not easily translate into other forms. *Grey Gardens* may, in fact, be a film that is impossible to remake: the fascination exerted so powerfully by the Beale women is the result of the film's precise form rather than the personalities and biographies of the Beales alone. In the musical of *Grey Gardens,* there is no acknowledgment that a documentary was ever made about the Beale women, nor are the Maysles brothers portrayed in the show itself. The musical's especially dull first act is largely devoted to Edie's childhood, a past more hauntingly evoked in the film through spoken language and photographs. Based on my one viewing of the show, I could discern no real reason for the first act at all, outside of allowing for the show's creators to take advantage of including a young Jacqueline Bouvier as a character. In spite of the Maysles brothers being erased from the musical, much of the dialogue in the show's second act is taken directly from the film. More than any other Maysles film, *Grey Gardens,* while available to be read in auteurist terms, gains even greater force from the sense of a collective voice arising from and around it. This collective voice does not belong only to those who created the film but also to those who have, since its release, viewed it, quoted it, and reworked it.

To begin understanding this phenomenon, one could hardly do better than to visit www.greygardens.com, a fan site devoted to the film, organized with categories for the visitor to click on: "What's New?" "Quotes and Maxims," "Essays," and "Links to Excavate." The site's founder, who simply calls himself David K., explains that the site is his attempt to "explore the *Grey Gardens* phenomenon from a psychological point of view." David K. wants to understand why *Grey Gardens* is a film that its followers view repeatedly, "memorizing the dialogue, singing the songs, and, dare I say it—donning the costumes?" There is nothing unusual about cultlike devotions to a film being expressed in this manner; that the film inspiring such passionate devotion is a documentary is another matter entirely. *Grey Gardens* is the most extreme instance of the Maysles brothers' ability to mobilize the structures, forms, and obsessions of fiction cinema (especially that of Hollywood) for the purposes of documentary. Consequently, I would like to use the film's enormous cult following as one of several threads in what follows here, as it throws into relief the most fundamental qualities of the film and the complex manner in which it has been received over the last three decades. This cult following also allows me to situate the film in relation to larger questions of cinephilia.

The term "cinephilia" has multiple meanings and connotations. It defines a certain type of fanatical relation to the cinema: at its most basic level, it refers to the "film buff" who fanatically sees film after film, all day long, sometimes anything so long as it *is* a film. Angela Christlieb and Stephen Kijak's documentary *Cinemania* (2002), taking as its subject five New York–based cinephiles who effectively live only for the activity of watching films, vividly captures this particular world. At another level, although by no means opposed to the first group, is the type of cinephilia nurtured by a somewhat "deeper" appreciation and understanding of the cinema's history and forms, expressed through film criticism and often put into film practice, as in the French New Wave, the New German Cinema of Wim Wenders and Rainer Werner Fass-binder, or the so-called film-school generation in the American cinema of the 1960s and 1970s. None of these kinds of cinephilia are of direct relevance to Maysles, least of all in terms of how the Maysles brothers themselves thought about the cinema. They claimed that they saw few films, and Albert Maysles has often stated that he has no interest even in documentary film history. Instead, the kind of cinephilia of interest in relation to Maysles (while not unrelated to these other forms) has its basis in a certain attitude about the motion picture image as such: what it can reveal, where its fundamental powers and properties lie, and what impact these kinds of images can have on spectators.

While *Grey Gardens* was released during a period when the mid-night-movie cult phenomenon was at its height, through such films as *The Rocky Horror Picture Show* (dir. Jim Sharman, 1975) and *Eraser-head* (dir. David Lynch, 1978), there is no evidence that *Grey Gardens* developed its following within this noisy, ritualistic, late-night atmo-sphere. The film's following developed more slowly, through scattered screenings over the years and through word of mouth. In a video inter-view on the Criterion DVD of *Grey Gardens*, the fashion designer Todd Oldham speaks of his discovery of the film in the mid-1980s through a friend's "very dupey" videotape—and the video format, rapidly expand-ing during that decade, was likely a primary way in which the film was discovered and re-seen by its admirers. (On the same DVD, another designer, John Bartlett, places his discovery of the film at around the same period as Oldham's.) But the cult followers of *Grey Gardens* (or the cult followers of other films) are not necessarily cinephiles. Often such cultism is fixated upon one individual film, and this kind of re-sponse does not immediately place the film's followers within the various larger communities of cinephiles. Nevertheless, the cult-film attitudes expressed toward a film such as *Grey Gardens* intersect and overlap with the broader discourses of cinephilia.

In its various permutations, cinephilia has been most strongly linked to mainstream narrative cinema, particularly Hollywood, since cinephilia often derives its pleasure from observing the ways in which institution-al forms and representations periodically break down. This perceived breakdown creates a space within which the cinephile may celebrate those moments that escape from the restrictions of dominant production and viewing practices. Paul Willemen has argued that cinephilia takes place when the viewer demarcates certain moments out of a film: an unusual shot, a look, a gesture, a line reading, or a camera movement, "when cinema, in showing you one thing, allows you to glimpse something else that you are not meant to see" (Willemen 241). Cinephilia is less likely to take place with films that are, by their nature, acts of demarcation, produced outside of the mainstream and generally dominated by their explicit immersion in countervailing aesthetic or political forms.

Documentary would seem to be resistant to cinephilia. Within documentary criticism, the endless agonizing over the ethics of the film image and the repeated insistence upon individual filmmakers being held accountable for their work is the antithesis of cinephilia's love of the marginal and its active search for pleasures that resist the moralism of entrenched discourses. However, cinephilia repeatedly celebrates not simply the image but the reality that gives birth to that image, hence its attraction to the indexical; its celebration of traces, fragments, and inscriptions; its love for flawed and incomplete films; as well as its overall fascination with the production process. Cinephilia is not fixated upon fictional characters so much as the actors portraying those characters; not so much with the hermeneutics of narrative structure as with quotable dialogue; and not so much with story as with style. Cinephilia is drawn to certain kinds of images not because they are sumptuously false, but not because they are transparently real either. Instead, the cinephilic image is caught up in a paradox of the real and the artificial in which the allure of each feeds off of and generates the other.

From the moment the Maysles films appeared, an atmosphere of provocation, scandal, and suppression surrounded them: Joseph E. Levine's initial refusal to allow *Showman* to be publicly screened (a state of affairs maintained to this day by Levine's son); Brando's refusal to do the same for *Meet Marlon Brando;* or the vitriolic reviews that greeted *Salesman, Gimme Shelter,* and especially *Grey Gardens* upon their initial release—reviews that suggested not only that were these bad films but that they were bad for you. The Maysles brothers seemed to not only transgress boundaries of documentary form but, in certain instances, to push the ethics of filming to their limit. For many spectators, the Maysles brothers filmed things that we were "not meant to see." Few things fuel cinephilic devotion more than a general perception that a film has gone too far, that its provocations push it outside of mainstream ideologies, and that to love it is, in itself, a form of scandal. There is a notorious moment in *Grey Gardens* when Mrs. Beale, wearing a bathing suit, gets up out of a chair, and we can briefly see her aging breasts, drooping down from the top of the bathing suit. For many viewers, this shot is the ultimate horrifying transgression, the moment when an already precarious film crosses a line from which it can never return. "'Aren't there times,'" Haskell cried in relation to *Grey Gardens*, "'when we should simply close our eyes?'" (qtd. in Epstein, "*Grey Gardens*" 11).

But this moment of Mrs. Beale briefly exposing herself, through its very extremity, epitomizes the emphasis throughout Maysles on slips, tears, holes, cracks. At one point in the film, the Beales fight over a photograph of Mrs. Beale that Edie wants to show to the filmmakers. "I want to show it to Al!" Edie screams. As the two women tussle over the photograph, the corner of the cardboard frame is ripped. "Look what you made me do," she says to her mother. This torn frame, held up by Edie for the benefit of the camera, is an emblematic image from the film and from the Maysles brothers' body of work. Within a cinephilic context, such a fascination with seductive flaws opens up Maysles to a world in which meaning is in a state of flux, perpetually and fetishistically suspended between fullness and absence, order and chaos. "I feel something slipping," Edie says as she nervously tugs at one of her revealing outfits. Throughout *Grey Gardens*, suspense is often created around the various scarves and creatively shaped towels with which Edie tightly covers her head. More than once, these head coverings threaten to slip, revealing her presumably thinning hair underneath, which she clearly wishes to remain covered. Occasionally, one glimpses what might appear to be a few strands of white hair peeking out of the top of the scarf. But the head is never fully exposed to the camera, and our curiosity is never satisfied.

The Maysles brothers often draw upon this state of slightly suspended knowledge and desire, perpetually filming their subjects on the edge of collapsing the order of their own presentation of self—and with this, the very order upon which their social environment is constructed. Christian Metz has argued that films with erotic subject matter often play with the edges of the frame, films built upon a structure of suspense, of incomplete revelations and perpetual striptease (77). Metz is writing

A torn image from *Grey Gardens:* Edie Beale
holding up a photo of her mother.

about cinematic works of fiction, and his arguments would be of more obvious use in writing about overtly erotic and fetishistic filmmakers like Alfred Hitchcock or Josef von Sternberg. But the Maysles brothers often put into play an erotics of documentary filmmaking, perpetually teasing the spectator, playing with the edges of the frame and the edges of the worlds that they are filming, nowhere more so than in *Grey Gardens.*

For the last three decades, *Grey Gardens* has sharply divided spectators, from those who wish to simply close their eyes to the horrifying spectacle to those who cannot tear their eyes away from it, who must look again and again, taking in the sounds and images until they have been absorbed into the body and mind of the entranced viewer.

I I I

Albert Maysles has described *Grey Gardens* as a film that appeals to people who are "on the margins, people who are outsiders" (DVD commentary track). Much of this appeal is directly traceable to the film's two subjects, who were taken to be (and certainly perceived themselves to be) outsiders within their own community. The Beales were not only living under limited economic means at the time that Maysles was filming them; as the film shows in its opening montage of newspaper headlines and articles, their behavior and manner of living had caused them to become pariahs within East Hampton, briefly subjecting the Beales to arrest.

As we have already seen, such an attraction to filming outsiders recurs throughout Maysles. The Burks, for example, are in some ways working-class versions of the Beales. The Burks refer to how they are ridiculed by their surrounding community, and, like the Beales, they speak of their difficulties with the law. The Burk family forms a self-enclosed world or village, the home of each family member close to one another, as though shoring itself up against hostile outside forces. Mrs. Burk says that even if her husband leaves her she'll have her children to comfort her. "I like all my kids to be around me." (In this regard, she is luckier than Mrs. Beale, whose two younger sons have moved away and, we are led to believe, do not continue to have extensive contact with their mother.) This idea of the family is repeated in *Lalee's Kin,* in which Lalee's children also live close by. "I love a house full of children," says Lalee. Still, in spite of these strong thematic links, neither *The Burk Family of Georgia* nor *Lalee's Kin* has achieved the canonical status of *Grey Gardens.* While the far more limited exhibition circumstances of the two later films may account for some of their marginalization, the articulation of these issues in *Grey Gardens* is of a different and far richer order than what we find in *The Burk Family* and *Lalee's Kin.*

In writing on the use of architecture and domestic space in *Grey Gardens,* John David Rhodes asks of the film: "Is this a domestic melodrama? . . . Is it an exercise in gothic horror? . . . Is it a musical?" (83). Rhodes's rhetorical uncertainty relates to a fundamental element of many cult films: their tendency to absorb several genres or modes at once, opening the films to multiple points of entry and to diverse possibilities for citation and appropriation. Rhodes's question, we should remember, arises in relation to a documentary; but the genres he invokes are associated with fiction cinema. We have already seen how Hollywood and theater hovers around much of the Maysles brothers' work. This evocation remains present in *Grey Gardens.* In terms of theatrical connections, Froemke has said of the film, "It's Tennessee Williams; it's Eugene O'Neill"

(DVD commentary track). And David Maysles has compared the film with Arthur Miller's play *The Price*—like *Grey Gardens,* a work about long-suppressed family bitterness and resentment played out amidst a ruined domestic environment (Epstein, "*Grey Gardens*" 11).

But as has been noted elsewhere, by scholars and by the filmmakers themselves, the structure of *Grey Gardens* is much less beholden to conventional theatrical and narrative models than *Salesman.* "Nothing happened" is Meyer's description of the activities filmed by the Maysles brothers (DVD commentary track). This was also the great challenge she and Hovde faced in editing the film. The footage did not easily lend itself to being shaped into a conventional narrative form, as the behavior and actions of the two women were endlessly repetitive rather than developmental. The solution to this problem was, says Hovde, to organize the film so that it was "psychological" in its development (DVD commentary track). To organize a film based on the principle of "nothing happening" is, of course, to participate in a long tradition of narrative modernism. This approach to the film has been explored elsewhere, and I have no desire to repeat those arguments here. What does interest me is that the very absence (or at least muting) of conventional narrative structure in *Grey Gardens* allows the film to be more directly experienced as a beloved cult and cinephilic object, freed from the restrictions of narrative anchoring. As Jean Epstein has written, "I want a film in which not so much nothing as nothing very much happens" (11). Nevertheless, if *Grey Gardens* is not organized in the manner of a conventional narrative film, it consistently evokes Hollywood in other ways, through spectacle, genre, and glamorous camera subjects.

At the center of the film, we have two "stars." The Beales are not really celebrities on the order of the subjects of the early Maysles films; but through their upper-class backgrounds and their connections to the Bouviers and the Kennedys, they are not "ordinary" people like the subjects of *The Burk Family of Georgia* and *Lalee's Kin.* Edie's outrageous and totally singular approach to wardrobe, for example, becomes part of the film's spectacle, every outfit as stunning in its way as what one might find in a Kay Francis vehicle of the 1930s. The Beales are no longer wealthy, but they do not live as though they are working-class. In fact (and unlike any Maysles subject prior to this), they do not work at all, in spite of their circumstances. They continue to live on their estate while paying a gardener to tend parts of the grounds. If "nothing" of major importance seems to happen in *Grey Gardens,* much of this emerges through the women's total detachment from the concept of work, of striving toward anything outside of their day-to-day existence. Work does not even seem to occur to them, regardless of their economic situation. Their fundamental sense of themselves as aristocrats remains intact, money or no money.

Like virtually all of the subjects of Maysles films up to this point, the Beales are performers. As performers, though, they are less than professional and more than amateur; we might loosely term them "frustrated" in that both women were, due to family and social circumstances, denied their dream of becoming professional performers. The comments that Mrs. Beale makes about her failure to have a show-business career strongly suggest that she was prevented by her status as an upper-class woman and the opposition of her former husband, Phelan Beale. She responds by staying at home, superficially fulfilling her maternal and matriarchal duties. But she does so in a perverse manner, never fully observing the rules of social conduct of her class, gender, or community. However grandly matriarchal she might be, Mrs. Beale, even allowing for her dire financial situation, is a disaster at presiding over and controlling her own domestic sphere. The house is not only rotting but is overrun by dozens of cats, sleeping with her on an old mattress encrusted with dirt. The cats urinate behind one of her portraits propped up against a wall, while, even more astonishingly, raccoons are slowly eating their way into the house.

Rhodes notes that rooms at *Grey Gardens* are used "for and against their intended purposes" (92). The women, for example, cook and eat in Mrs. Beale's bedroom. (The only time we see the kitchen is when Mrs. Beale has a birthday party, with two guests in attendance.) While the mother's partially bedridden state no doubt served as a precondition for this situation, and it is not uncommon for one or two people living in a very large home to confine themselves to a limited number of rooms, the spectacle of this in *Grey Gardens* remains quite strange. The Beales live in a mansion but behave, at times, as though they are living in a tenement. And the food itself (some of it offered directly to the Maysles brothers while they are filming) is a mixture of the frugal and the luxurious: canned liver pate, various types of hors d'ouvres, boiled

Grey Gardens: The hole in the wall created by raccoons.

ears of corn lathered with margarine and prepared by Mrs. Beale on a hot plate next to her bed. Mrs. Beale is at once the mother, surrounded by products of nurturing and domesticity, and the bedridden aristocrat, haughtily surveying her domain and ordering people about, especially her daughter.

The eccentricity of both women evokes the trope of the "madwoman in the attic," familiar from nineteenth-century literature and famously analyzed by Sandra M. Gilbert and Susan Gubar. Gilbert and Gubar's description of these nineteenth-century women is strongly echoed by the twentieth-century Beales who are, in their own way, "imprisoned in men's houses" and "locked into male texts, texts from which they could escape only through ingenuity and indirection" (83). For Gilbert and Gubar, in the "paradigmatic female story," a haunted mansion, dominated by a family's dark past, plays a central role. These tales explore the "tension between parlor and attic, the psychic split between the lady who submits to male dicta and the lunatic who rebels" (86). The parlor is the traditional nineteenth-century space of socializing. And while a parlor was undoubtedly part of the Beale home, it is never shown in *Grey Gardens*. Instead, the film (either through the choice of the film-makers or because this was how the Beales were living by this point) emphasizes the upper floors, from the bedrooms to the sundeck to the attic. In effect, the film moves everything away from collective social spaces to private ones—in the realm of the gothic, spaces traditionally connected to enclosure and repression.

While there have been numerous film adaptations of gothic, female-centered literature, *Grey Gardens* especially evokes modern-day variations on the basic themes and iconographies of this genre. In particular, *Grey Gardens* evokes *Sunset Boulevard* (dir. Billy Wilder, 1950) and *What Ever Happened to Baby Jane?* (dir. Robert Aldrich, 1962), two films revolving around eccentric (and eventually mad) women living in decaying mansions and in which the animals inhabiting these mansions become symptoms of the madness and decay on display: the dead pet monkey of Gloria Swanson's Norma Desmond in *Sunset Boulevard,* receiving its own ritualistic burial in the back yard, or the rats in both films, scampering about in the swimming pool in Wilder's film or served as a mock dinner to Joan Crawford's Blanche Hudson by a malicious Bette Davis (the Baby Jane Hudson of the film's title) in the Aldrich. Both the Aldrich and the Wilder films are set in Hollywood and deal with aging women who, while once great stars, have largely been forgotten and are making one last attempt to return to performing. The women in these films (including *Grey Gardens*) are essentially fallen aristocrats.

Like Edie, Norma is a follower of astrology (as is, presumably, Jane Hudson, who has a large astrology chart pinned to her kitchen wall), a gesture that at once puts their behavior at an ironic remove (they are caught up in "frivolous" metaphysics) while also aligning the women with ancient and pre-Judeo-Christian thought, as though the forces that drive them cannot be explained within accepted discourses, religious or otherwise. In one major sequence of *Grey Gardens,* the Beales listen to a radio broadcast of Norman Vincent Peale, each of the women lying on a single bed, a cat sitting on a table between them. Peale's enormously successful "power of positive thinking" emerged out of his reformed Dutch Protestantism, which he ingeniously crossed with simple American ideas of social and economic success. While the Beales were Roman Catholic, they appear to have listened to Peale regularly, especially Mrs.

Beale, who has to defend her love for him against Edie's suggestions that embracing Peale makes her mother a bad Catholic.

There are several interesting elements to this sequence. First is the gap between how Edie appears to respond to Peale's sermon in comparison with Mrs. Beale. The sequence is edited in such a way that Mrs. Beale seems to be genuinely moved and impressed by Peale's admonitions. She listens intently to everything he says, at one point even rhythmically nodding her head in relation to the rhythms that Peale imparts to his words. But the contradictions throughout the sequence between the ideology of Peale's sermon, with its banal ideas about success, ambition, and self-love, and the spectacle of the aging Beale women, whose own ambitions were thwarted and who now lie sprawled on dirty mattresses, are painfully enormous. (In this regard, Peale's sermon has a clear relationship with the "inspirational" speech delivered by Melbourne I. Feltman in *Salesman*, which, like Peale's here, conflates American principles of hard work and economic success with a pop form of Christianity.)

While the women do not express any overt hostility or criticism toward Peale, their behavior and the manner in which the sequence is assembled point toward an implied exposure of Peale's false optimism. Peale tells his listeners to "get on top of things and stay there, or things will get on top of you," prompting Edie to turn toward the Maysles brothers and say, "Isn't he terrific?" But the enthusiasm of her words is belied by her body language. As Peale talks, Edie fidgets, as though bored; she smiles and poses for the camera or fusses with her outfit. At one point, she picks up a white high-heeled shoe and begins to carefully examine it, inside and out, as though not even listening to the radio. Peale tells his listeners to "try, really try." Edie promptly mimics the line, but her uninflected delivery of this pearl of wisdom unwittingly satirizes Peale. When Peale uses the word *dispassionate* in one of his sentences, Edie immediately loses interest in the content of the speech and instead says to her mother and the Maysles brothers, "Dispassionate! That's the word I wanted the other day. I couldn't think of what it was." Even Mrs. Beale is moved to rhetorically ask in relation to Peale's injunctive to "get on top," "Does that mean women, too?" At this moment, Mrs. Beale possesses a far greater awareness of the structures and complexities of language than Peale. At the end of the broadcast, Edie (possibly to humor her mother) gives Peale a backhanded compliment: "That was very good—very long. He knows how to go on and on." This sequence concisely shows how the Beale women are at once "locked into male texts" while also managing to escape through "ingenuity and indirection," even if they are not necessarily aware of the full weight of their ingenuity or of how strongly the ideology of figures such as Peale is part of the forces of their own oppression.

Sunset Boulevard and *Grey Gardens* emphasize the vision problems of their subjects, a common strategy in female-centered melodrama. Our first view of Norma Desmond is through a window, the cracks in the blinds opening just enough to show her eyes, largely hidden behind a pair of sunglasses. Her pupils, barely visible behind the glasses, are represented by two tiny white points as they zero in on her prey, Joe Gillis (William Holden), a failing screenwriter. As the camera zooms in to Norma's sunglasses, the tiny points of light suggest madness and acute vision. In *Grey Gardens,* there are references to Mrs. Beale's eye operations (one of them taking place during World War II, requiring Edie to live at home and care for her while her friends went overseas as part of the war effort), and the film contains numerous close-ups of Mrs. Beale displaying her extremely thick bifocal lenses. She usually wears these glasses at a skewed angle, giving her a slightly demented look. Edie doesn't wear glasses (at least not for the camera) but reads her astrology book with a magnifying glass and has to use binoculars to read her weight on the bathroom scale. And in all three films, the women are surrounded by images of themselves from their glorious pasts (films and photographs that focus on moments of public performance or display) while they simultaneously turn their domestic spaces into performance spaces. Norma stages "The Norma Desmond Follies" in her living room for the amusement of Gillis, while Jane Hudson in her living room performs a hit from her child-star days, "I've Written a Letter to Daddy."

In spite of these important links, though, *Grey Gardens* diverges from these earlier films in some fundamental ways. *Sunset Boulevard* and *Baby Jane* remain more firmly part of the female gothic tradition, even while they update and reimagine this tradition. Within the logic of both films, madness and death are the only logical culmination for the issues at stake in relation to these women, repressively trapped within their own homes. The resolution to *Baby Jane,* for example, relies on the melodramatic staple of the deathbed confession, given by Blanche to Jane, in which she confesses that she drove the car that caused the accident that crippled Blanche, an accident long blamed on Jane. While Jane listens to the confession, her mental state has already substantially disintegrated, and the final shots of the film show her cavorting on the beach, regressing to an infantile state as her sister's body lies on the sand. While the basic shell of this structure is present in *Grey Gardens,* it does not carry the same weight it does in the earlier films.

The one major violation of the chronology of the events filmed by the Maysles brothers in *Grey Gardens* is the placement of Edie's tearful monologue in the pink room. Edie delivers this monologue directed largely into the camera, detailing her unhappiness over her mother's interference with her suitors, an interference Edie claims to have largely been responsible for her failure to find a husband. This moment was filmed fairly early on in the shoot but was placed near the end of the film by the editors, who felt that it gave a sense of development and climax to the film that it otherwise lacked. What is observed here by the filmmakers is a certain convention of dramatic (and melodramatic) form, this moment serving as the big "confession" in which all pent-up repressions are let out. But however conventional the placement of this sequence is, it does not override a larger sense that moments of breakdown and confession here no longer represent a cataclysmic intensification and ultimate breaking through of repression. The relationship between Mrs. Beale and Edie continues after Edie's hysteria, very much the same as before. Melodrama is evoked in this sequence and then, within the larger context of the film, elided.

Norma Desmond and Jane Hudson both perform in their living rooms, areas in the home that historically have been set aside for amateur performance. The Beales, in a strategy typical of their brilliant resistance to social norms, turn the private or transitional spaces of the house into public spaces of performance. *Grey Gardens* is, among other things, their moment of vindication, an opportunity to sing and dance for the public, and there are as many moments of singing and dancing in *Grey Gardens* as there are in *Top Hat* (dir. Mark Sandrich, 1935) or *Singin' in the Rain* (dir. Gene Kelly and Stanley Donen, 1952). The film's relationship to the musical transports *Grey Gardens* out of the morbidity of the gothic and into the celebratory and transformative realm of a very different genre.

Mrs. Beale, for example, can now be seen as someone who ceases to be a victim of male dominance and assumes a greater degree of autonomy, someone who has made certain active choices and is now peacefully living with them at the end of her life. "I've had my own cake, eaten it, masticated it, and enjoyed every minute of it," she says.

Central to the impact of the singing and dancing here is its moving and poignant failure—as opposed to the stage musical of *Grey Gardens*, in which everyone performs in a professional manner, thereby negating one of the crucial elements of the Maysles film. Virtually every time the women perform they struggle to perform "beautifully" and "correctly," as Mrs. Beale phrases it. But through this struggle, they achieve a level of expressivity not possible through more polished means. The success of performers in American popular song and dance has always been less a matter of technical skill than of selling a song or dance through the sheer force of personality and style. I can think of no better illustration of this than the moment in *Road House* (dir. Jean Negulesco, 1948) when a smokey voiced Ida Lupino sings "One for My Baby" in a nightclub, her idiosyncratic performance prompting a nightclub employee (Celeste Holm) to respond, "She does more without a voice than anybody I've ever heard." Style masks and exposes technical limitations. The performer is someone special, magical—through her talent and her style, which put her above the "ordinary" spectator. But she is also fundamentally human due to her technical flaws as a performer, making her seem not that much different from her adoring audience. With the Beales, this relationship between genuine talent and charismatic personality is simply wider than normal, personality winning out over skill.

For both women, musical performance is connected to a past they wish to reclaim and thereby finally achieve the measure of success they were hoping for (but had been denied) in earlier years. "I have to get my voice back exactly the way it was when I was forty-five years old," says Mrs. Beale, sitting up in bed wearing a large sun bonnet, as though about to promenade like a showgirl from a 1920s musical.[11] She first attempts to sing along with a (most likely private) recording she had made in the 1930s, "We Belong Together," which Edie places on the phonograph for her. But the defects of the scratched and dusty record prevent Mrs. Beale from finishing this performance. She then attempts to sing along with an Andre Kostelanetz orchestral recording of "Tea for

Two." Her rendition is an utterly singular hodgepodge of archaic trilled r's, screeched high notes, and talk singing. A bit later, in another part of the house, Edie's solo dances for the Maysles brothers attempt to demonstrate what she believes to be her enormous and largely untapped skills as a dancer: "I do terrific dances."

Edie's big number in the film, her dance to the "V. M. I. March," is not quite a march and not quite an interpretive dance. She performs it twice in the film, once as a rehearsal, dressed in red, without musical accompaniment on the porch, the dance steps taken at a frantic pace; and then later in the film she performs the finished version in the foyer, marching down a flight of stairs while brandishing a small American flag as a full orchestral recording plays. For this performance she wears what appears to be a black rehearsal outfit—black hose, white, low heels (probably the same ones she was examining so closely during Peale's sermon), and her hair covered (as usual) in an ornate scarf. She doesn't so much dance as walk backwards and forwards and in circles to the music, periodically waving the flag into the lens of the camera, suggestively wiggling her hips and doing an occasional spin. Virtually everything she does is played directly into the camera, with a self-satisfied smile on her face. Not by any traditional standards is this great dancing, but it's a mesmerizing performance nonetheless—a combination of a showgirl descending a staircase in a Ziegfeld revue and Judy Garland singing "Over the Bannister" while seducing the boy next door on the stairs of her family home in *Meet Me in St. Louis* (dir. Vincente Minnelli, 1944).

What gives these moments of musical performance by the Beales their considerable impact—at once funny, embarrassing, and deeply moving—is the enormous investment and brazen self-confidence they display. At such moments, *Grey Gardens* taps into one of the fundamental discoveries of the modernist musical: one need not possess professional and accomplished musical skills to be a compelling performer. In fact, being a committed amateur may allow one to achieve an even greater emotional power: *Distant Voices, Still Lives* (dir. Terence Davies, 1988), for example, or *Haut/Bas/Fragile* (dir. Jacques Rivette, 1996). Within a cinephilic context, these films allow the spectator to not so much marvel at the technical brilliance of the performance as to observe that performance's traces, its marks of enunciation in which one can see all too clearly the process and the labor by which it has come to life. In terms of genre, *Grey Gardens* is like a two-sided mirror that keeps slowly spinning around, with a gothic melodrama played out on one side and a musical comedy played out on the other side.

The Burk Family of Georgia and *Lalee's Kin* draw upon some of the same issues but with different emphases and implications. The presentation of women carrying out their domestic duties in an indifferent manner returns in *The Burk Family*. While the father sits in the next room watching television, waiting for dinner to be served, one of his daughters, Peggy, prepares the food, a mix of seemingly incompatible items: biscuits, spaghetti (served with Ragu sauce), fried potatoes, and canned mixed vegetables. When the biscuits are hot and ready to be eaten, she carelessly empties the tray onto the supper table, the biscuits falling where they may, as though she could not care less about the niceties of presentation in feeding and serving her family. When the food is finally served, her husband complains about the total absence of salt in any of it. By contrast, in *Lalee's Kin,* as Lalee cuts up bologna into some kind of sauce for her grandchildren, she explains to the camera that being a "chef cook" was a dream of hers. Aside from the $494 a month she earns on disability, she now makes her living preparing low-priced chicken and beef lunches to local cotton workers, which she sells from her son's van.

The differences in attitude toward cooking in these two films relate fundamentally to questions of work. The Burk women have jobs, mainly at the local carpet mill. Cooking and housework are done in addition to regular labors, which may account for the resentment and indifference with which food is served. Lalee's status for years as a cotton worker, however, ties her not simply to labor but to a type of slavery, a world in which work has no redemptive capacities whatsoever. As Lalee states, "When they said we ain't gonna pick no more cotton, I jumped, 'Hallelujah!'" Work only leaves Lalee exhausted and with little dignity left. Her situation is even worse than that of the Burks, who are at least able to insist on their basic dignity in not taking welfare funds and always earning their own way through life. As one of the Burk daughters proudly explains, "Mother's never been on welfare. They've always made it on their own." Moreover, the extremely low wages and long hours that Lalee and other African Americans suffered in the Delta is tied to a regulated and enforced ignorance that had been in place for many years. "All of us slaved till a few years ago," Lalee says. Keeping the cotton workers ignorant assures the owners of their incapacity for fully grasping the implications of their situation or for discovering methods of resistance. As Lalee states, "When you've got your education, you don't have to stoop too low." Cooking at least gives her a measure of autonomy and satisfaction that she never had as a cotton worker.

The subjects of *The Burk Family* and *Lalee's Kin* lack the capacity of the Beales to transform their surroundings through performance. The world of show business never firmly touches these two southern environments. One of Lalee's daughters says that she loves to dance, but the film never shows this love being put into action; the Delta in this film is untouched by the aesthetic or theatrical. It is television that dominates the world of the Burks. (By contrast, the Beales do not appear to even own a television set but instead listen to the radio, like a family out of the 1930s.) One of the Burk grandchildren is named Robert Blake, after an actor on his mother's favorite television show, *Baretta*. But this love for television does not seem to inspire the Burks to achieve any heights of performance themselves. One of the most memorable moments in the film takes place when the father is watching a boxing match on his set. The excitement of the match causes this rather quiet, passive man to writhe about in his seat, occasionally raising himself up in excitement, as though wanting to give full physical and emotional vent to his responses, to leave behind his role as a passive spectator in a manner otherwise repressed in his day-to-day existence.

Unlike the Beales, the Burks are not "natural" camera subjects. In particular, some of the men of the family, as well as Mrs. Burk, give the impression of being distinctly uncomfortable while being filmed. At times, it looks as though they are being gently prodded into talking to the Maysles brothers. Their stiffness and formality before the camera suggests something closer to a newsreel or socially conscious documentary of the 1930s, with subjects who are looking at a motion-picture camera for the first time and not fully understanding what is being asked of them. In one sequence, a family member reads haltingly out of a *World Book* encyclopedia, apologizing that he can only read "the little bitty words." For a Maysles film, this moment feels unusually set up, done strictly for the benefit of the camera. (Where did this man get an encyclopedia?) He is not subjected to ridicule, and the moment has its pedagogical function for the viewer in demonstrating the near-illiteracy of the Burks. But the sequence is symptomatic of the difficulties the filmmakers seem to be having in animating or relaxing some of their subjects. Unlike the Beales, the people we see in *The Burk Family of Georgia* and *Lalee's Kin* never transcend or complicate their status as social subjects in a documentary. At the end of the film, Mrs. Burk declares that she was born poor, lived poor, and most likely will die poor. In this manner, these families are more fixed and definite than the Beales, less fluid and available to be read on multiple levels, in spite of the numerous points of contact among them.

Due to accents and local vernacular, both films are partially subtitled. Maysles has vacillated over the years in terms of his attitude toward subtitling, in his interview with me regarding it as necessary but in earlier interviews criticizing it, as though it were imposed on him and his collaborators.[12] Through subtitling, these American subjects become, in essence, "foreigners," and the film is turned into a kind of ethnographic expedition. Literacy and education are addressed in both films, either directly or indirectly, as in the "little bitty words" *World Book* sequence from *The Burk Family*. In another early sequence from the film, we see one of the Burk daughters in school reading haltingly aloud from Mark Twain, in which she must stumble through a literary version of the southern vernacular she more naturally speaks.

The implications of such moments are clearer when placed in relation to *Lalee's Kin*, in which literacy is a central project of the film and of Barnes's ambitions for his school district. "The students," Barnes declares, "have weak vocabulary skills, and they don't understand the language." He adds, "We got kids in kindergarten who don't know their own names." Statements like these are later implicitly juxtaposed with such moments as the community manager Robert Jamison teaching the old woman Sadie to write her name on a form. To lack language skills and education is strongly bound up with oppression in this world. Lacking these skills makes one less than human or less "civilized," a slave, something animal-like—although even an animal (or at least a pet) will usually recognize the sound of its own name.

At the same time, within this culture one hears the kinds of creative reimaginings of language typical of the vernacular and dialect that spring up in isolated communities. When Sadie tells Jamison about a husband who abandoned her, her words are, "He got gone." Her ingenious refraction of the rules of English grammar is the type of gesture that would most likely be done away with once Tallahatchie improves its "vocabulary skills" and begins attempting to match them to national standards. This may be a fair price to pay for breaking out of the cycle of poverty and oppression, even if in the process some vital elements of a community's indigenous culture are erased. As Barnes says early in the film, "The Delta has a heritage, a history which defines but also limits it."

| | |

For Umberto Eco, one of the fundamental elements of a cult film is that it is outside of the conscious control of those who created it: "Its addressee must suspect it is not true that works are created by their authors. Works are created by works, texts by other texts, all together they speak independently of the intention of their authors" (199). While this argument is only partially correct (there are numerous auteurist cult films, for example), it does relate to some interesting elements of *Grey Gardens*, although even here some caution is required. If *Grey Gardens* is a film that is "larger" than the Maysles brothers and the sum of their conscious intentions, it is also unimaginable without them. Hovde has spoken of the spell the Beale women cast over the brothers while they were shooting the film. Both men were so taken with the personalities of the Beales that, according to Hovde, they could not articulate what they found so fascinating about these two women.

Rather than attempting to fully address their feelings toward the Beales, the Maysles brothers simply filmed and filmed, as though enraptured but without a clear purpose outside of the desire to simply document their encounters with the Beales. While Albert Maysles has often stressed the importance of developing close ties with his camera subjects, the dynamic the Maysles brothers developed with the Beales exceeds this conversational-partner relationship. This emerged partly due to practical considerations. Like the Beatles in *What's Happening*, the Beales would not stop acknowledging the camera and performed for it virtually nonstop. The Maysles philosophy of not strongly intervening in the situations they are filming led, as in *What's Happening*, to this strong element of direct address. But the Beales go one step further than the Beatles ever dared to go: they interact with the filmmakers as specific individuals, not only playing to the camera but playing to Albert and David individually.

The early auteurist practice of cinephilia, to a large extent fixated upon classical Hollywood, often attempted to locate the elusive source of inscription within films that were, on a practical production level, collaborative. Serge Daney has referred to this type of cinephilia as one in which the presence of the auteur is glimpsed in "a void between two words, two letters" (French 21). Offscreen space in cinephilia is highly fetishized and assumes a number of different forms. This fascination with the offscreen in auteurism reflects its concern with the presence and absence of the filmmaker. The filmmaker's style must be fully present and recognizable within the editing and mise-en-scène but absent from the images to give them life; however, the filmmaker (we believe) is also there, at the moment of filming, just on the other side of the camera but unseen. Actor-directors (Orson Welles being the preeminent example) are still caught up in this fantasy of presence and absence, albeit in somewhat different terms, since to cross over to the other side of the camera, they must often assume fictional roles. More than any documentary practice before it, cinéma vérité (in terms of the technical equipment it uses and the consequent close physical ties between filmmaker, camera, and his or her subjects, as well as in terms of its general ethos) introduces the real possibility of the filmmaker's physical presence being brought into the image, even if all films of this school do not necessarily deliver on this possibility. The literal presence of Jean Rouch and Edgar Morin in *Chronicle of a Summer* is crucial to the interventionist nature of the project in which Rouch and Morin, as Fereydoun Hoveyda writes, "enter the arena, to put themselves on stage (and into question)" (251).

In the purest type of direct cinema, as in classical cinema, theoretically the traces of authorial inscription are least apparent. When David Maysles claims that he and his brother never ask their subjects to move so that the light or composition will be better, he is refusing (at least officially) the conventional role of the controlling *metteur-en-scène* and insisting upon the ability of the camera and microphone to record spontaneous events. But whatever their publicly expressed devotion to pure direct-cinema goals and humility before their subjects, the Maysles brothers make themselves physically present in their films more extensively than any other American direct-cinema practitioners. Nevertheless, one can sense their reluctance to cross from behind to in front of the camera; and so they play a game of presence and absence. For the viewer, the fleeting physical presence of the auteurs becomes part of the cinephilic love for spotting something you are "not meant to see," but which is also clearly there to be seen.

What is distinctive about *Grey Gardens* is simply its extremity in terms of the physical presence of the Maysles brothers within their own film. (It is true that in *Gimme Shelter* David Maysles and Charlotte Zwerin are physically present within the film itself, as they screen footage to Mick Jagger and Charlie Watts. But they are positioned as being in control of that particular situation, with Albert Maysles remaining invisible within the images he has been so central in creating.) The Beales will (often literally) pull the Maysles brothers out from behind their camera and recording equipment. Edie, in particular, has a tendency to step too close to the lens and confide in the brothers.

In spite of the ostentatious behavior of the Beales, the film never quite slides into the documentary mode Bill Nichols has identified as "interactive," with its strong reliance on not only the interview but also on frequent and explicit exchanges between filmmaker and subject (44–56). For the Beales, exchange with the Maysles brothers is of secondary importance to the possibility of having a captive audience. In this manner, the film is closer to documentary and nonfiction portrait films of the 1960s, such as *Portrait of Jason* and *Blonde Cobra* (dir. Ken Jacobs and Bob Fleischner, 1962). Here the camera does not simply reveal something about the subject; the subject seizes the moment and performs in excess of the conventional needs of the filmed portrait. We move beyond revelation to a kind of exhibitionism in which the spectator's own responses are implicated. In *Chronicle of a Summer,* Morin states: "When sincerity is a bit more than life size, it's called ham. Or else exhibitionism. If they are thought actors or exhibitionists, our film is a failure." In *Grey Gardens,* the Beales are actors and exhibitionists (or "hams"), but such exhibitionism is the mark of this particular film's strength, not its failure.

While the women at the Paris theater in New York were correct in noting that the relationship the Beale women established with the Maysles brothers would have been unimaginable had the filmmakers not been men, their objections to this gender dynamic are misplaced. Edie is is not engaging in simple exhibitionism or sexual desperation brought on by the entrance of two eligible men in her life. It is as though she wants to obliterate the distance between her status as a camera subject and the Maysles brothers' status as filmmakers. Taking the logic of auteurism to its absolute limit, Beale wants to appropriate the filmmakers directly as love objects while they are still attached to their filming equipment.

However, as Hovde and Meyer (and the Maysles brothers themselves) have noted, the filmmakers' closeness with their subjects was due not simply to the force and charisma of the Beales nor to their insistence on interplay with the filmmakers. Meyer has drawn links between the Maysles brothers and the Beales, arguing that all of them were involved in dependency relationships with one another (*Grey Gardens*, DVD commentary track). The two women were not mere subjects for the men behind the camera but extensions of them—and vice versa. Most likely as a result of this mirroring effect, *Grey Gardens* avoids (or at least considerably mutes) the more typical Maysles structure of the clash between worlds. Like *Salesman*, *Grey Gardens* allows the Maysles brothers to project their own Jewish working-class family and social situations onto subjects who are, in so many other ways, very different from them. Albert Maysles has said, "The Beales were aristocracy and we're from Russian Jewish stock. To make a close friendship with people of that social level is a long journey" (Pryluck, "Ultimately" 9). The acts of transference and displacement that occur in *Salesman* are repeated here in a different form. The transference of the traveling-salesman archetype from Jewish American working-class to Irish Roman Catholic working-class in *Salesman* undergoes a set of even more complex permutations in *Grey Gardens:* not only from Jewish to Catholic but from working-class to upper-class, and from two male figures (the Maysles brothers) in the earlier film who project onto and identify with an Irish male figure (Paul Brennan) to, in the later film, the Maysles brothers projecting onto two female figures.

Timothy Corrigan has argued that "cult movies are the products of a viewer who acts out simultaneously the vision of child and adult" (26). All cult films for Corrigan "are adopted children" (28).[13] *Grey Gardens* enacts this familial metaphor with a particular vividness. Hovde and Meyer claimed that they were able to maneuver the brothers into ad-

David and Albert Maysles with Mrs. Beale (left)
and Edie. Courtesy of Maysles Films, Inc.

mitting that Albert's fascination with Mrs. Beale was strongly based on her evocation of his recently deceased mother—a powerful matriarchal presence in the lives of her two sons. In one sequence, Edie holds up a portrait of her mother and begins to analyze her features. Edie claims that they connote "British blood, maybe Jewish in the Leman family. I'm not sure. Scotch blood—the Ewings. But it's just a girl from a good French family. It's a very beautiful face." Later in the film, Mrs. Beale adopts an Irish brogue in imitation of a priest, Father Murphy, who had bemoaned the young Edie's lack of discipline: "She sure needs a very strong hand, yer daughter." Like Paul Brennan, Mrs. Beale (regardless of her actual origins) encompasses the Jewish/Irish divide and connection that is so central to the Maysles brothers' own background and to *Salesman*.

In the case of David, according to Hovde and Meyer, Edie's family situation reminded him of his own status as a child—like Edie, he delayed marriage due to a strong attachment to family (Rosenthal, *Documentary Conscience* 377). At the time of *Grey Gardens*, both brothers were still unmarried, and while younger than Edie, they were beginning to approach middle age. Hovde has said of David's relationship with Edie: "He saw her almost as himself" (DVD commentary track). It is clear that, regardless of her fondness for Albert, it is David to whom Edie is more strongly drawn, even going so far as to actively flirt on-camera with him. "Darling David, where have you been all my life?" she exults, as she dances about. "Where have you been? Where have you been?" Early in the film, just before the frequently quoted moment when Edie presents and describes her "costume for the day" to the Maysles (a skirt worn upside down with pantyhose underneath, a head wrapped up in a towel, clipped with an expensive pin), she looks at what David is wearing. "David, you look absolutely terrific, honestly. You've got light blue on." She then looks over at Al and at his presumably drab outfit. "Well, Al, you're still, uh, mother says you're very conservative." David and Edie here become linked by their concern with fashion—although David, like Al, remains off-camera, the physical appearance of the brothers clarified for us through a black-and-white photograph inserted into the sequence's opening shot. Al is implicitly linked with the mother, becoming the "good" son who dresses conservatively.

But the linkage between the Beales and the Maysles brothers is broader than this playing out of family situations. In their refusal to be well behaved direct-cinema subjects, the Beales not only directly address the camera but also appear to determine much of the shape and direction of the individual sequences. In a more obvious manner than in any of their other films, their subjects lead the Maysles brothers around, the Beales implicitly becoming the *metteurs en scène* of their own film, performing the function in front of the camera that the filmmakers simultaneously perform behind it. Edie's statement at the time of the film's release ("'Only we, together, could have made this film'") shows that she clearly understood this (qtd. in Epstein, *"Grey Gardens"* 10). Edie's fashion sense and her love for doing collages tie her to the world of visual aesthetics, while the command of language exhibited by both women allows them to be the unofficial writers of the film's "dialogue."

In the "pink room" sequence near the end of the film, Mrs. Beale says that she cannot open the seat to her bathing suit in front of the camera, as there is no back to it. David's voice can then be heard: "We won't look." The camera pans left, away from Mrs. Beale, catching the Maysles brothers themselves in a large, cracked mirror on the other side of the room, Albert with the camera on his shoulder facing forward, and David in profile, sound equipment on his shoulder and headphones over his ears. Rather than keep the camera completely on themselves at this moment, though, Albert slowly pans and zooms past himself and his brother, focusing his camera on a watercolor of a young and very pretty Edie pinned to the wall. This shot beautifully condenses the complex relationship between the two families. The Maysles brothers share a space with this "aristocratic" family, a feminine space marked by the color pink. But they share it at a slight remove, from behind their camera equipment, their virtual image caught within a mirror, almost like specters that materialize and then disappear. In averting their eyes from the mother's state of partial undress, the filmmakers catch themselves in the mirror, an image they must also look away from, instead finding an image within this image—that of Edie. The camera, though, does not seem to be embarrassed here, either by the possibility of seeing Mrs. Beale's exposed rear end or by the sight of the filmmakers in the mirror. The camera pans only because it is taking its cue from Mrs. Beale. The slow zoom in to the portrait of young Edie, after the camera has caught the

Grey Gardens: Albert and David Maysles film themselves in the mirror of the Beales' Pink Room.

brothers themselves in the mirror, gives the impression of a measured consideration of what is at stake: a reciprocal fascination between the two families, but one in which the Beales, the ultimate subjects of the film, must finally assume dominance.

But the presence of the Maysles brothers also relates back to questions of women and genre. When Bette Davis sings "I've Written a Letter to Daddy" in *What Ever Happened to Baby Jane?* the "Daddy" she is referring to is dead and the letter is being sent to his address "in Heaven above." This type of female-centered project (most frequently gothic or melodramatic in nature but not exclusively—see George Cukor's 1939 version of the comedy *The Women*) often depends for its structure on the marginalization or absence of strong male figures. This absence leads in turn to an "excess" in the representation of these female figures—women behaving in an extravagant manner, their physical presence sometimes doubled or multiplied within the film through familial relations or extremely close friendships. The men are at once expendable, coming and going, and essential in that even in their absence they continue to shape the lives of the women—through their economic and social power and/or through their function as objects of desire. This structure is repeated in *Grey Gardens*, in which absent male figures (father and husband Phelan Beale, the two Beale sons, Mrs. Beale's former accompanist Gould, Father Murphy, Edie's various suitors, Max Gordon, the theatrical agent who discovered Judy Holliday but who told Edie that she was "much funnier") are frequently at the center of conversations. (One is reminded of the original posters for *The Women,* which announced: "*The Women:* It's All about Men!")

The figure of the young Jerry, a kind of handyman in jeans, t-shirt, and painter's cap who regularly visits the women, is interesting in this regard. Edie gives him the nickname of the "marble faun," a reference to Nathaniel Hawthorne's novel, which Edie is seen reading in paperback early in the film as Jerry walks up to her on the porch. The title of the novel refers to the Faun of Praxiteles and to a character within the novel, a young Italian count, Donatello, whose innocence is eventually destroyed through his contact with several American artists. Jerry's innocence is of an altogether different nature—slightly vacant and not especially articulate (at least insofar as the film presents him). For Mrs. Beale, he represents young male company she can enjoy while simultaneously using him to taunt Edie, making her jealous, as though he were her lover and her child. But she also constructs him as a lover for Edie, at one point claiming that he is "madly in love" with her even while mocking her for the huge discrepancy in age between them. "Jerry's out every night with a different girl," Mrs. Beale matter-of-factly declares.

In reality, Jerry Torre's evenings outside of those at Grey Gardens were often spent at local gay night spots, and he would sometimes dance in his jockstrap on the bar of the Anvil, a gay sex club in Manhattan. Two years after the film was made, he was voted Mr. Club Baths of 1977 (Green 29–30). The film never touches on this part of Jerry's life, and most likely the Maysles brothers did not know or were not interested in the reality of Jerry but rather in what Jerry meant to the two Beale women. However, his male presence in the film is feminine as much as masculine. With his head of long and full curled hair, he looks like a pre-Raphaelite slacker. (In *The Beales of Grey Gardens,* a sequence in which Mrs. Beale discusses Jerry's face leads David to compare his looks to the Medicis.) His feminine appearance is noted by Mrs. Beale, who tells him, "You have a beautiful face, like a girl," while also regarding him as the "absolute image" of her own mother. A male figure enters Grey Gardens only to be turned into something at once male and female.

In different ways, the absence and marginalization of male figures in *Grey Gardens* is also true of *The Burk Family of Georgia* and *Lalee's Kin.* Most of the men in *The Burk Family* are defined by alcoholism, failure, or death. At the beginning of the film, Charlotte says, "Every time we turn around it seems like somebody's getting hurt or dying." But what mainly dies or is hurt in this film are the men, with special significance given to two sons who were killed at a young age (one was sixteen and the other twenty-three). Discussion of them dominates the first two sequences of the film, their death positioned as a kind of mystery that the film will presumably answer at some point. (At the beginning of the film, when David Maysles can be heard off-camera asking Mrs. Burk to talk about her sons, she says that she "doesn't want to bring that up no more.") In the opening sequence involving Charlotte and the one involving Mrs. Burk, the women speak to the filmmakers while their husbands are positioned as spectators. Neither Charlotte's husband (who passively sits with his shirt off, listening to his wife) nor Mr. Burk contributes anything to the discussion, and the only image of Mr. Burk in the opening sequence is of his back, walking away from the camera as the topic turns to that of his two dead sons. Mrs. Burk is clearly the dominant figure in the family, while the behavior of the father (like that of his sons) is marked by alcoholism and the inability to maintain steady employment.

While the failures of the male figures dominate *The Burk Family of Georgia*, in *Lalee's Kin* it is the absence of males that is most strongly felt. Lalee never knew her biological father and confesses that she has never been in love—despite the fact that she has given birth to eight children. Men, she declares, "they ain't no good." The basic drive in Maysles toward the maternal is given explicit voice when one of Lalee's daughters declares, "When you ain't got no mama, you ain't got nobody." Nevertheless, the film's parallel editing structure, frequently cutting away from Lalee and her family and returning to Reggie Barnes's attempts to save the school district, supplies a stronger male presence in the film than in either *Grey Gardens* or *The Burk Family*. In a sequence near the end of the film, one of Lalee's grandsons, Main, has a meeting with his mentor from a social-work project. The older and younger males compare hands. "You've got a little, small hand," says the mentor. "My hand look real big to you, don't it? Well, there's hands out there even bigger than mine." Main responds, "When I grow big, my hand gonna be big." On its own terms, this is a touching, lyrical exchange (while also harkening back to the emphasis on the hand and gesture in *Salesman*). But its placement near the end of the film shifts the film's concerns away from the matriarchal world of Lalee toward the "outside" world of men, the very beauty and lyricism of this scene also implying the necessity for Lalee's grandson to get away from her to more successfully cope with the harsh realities of his social environment. While Edie's needing "a strong hand" is treated ironically by Mrs. Beale, in *Lalee's Kin* physical and moral strength is split between the majestic Lalee herself, who repeatedly threatens to "whup" her grandchildren for misbehaving, and figures like Barnes and Main's mentor, who more benignly hold out their hands to the children of Tallahatchie. (Barnes, at one point, apologizes to a gathering of the children in an auditorium for yelling at them, a gesture unimaginable from Lalee, who is made of loving but much sterner stuff.) Whether the approach of men like Barnes constitutes a real alternative to the difficulties of life in Tallahatchie and a possible way out of years of oppression is an issue the film does not resolve.

If many cult films are about family, they also, by extension, speak to microcosmic communities that bond together as a source of refuge from and defense against the hostility of the dominant cultures. This is literally represented in all three Maysles films discussed in this section. But the cult following for *Grey Gardens* suggests that that film's specific inflection of the issue of community has especially resonated with certain spectators. Part of this is traceable to the film's treatment of the bodies of the Beale women. Responding to Goodman's attack on the film in the *New York Times,* Edie Beale told a journalist, "'Mr. Goodman tore me apart saying that I had heavy thighs and was unattractive. He said really brutal things. He found the film completely distasteful.'" Beale's analysis of the nature of Goodman's attack is typically insightful: "'The film portrays age. Age portends death. Death brings God and Mr. Goodman cannot face God'" (qtd. in Epstein, *"Grey Gardens"* 10).

This notion of the presence of God amidst death and decaying flesh suggests a relationship to Roman Catholicism (the Beales were devout Roman Catholics) and the concept of revelation so central to cinephilia in general but especially to the *Cahiers du cinéma* version of it, within which Roberto Rossellini was a central figure. Ingrid Bergman and George Sanders in Rossellini's *Viaggio in Italia* (1953) looking at a skeletal couple unearthed from the ruins of a volcanic eruption and locked in an embrace, causing Bergman and Sanders to come face to face with their own self-absorption and mortality, is an emblematic moment within this type of cinephilia. However, Christianity in Maysles is often positioned as another source of cultural decay and irrelevance, epitomized by the outrageously overpriced Bibles the salesmen hawk to lower middle-class people who cannot afford them; or by the "inspirational" sermons spoken by the likes of Melbourne I. Feltman and Norman Vincent Peale.

While *The Burk Family of Georgia* was cosponsored by the United Church of Christ and the United Methodist church (along with Westinghouse), the church is only referred to in passing in the film and discussed by the Burks as though it were more of a social activity than a religious one. Within such a context, the Beales' Catholicism acquires a sincerity bordering on camp, as when Edie declares that her three favorite things in the world are "the Catholic Church, swimming, and dancing." Nevertheless, a quasi-religious cultlike fascination with the body is often present in the film. "My body is concentrated ground," Mrs. Beale declares. And while David Maysles corrects her by using the word "consecrated," this is likely not a slip on Mrs. Beale's part; like her daughter, she possesses a magnificent command of language. For Mrs. Beale, her body is abundantly physical. She is never ashamed of a body that for her must be concentrated before it can be consecrated.

We often find Maysles's camera drawn to human subjects because they seem to be connected to a theatrical vitality that makes them naturally photogenic. At the same time, these subjects are often presented in such a manner that they are connected to aging and decay, nowhere more so than in *Grey Gardens*. The body becomes heavier here, the skin flabbier, as it slowly, visibly announces it movement toward death. Such a fascination with decay links these Maysles films with the concept of decadence that was so popular in the 1960s and 1970s. The dominant social orders are now faced not simply with decline but with the possible birth of new social orders. However, in these Maysles films, the older generation attempts to hold back the younger, projecting its awareness of aging onto later generations, dragging them down. As one Burk daughter says, "Mama and Daddy wants us to be old, like them. They want me to act as old as they do 'cause I got two kids." And Lalee's granddaughter is given the nickname Granny because when she was little, according to Lalee, "she act like a old lady . . . crawl like a old lady." We have worlds here in which bodies, objects, and social environments are falling apart almost from the moment of conception. Lalee excitedly awaits the arrival of her mobile home from the government. When it does arrive, though, this "new" trailer has clearly seen better days, with visible signs of rodent and roach infestation, a mobile home that Lalee cannot even hook up to running water.

Corrigan refers to the most important motif in cult films being "the debris and excess that define characters and environments" (28). In muted form, these films (especially *Grey Gardens* and *The Burk Family of Georgia*) often suggest a relationship to the surrealist documentary in which modernity is defined by this type of debris rather than by its energy and capacity to renew itself. "Debris and excess" marks the mise-en-scène of these films, in which objects that have long exhausted their function clutter up the lives of these subjects. Maysles's camera frequently calls attention to certain off-kilter details and sharp contrasts: A young girl at the beginning of *Lalee's Kin* scampers down the road in street clothes and a pair of rabbit-eared bedroom slippers, passing wrecked cars and a rusting Coca-Cola refrigerator; or Mr. Burk gets up from a chair and places a gun next to a plastic radio, the juxtaposition emphasized though a close-up; and Edie's eye for sharp contrasts in her own ensembles suggests an untapped surrealist eye. The lives of the Burks are cluttered with useless objects: cars seemingly damaged beyond repair sit scattered across the front lawn, along with an unused washing machine. One may be reminded here of the opening of Georges Franju's classic surrealist documentary *Blood of the Beasts* (1949). In Franju's film, various relics are sold at the gates of Paris, such as mannequins missing their arms, an ancient gramophone, or a lamp its owner draws attention to by hanging it from a tree. By placing these items intended for indoor use in a natural setting, Franju's film not only underlines how these objects have exhausted their modern use value but also paradoxically links these artificial, manufactured items with the natural world. Mr. Burk performs a similar gesture when, instead of cutting up wood for heat, he cuts up a tire and feeds that to the stove. There is a memorable shot early in the film as one of the sons exits the house. As he leaves, he thoughtfully closes the door behind him. But this gesture of social decorum is slightly undercut by the fact that the door has no knob, a detail underlined through a zoom into the hole with the son's finger still in it.

The anxiety on the part of *Grey Gardens'* early reviewers about heavy thighs and sagging flesh highlights the degree to which within cinephilia the love of gesture and surface often translates into a larger fascination with corporeality—with strange, overweight, or misshapen bodies—suggesting a relationship to the worlds of carnival and naturalism, the human as animal: *Freaks* (dir. Tod Browning, 1932) is the classic example here. For all of the theatricality and artifice of the Beales, *Grey Gardens* repeatedly links the women with the natural world and with the cycle of life and death. The film's opening and closing credits are white letters against a green background. This green becomes a color motif throughout the film, strongly tied to nature. In spite of the fact that the Beales have a gardener, Grey Gardens overwhelmingly appears as an environment being swallowed up by trees and other plant life—a sense of nature run amok that no gardener could possibly control. When Edie loses her scarf outside the house, she refers to these grounds as a "sea of leaves," linking the plant life with the ocean that her home looks out on and in which she swims every day. (The film's use of extreme long shots to show Edie swimming suggests that she is being symbolically swallowed up by this natural environment.)

In contrast to *Grey Gardens*, *The Burk Family of Georgia* does not so strongly equate the animals in the film (primarily dogs, chickens, and cats) with its human subjects. While their physical presence appears to be no less strong in this environment than on the Beales' estate (and the film's soundtrack is often overwhelmed by the sounds of roosters crowing), the film is not so insistent on drawing links between animals and humans. Clearly, if it had done so within this context it likely would have implicitly equated the lower classes with an animal state. Instead, the existence of the animals is treated as a fact rather than a symptom or symbol. Edie spends much of *Grey Gardens* speaking of her desire to leave the country and move to New York, its urban noise and chaos something she embraces, in marked distinction to her response to the country: "I can't stand a country house. In the first place, it makes me nervous. I'm scared to death of doors, locks, people roaming around in the background, under the trees, in the bushes. I'm absolutely terrified." At the same time, her choice of language in describing her desire to return to New York links her to the natural world from which she wants to escape. She says that she will accept any apartment in Manhattan, no matter how small. But she refers to these hypothetical apartments as "rats' nests" and "mouse holes." And for someone who professes to be terrified of the outdoors, she is intent on bringing the outdoors into Grey Gardens. At no point does the film ask her to explain why she performs the bizarre act leaving enormous loaves of white bread in the attic for the raccoons, even while complaining about their invasion of the home. Does Edie derive pleasure from watching these animals destroy Grey Gardens, a space she explicitly identifies at the end of the film as "my mother's house?"

The "freak" in much of cinephilia and cult cinema is at once an outsider and someone who, individually or collectively, threatens to overturn conventions within the dominant culture. In this regard, central to any understanding of the *Grey Gardens* cult is the film's large following among gay spectators. While this following does not constitute the only basis for the film's cult appeal, it is nevertheless a crucial element of it. This gay cult is something of which Albert Maysles is well aware (as he indicates in the interview in this book), although it is unlikely that anyone connected with the production of the film would have anticipated the powerful connection *Grey Gardens* would ultimately make with gay audiences. Why this cult exists is a complex matter, and I cannot do full justice to it here. But let us briefly return to Haskell's denigration of the Beales as "travesties of women." Within Haskell's essentialist and moralizing feminist discourse, the Beales are not "real" women; they are too extreme and flamboyant, caricatures rather than inspiring and "mature" role models. To be a travesty of a woman is to fail at fulfilling a conventional gender role. Mrs. Beale's indifference to being a "normal" wife and mother, to looking after the upkeep of her own home, and Edie's failure to marry, settle down, and become a typical upper-class matron establishes a foundation for their otherness, their status as feminine travesties. Doubtless for many viewers, Edie's improvised outfits, assembled through a number of seemingly incompatible elements, are pathetic attempts at being fashionable. In fact, everything about the Beales' style of dress, their manner of speaking and eating, and their performative impulses marks them as being outside of standard modes of social behavior. But it is precisely these areas of excess, of otherness, within which gay subjects have found a space of empathy, if not identification.

On one level, the Beales are consistent with a long line of female celebrities whose artificial manner of behaving lends itself to camp reading strategies. The performances of Gloria Swanson in *Sunset Boulevard* and Bette Davis and Joan Crawford in *What Ever Happened to Baby Jane?*—both films that are major gay cult items—are two obvious examples. When Eco writes that within cult cinema, "its characters are psychologically incredible, its actors act in a mannered way," his general description could be stretched to include the type of performances that have historically been celebrated within various gay cultures (Eco 197). The flamboyance of the Beales, like the flamboyance of Davis or Swanson, immediately lends itself to quotation. The performances of Davis and Swanson are not read by gay spectators as being "natural" but as something constructed. At the same time, this artificiality is celebrated for achieving an emotional authenticity that bypasses (or even surpasses) the performance codes of naturalism. But while stars such as Davis and Swanson are clearly playing roles, the Beales are "playing themselves."

With the Beales, the Maysles brothers find yet another instance of reality validating what is more generally perceived to be the artifice of Hollywood. If movie stars become direct-cinema subjects through a dialectical process of "unmasking" and reglamorizing within the context of documentary form in *Showman* and *Meet Marlon Brando*, in *Grey Gardens* two non–movie stars behave and are filmed in a way that engenders a cultlike response more typically associated with Hollywood celebrities. The Maysles brothers must have had some awareness of this connection to Hollywood even before their film began to assume its cult status. They were savvy enough when it opened to make an "old Hollywood" connection in its publicity by arranging a luncheon with Edie at the Russian Tea Room in New York, in which her two companions were Lillian Gish and Anita Loos. Among other things, Loos told Edie that the character played by Clark Gable in Loos's 1936 screenplay for *San Francisco* was based on Beale's uncle. (A slightly confused Beale at one point called Loos, "My dear Miss Gish.") The event was covered by the *Village Voice*'s openly gay columnist, Arthur Bell (129).

One may consequently be tempted to situate the gay cult response to *Grey Gardens* within a tradition of camp, but I am not certain that this takes us very far. It is striking, for example, that neither Oldham nor Bartlett discusses the film as though it were a camp object. For these two designers, the Beales, far from being treated ironically, are spoken of with the utmost respect. Edie's methods for assembling her daily outfits are regarded as indicative of her true fashion sense, so much so that both men claim to have been inspired by her in their own designs. Oldham speaks with disdain about a fashion spread done by the photographer Steven Meisel (whose name is conspicuously never mentioned) in which a model literally re-creates Edie's look in a tongue-in-cheek fashion, making ridiculous faces as she does so. It is as though Meisel has defaced a sacred object. The same is true of the *Grey Gardens* website and other sites devoted to the film or to the Beales. While not entirely without humor, what is especially moving about them is their straightforward and almost innocent investment in the Beales and in the film. (One site devoted to Edie is entitled, without any apparent irony, "Goddess!") The

Beales, in being so profoundly and eccentrically performative, move beyond camp and touch a major chord. These "travesties of women" to whom we should close our eyes majestically and unashamedly enact their otherness before the camera, celebrating themselves in the face of years of contempt and ridicule.

Like many fans of *Grey Gardens*, Oldham quotes several favorite lines of dialogue from the film, some of which he claims that he or his colleagues use at work in relation to certain situations. But Oldham unintentionally misquotes them. Edie's line, "This is the best thing to wear for the day," becomes, in Oldham's version, "This is the best outfit for the day." Or (from a newspaper clipping shown at the beginning of the film), "It was the most disgusting, atrocious thing ever to happen in America" becomes, "This is the most horrible thing to happen to anyone in America!"

These slips on Oldham's part, though, are entirely consistent with the film itself. It is *misquotation* and not quotation that is the order of the day in *Grey Gardens*. Edie stumbles over lines from "The Road Less Taken" (the end credits quote the poem in its entirety, correcting Edie); Mrs. Beale searches for the correct lyrics to "You and the Night and the Music" ("The words are wonderful," she says) and asks the Maysles brothers for help (they offer it, but she cannot resist correcting them); Edie tries to remember the lyrics to "Lili Marleen" but gives up and says, "If I only knew the words"; and a long section is given over to Edie's performance of "People Will Say We're in Love," whose title is misidentified as "Don't Throw Bouquets at Me," and neither Edie nor Mrs. Beale can completely remember the lyrics. Again, though, this does not stop Mrs. Beale from her impulse to correct. "Oh no, you're way off there!" she barks at Edie as Edie attempts to sing. The Beales are constantly searching for the right word, the exact quotation, the correct way of doing things. But their innate idiosyncrasies compel them to swerve off course, to offer not so much an exact quotation as an *interpretation* that is often as interesting as the texts they are struggling to remember.

What these women say and the manner in which they say it has become central to the fascination that the film has exerted over the last three decades. On one level, the emphasis on language in *Grey Gardens* is simply another manifestation of the larger fascination with language that runs throughout the history of cinéma verité and direct cinema. But the film moves beyond the basic direct-cinema fascination with language that can "breathe." *Grey Gardens* has become a highly quotable work, closer to the way that a Hollywood cult film would be experienced than a documentary. Cinephilia's obsession with the contingent has often been expressed through a response to performance, not only through gesture or facial expression but also through idiosyncratic line readings and accents that cause language to swerve off course, rendering it transparently artificial and instantly quotable.

In *Sunset Boulevard,* Joe Gillis tells us in the voiceover narration, "Audiences don't know that someone writes a film. They think the actors make it up as they go along." In *Grey Gardens*, the "actors" literally do make the dialogue up as they go along, in language that, as many commentators have noted, evokes the literary and theatrical. The inflections that the Beale women bring to their utterances (impossible to reproduce on the page) are much of what makes them so quotable. In the "woman's" melodrama *Caught* (dir. Max Ophuls, 1949), the entrée the protagonist Leonora (Barbara Bel Geddes) desires into the world of the upper class initially occurs through her enrollment in a charm school in which the women learn, among other things, the proper way to pronounce the words *mink* and *Thursday*—the latter being pronounced exactly the way that Edie pronounces it in *Grey Gardens*. In the finishing-school world of *Grey Gardens*, with everything crumbling about them, *skirt* is still pronounced "skuurt" and *Thursday* is pronounced "Thuhs-day." The Beales sound like figures out of an elegant comedy of manners from the 1930s, incongruously placed within a 16mm documentary. The language they speak and their manner of speaking it is, like everything else around them, decaying—although this contrast is not necessarily as strange as it might initially appear. As Corrigan argues, a cult film is often a type of home movie (27). But as *Grey Gardens* shows, literacy and command of language are no guarantees that one will be perceived as belonging to a dominant culture. One's individual and collective status as an outsider is the result of a network of factors in relation to social behavior, history, economics, class divisions, sexuality, and gender that cannot be transcended by accurately quoting Robert Frost or by reading aloud from the encyclopedia.

The beginning and end of *Grey Gardens* are framed by images of a hole created by raccoons that are slowly eating their way into the Beale home. The small hole at the beginning of the film has, by the conclusion,

The end of *Grey Gardens:* The giant gash in the wall created by the raccoons.

The end of *Grey Gardens:* A sleeping Mrs. Beale.

become a giant gash, as though the entire house is being devoured. At the end of the film, the images of Mrs. Beale, half-asleep on a mattress caked with dirt, singing "Night and Day" and surrounded by sleeping cats while her daughter dances alone downstairs in the foyer, uncannily anticipate Mrs. Beale's own death (which took place not long after the film opened). Mrs. Beale seems to be returning to the earth, amidst the decay of her once aristocratic lifestyle. Cinephilia, at its most extreme, has been attracted not simply to the image but to the image's disembowelment, to the moment when the screen and the frame disappear, and the film, now transformed, begins to inhabit the viewer. That giant hole at the end of *Grey Gardens* is terrifying and thrilling—terrifying in that it portends the destruction of one world, but thrilling in that it also could open up to new worlds and new ways of seeing.

Democratic Art Forms:
A Visit with Truman Capote, A Journey to Jerusalem,
Muhammad and Larry, Ozawa, Vladimir Horowitz:
The Last Romantic, Horowitz Plays Mozart,
Soldiers of Music: Rostropovich Returns to
***Russia,* and the Christo and Jeanne-Claude Films**

> People desire to understand that which they cannot understand. . . .
> People desire to understand that which they cannot understand.
> —*Muhammad and Larry*

> Did you meet Cassius Clay?
> —*Salesman*

In 1973, the Maysles brothers were asked by the Bulgarian artist Christo Javacheff and his collaborator and wife Jeanne-Claude to film them at work installing their latest project, *Valley Curtain in Rifle, Colorado*—a mammoth orange canvas stretched across a valley in a small Colorado town. *Christo's Valley Curtain*, running only twenty-eight minutes, is one of the most widely praised of the Maysles brothers' films. It is a visually beautiful work, masterfully edited by the codirector, Ellen Hovde. While made between *Gimme Shelter* and *Grey Gardens*, *Christo's Valley Curtain* more properly belongs to—and in some ways initiates—the later phase of Maysles: films attempting to capture the process by which artists and performers work. *Christo's Valley Curtain* has been followed by several other Christo and Jeanne-Claude films, including most recently *The Gates* (which was unavailable for viewing as of this writing). In addition to the Christo and Jeanne-Claude films, other Maysles films about artists include *Ozawa* (focusing on the conductor Seiji Ozawa, codirected by Susan Froemke and Deborah Dickson), *Vladimir Horowitz: The Last Romantic* (1985) and *Horowitz Plays Mozart* (both dealing with the pianist Vladimir Horowitz, the former codirected by Froemke, Dickson, and Patricia Jaffe; the latter codirected by Charlotte Zwerin and Froemke), *Muhammad and Larry* (1980; the boxers Muhammad Ali and Larry Holmes preparing for a fight—although it may be a stretch to consider boxing an art form, it is a type of public performance) and *Soldiers of Music: Rostropovich Returns to Russia* (1991; documenting Dimitri Rostropovich's return to the Soviet Union after an exile of sixteen years). Also relevant to this group, although preceding and in some ways standing apart from it, are *A Visit with Truman Capote* (largely a filmed interview with Capote after the publication of *In Cold Blood*) and *A Journey to Jerusalem* (Leonard Bernstein's visit to Israel after the Six Day War to conduct Mahler's "Resurrection" symphony).

Assessment of the value of these films (as well as the numerous others produced by Maysles Films profiling musicians, choreographers, dancers, and composers) within the context of Maysles's entire body of work is a complex matter. In spite of many effective moments, none of them are equal to the best of his work, from *Showman* through *Grey Gardens.* The limitations of these later films have largely to do with their status as commissioned works, which, unlike in earlier commissioned films as *Meet Marlon Brando, What's Happening* or *Gimme Shelter,* the Maysles brothers were unable to completely transcend. This is particularly evident in the films initiated, produced, or coproduced by Peter Gelb of the classical division of Columbia/Sony Records. These films came about after Gelb became acquainted with Albert and David Maysles at a party in the early 1980s, when Gelb was vacationing on Fisher's Island, near Manhattan. Gelb offered them the opportunity to make a series of films for Columbia's (and, later, Sony's) classical music division. Many of these films, whatever their virtues, are designed to essentially flatter their subjects as well as sell music products—the films become not only an extension of the marketing process but, at times, even interchangeable with it. For example, an Air France commercial done by Maysles Films uses footage from *Christo in Paris* (1990) of young lovers kissing along the Seine, the commercial even recycling the same underscoring used for the opening of *Christo in Paris:* Edith Piaf's recording of "La vie en rose." Of course, the shooting of the commercial may have preceded the film or occurred simultaneously with it, but this in itself is a symptom of the overlapping in later Maysles between the commercial and the noncommercial. An even more extreme example would be *The Met in Japan* (1989), a promotional short done for the Metropolitan Opera's 1988 tour. In addition to documenting the standard meeting of East and West (the conductor James Levine is asked by interviewers if he likes Japanese food, and a Japanese woman declares that Western music "has more feeling" than Japanese music), the film devotes an extensive amount of footage to the opera stars Placido Domingo and Kathleen Battle doing commercials for such lucrative Met sponsors as Nikka whiskey and Asahi beer. On the Maysles website, the still used for *The Met in Japan* in the filmography is, in fact, taken from Battle's whiskey commercial, a commercial that is done, as Battle puts it in the film, "with such great style and taste."

As in their television commercials, the Maysles brothers skillfully employ their direct-cinema style on these commissioned films, showing personal or backstage material, the performers relaxing with family and friends or engaged in sometimes intense aesthetic debates. But only occasionally is there a feeling that the subjects have been deeply revealed by the camera or that we are being invited to observe a process of working that the artists would not want us to see. It is perhaps significant in this regard that there is a sequence in both *Running Fence* (1978) and *Ozawa* when their subjects, at moments of particular emotional intensity, ask the Maysles brothers to stop filming, a request with which they comply. Even if one is able to appreciate their ethical delicacy in not wanting to violate the privacy of their subjects at these moments, such a gesture is inextricably bound up with the atmosphere of caution that surrounds these films.

Two films I shall not otherwise discuss in this section will serve as brief examples of the kinds of limitations that crop up in many of these later works. In *Baroque Duet* (1992, in collaboration with Froemke,

Gelb, and Pat Jaffe), the famously temperamental opera singer Kathleen Battle is presented as warm and gracious, much loved by colleagues and family. It is possible, as Maysles maintains in my interview with him, that this is the only element to her personality that Battle presented to the camera. (And, of course, it is also possible that Battle's reputation as a difficult person is inflated. I wouldn't know.) Still, in such instances one can only ponder the enormous gap between what is known about the behavior and personality of the subject and the selective nature of what we observe in the finished product. Direct cinema here does not so much reveal as obfuscate. In a similar fashion, there is *Jessye Norman Sings Carmen* (1989, in collaboration with Froemke, Gelb, and Zwerin), which deals with that opera singer's attempt to break out of the heavy, German repertoire with which her reputation was established through a recording of Georges Bizet's *Carmen*. The film is given a by-now familiar early direct-cinema structure of conflict and the overcoming of obstacles: will Norman triumph with this bold, new direction in her work? The film implicitly answers in the affirmative through its celebratory presentation of her performance in the final sequence. But Norman's recording of this opera was not a great triumph for her, a fact that the film is able to conveniently avoid by focusing solely on the recording process and not showing the response to the final product. The basic drive toward optimism in these films—the sense that these subjects are fascinating, wonderful personalities who create great art—is not far removed from a celebrity profile in *Vanity Fair* magazine. While *What's Happening* and *Gimme Shelter* have a weight and power as documentary films that are not predicated on audiences being admirers of the Beatles or the Rolling Stones, *Jessye Norman Sings Carmen* is unlikely to appeal to anyone outside of fans of the singer.

A Maysles film achieves much of its distinction from the sense of a sustained encounter with its subjects, drawing out complexities and nuances in personality and behavior in relation to carefully defined social settings. But with their elliptical structures and tendency to celebrate the most widely known facts about their subjects, these later films mute what is most distinctive about Maysles. In these films, Albert Maysles and his collaborators are too obviously "salesmen," and the act of selling is never seriously questioned, as it is in the most interesting Maysles films. That Maysles Films has almost entirely devoted its time and energy over the last two decades to this kind of work only magnifies the disappointment. The days of *Salesman* and *Grey Gardens* now belong to an unreachable and unrepeatable past. At the same time, none of these later films are without interest. All of them are, within their carefully delimited formats, accomplished and even moving works. In this manner, one may think of these films as poised between the television commercials (in which the Maysles brothers' direct-cinema style is applied to pure selling) and the more personal projects.

| | |

Most significantly, a number of these films take the subject of work, treated so richly in *Showman*, *Meet Marlon Brando,* and *Salesman,* and shift it to the realm of aesthetic production. The Christo and Jeanne-Claude films treat work in relation to aesthetics in the most extended manner. It has been argued that what we observe in the Christo and Jeanne-Claude films is a process of production (their large-scale art projects) that has clear analogies with the Maysles brothers' own method of work. Jonathan Vogels has drawn some links in this regard, in particular noting Christo and Jeanne Claude and the Maysles brothers' shared belief in setting a production process in motion and then letting that process takes its course. In an essay on *Christo's Valley Curtain* and the second of the Christo and Jeanne-Claude films, *Running Fence,* Nancy Scott draws similar links, seeing in the Christo and Jeanne-Claude works "the sort of ambiguous catalyst of unplanned moments and of unfolding layers of meaning [the Maysles brothers] so admirably capture on film" (61). At the beginning of *Christo's Valley Curtain,* Christo states, "Generally, the artist is the supreme master in the studio. . . . For me, the excitement . . . really begins when I leave the studio. . . . So what happens in the real world changes my idea and the drawings themselves."

I am not entirely convinced of the analogies with Maysles here. The importance given to studio preparation (design and construction of the raw materials of the project) by Christo and Jeanne-Claude, which is then tested against enormous natural settings and mammoth physical constructions, requiring, in some cases, hundred of workers and collaborators, is in some ways the opposite of how the Maysles brothers usually work. What Christo and Jeanne-Claude put together has more in common with a Hollywood superproduction than it does direct cinema:

the marshalling of millions of dollars in funds and resources, the tremendous act of physical labor involved, and the "invasion" into a location in which something at once natural and artificial is constructed, but only for a temporary period. In *Islands* (1986), Christo complains of his difficulties obtaining permission to construct his project: "If [the *Islands* project] was the backdrop to some multimillion-dollar Hollywood production, there would be no problem." But in effect, the Christo projects, whatever their aesthetic and social merits, function as giant location sets that are promptly dismantled at the end of the shoot. While chance and the vicissitudes of the natural world play a role in the construction of the work, Christo and Jeanne-Claude are driven to produce a finished project that more or less conforms to their predetermined vision, in spite of Christo's statement that "what happens in the real world changes my images and my ideas" (Scott 62). At the end of *Christo's Valley Curtain,* as Christo and Jeanne-Claude stand back from the finished work and look at it with pride, Christo says, "Incredible. Just like the drawing." With Maysles, the philosophy of nonintervention, of the artists refusing to impose themselves on the "reality" being filmed, stands in contrast to Christo and Jeanne-Claude, who transform reality and the natural world. "Art is about transformation," Christo states explicitly in *Christo in Paris.* But for Maysles, art is about revelation experienced through more immediate contact with—and appreciation of—various social worlds and their human subjects.

The Christo and Jeanne-Claude films are not so much allegories about Maysles's filmmaking practice in relation to realism and spontaneity as another instance of the paradoxical relationship much of Maysles has with Hollywood-like spectacle. Like a Christo and Jeanne-Claude project, the success of a Maysles film implicitly depends on the harmony of a collaborative atmosphere in which everything is, so to speak, for the good of the show. More than any other Hollywood genre (or subgenre), the backstage musical has articulated this ideal of collaboration, of an ensemble working together (usually under the strong but not overly dominating leadership of a director) to create a spectacle that also gives life to American ideals. It is difficult not to think of the musical genre in *Running Fence,* as all of the workers come together to construct the fence against a pressing deadline, while a recording of "Take It to the Limit" redundantly plays on the soundtrack, the collective physical actions of the workers coming close to resembling a dance ensemble. Everyone in the Christo and Jeanne-Claude films becomes a kind of artist by mere contact with the projects, and everything they do, everything they work at, may be seen as art. In *Running Fence,* when a local housewife speaks at a public defense of the project, she argues that its temporary nature in no way disqualifies its status as art. She herself has created meals for her family that she thought were "masterpieces" but were then consumed and forgotten.

Christo has denied the theatricality of his own work, claiming that "some people say I make theatre art, but it is *not* theatre, because there is not one element of make-believe anywhere. All is reality. Everything really happen[s]" (Tomkins, Bourdon, and Gorgoni 34). But in observing the workers assemble his valley curtain, the theatrical evocation of a stage curtain must surely be obvious to everyone but Christo himself. In *Running Fence,* a local artist who opposes the project describes it as using "agriculturally zoned land for what amounts to advertising for their [Christo and Jeanne-Claude's] books and movies and happenings and theatrical gestures." In the beautiful final shot of the film, the white nylon fabric of which the fence is composed flaps in the wind and then spreads itself across the lens of the camera, like a curtain being pulled across the frame, bringing the film to a theatrical close.

Apart from the projects themselves, Christo in the films often behaves like a temperamental director whose vision is not being realized to its fullest extent. At the beginning of *Christo's Valley Curtain,* he refers to his resistance to being "the supreme master" of what he creates. Nevertheless, his occasional outbursts may be seen as those of someone who wishes to control his work in the manner of a supreme master while also being forced to continually subdue and modify that vision in relation to the demands of the collective. Throughout Maysles, the "show" (be it a Christo and Jeanne-Claude project, a boxing match, or the conducting of a symphony) is one in which democratic ideals prevail over threats to those ideals. Here the work of art, produced collectively but shaped and controlled by a strong visionary figure, serves as a magnificent embodiment of what can be produced within a democracy, however flawed certain individuals or political figures might be in their refusal to appreciate aesthetic innovation. Moreover, what is good for the makers of art also serves a public function, bringing people together (however contentiously) as spectators. Near the end of *Christo in Paris,* as Parisians gather on or near the Pont Neuf and angrily debate the covering of the bridge by Christo and Jeanne-Claude, one man says, "If the bridge weren't wrapped, we would never have spoken to each other." And at the end of *Christo's Valley Curtain,* one of the workers makes a reference to the project coming together due to "everybody workin' together." David responds by noting, "It's a democratic art form."

Democracy (particularly in its American practice) underlies a number of these films dealing with artists and is often positioned over and against Communist or other nondemocratic social and political forms. Within the ideology of these films, democracy creates a space within which artists have the freedom to create. Throughout *Ozawa,* there is an emphasis on Seiji Ozawa's physicality, his spontaneity and almost childlike nature. He touches his students, coaching them in the proper manner of conducting, with special emphasis given to a young Japanese male student who must be, in Ozawa's words, "loosened up." This physical and emotional stiffness is not simply one which this individual student possesses but, so the film would have us believe, is innate to Japanese culture—an innateness that Ozawa, now happily conducting the Boston Symphony, has transcended.

Soldiers of Music makes this conflict between Communism and democracy overt in that it addresses the return to Russia by Dimitri Rostropovich (now the conductor of the National Symphony in Washington, D.C.) and his wife, the opera singer Galina Pavlovna, after their political exile due to their support of Alexander Solzhenitsyin. In sequence after sequence, we are told of the enormous suffering of artists in the Soviet Union prior to perestroika, with Solzhenitsyin's ongoing exile continuing to cast a pall over the official jubilance of the proceedings. Near the end of *Soldiers of Music,* as Rostropovich is conducting a Shostakovich symphony, in the voiceover narration he says that Shostakovich once told him, "We're all soldiers of music. There are no generals among us." Both Ozawa and Rostropovich must leave their countries of origin, however painful that process of separation, and become, if not exactly American, significantly affected by the comparative freedom offered to artists within American culture. This notion of an artist fleeing the repressions of Communism underpins all of the Christo films but is made most explicit in *Christo in Paris,* in which Christo discusses leaving Eastern Europe in the late 1950s, which was then in what he calls its "high period of Stalinism" and marked by a "poverty of creativity."

The conflict between worlds, a structuring element central to so much earlier Maysles (and muted in *Grey Gardens* and *The Burk Family of Georgia*), returns here. But it is often played out on a massive physical scale, a spatial idea as much as a dramatic or human one. The films often show large, collective spaces: nations, cities, or overwhelming natural environments. If in such films as *Salesman, Gimme Shelter,* or *Grey Gardens* the laws of time and the natural world enter into and contaminate the spaces and bodies of the film's subjects, many of the Maysles films dealing with artists concern themselves with the reverse: artists go out into the world and control space and nature, symbolically or literally taming environments and bringing them into the service of the artist. *A Journey to Jerusalem* spends much of its running time showing Bernstein driving through what he experiences as a new, optimistic Israel. Space here is comparatively open in the aftermath of the war. "Of all the times I've been to Jerusalem, I've never been allowed past this Mandelbaum Gate," he says as he is about to drive through it. In *Salesman,* Paul Brennan gets lost in the "Muslim district" of the small Florida town in which all the street signs have Arab names. But in *A Journey to Jerusalem,* Bernstein drives freely and happily through a world in which he sees Jews and Arabs intermingling. "Now I have a feeling of really being in the Orient," he says as he drives past Arabic stores. Bernstein's fantasies of a harmonious Arab/Israeli paradise show no apparent bounds. When visiting the Mosque of Omar, he declares, "This can become a model for the world."

In *Christo's Valley Curtain,* local golfers comment that the construction is taking more time than they had imagined. The film places great importance on the two remaining hours the workers have in which to get the curtain up before the winds change direction, thereby threatening not only the completion of the curtain but the lives of the workers. But time here is simply a question of deadlines to be faced—a classical overcoming of obstacles, successfully achieved in all of these Christo and Jeanne-Claude films, which, with one exception, end on a note of triumph. These films return to a variation on the crisis structure of the Robert Drew films from which David and Albert Maysles had originally wanted to break away. In these instances, though, the crises are self-induced (Christo and Jeanne-Claude enter into these projects with a full awareness of the various problems that lie in wait) rather than arising out of social and political situations that get out of control, as in the Drew films. When the covering of the Pont Neuf in *Christo in Paris* appears to be going smoothly, David Maysles can be heard off-camera, gently taunting Christo by saying, "What are you going to do with no crisis, Christo? It's so easy." This self-induced crisis becomes part of a staging of the romantic agony of the artist.

The lightness of these films is part of their charm, even while it limits them, particularly in comparison with early Maysles. In this manner, *Running Fence* becomes an optimistic reworking of *Gimme Shelter* and *Salesman*—complete with a happy ending. As in *Gimme Shelter*, Europeans come to California and attempt to transform an American space through their art of "theatrical gestures." But they must first go door to door, working like salesmen to convince the local farmers to agree to the installation. Scott has drawn attention to Christo and Jeanne-Claude's goal of making art that "bears a relation to the real world, underlining the important interrelation of art, nature and society" (65). This dialectical goal in turn affects the structure of the films and their "constant use of oppositions" (65). Such oppositions occur within the images themselves and in their montage structure, with its reliance on parallel editing. This editing strategy becomes increasingly scattered with each succeeding film, from Hovde's simple and expressive cutting in *Christo's Valley Curtain* between the quiet of Christo and Jeanne-Claude's studio to the comparative chaos of the Colorado work site, to the increased reliance in the later films on cutting between multiple spaces, cities, and time frames. (*Islands* and *Christo in Paris* even overlap some of the same footage.)

Far more impressive than the sometimes obvious crosscutting of the later films is the camera's capacity for drawing attention to this element of dialectic and contrast within individual shots. Some of these relate directly to filming the work itself: in *Christo's Valley Curtain*, the juxtaposition of a golfer, calmly making a putt, with the massive orange curtain visible many yards behind him; or in *Running Fence*, when the fence itself is opened just wide enough for a herd of sheep to pass through. These images, in tandem with the almost silent soundtracks at these specific moments, implicitly suggest an absolute harmony between the art works of these "city slickers" (as Christo and Jeanne-Claude are called in *Running Fence*) and the natural environments within which these works have been thrust.

The one Christo and Jeanne-Claude film that climaxes on a note of anything less than triumph for the artists and workers is *Umbrellas* (1996, codirected by Henry Corra and Grahame Weinbren). Here the installation of large umbrellas across two mountainous valleys, one in California and the other in Japan, ultimately resulted in the deaths of two individuals, a woman in California and a man in Japan, due to weather conditions. The crises of *Umbrellas* go beyond self-inducement, as nature overwhelms Christo and Jeanne-Claude's confidence that they are able to peacefully coexist with the natural world. "Whenever you add something artificial to nature," states a Japanese shop owner in the film, "there are consequences." The camera in *Umbrellas* loses its prior omniscience once the deaths occur; our only views of Christo and Jeanne-Claude from this point on are through television broadcasts. The film ends on a note of pathos, with the film dedicated to the two people who died as a result of the project.

Even this ending, though, does not negate most of what precedes it, nor are the deaths positioned within the film as a culminating point of violence and decadence, as with the death in *Gimme Shelter.* Gone from *Umbrellas* are the conflicts in *Running Fence, Islands,* and *Christo in Paris* between politicians and "ordinary" people unable to appreciate the art. Instead, the film shows virtually everyone in Japan and California embracing the installation and profoundly moved by the final result. The same Japanese shop owner who warns about the dangers of mixing the natural with the artificial describes the umbrella project as one in which "dream and reality have come together," while in California a woman is moved to tears by the sight of the umbrellas. "It was truly a blooming," she declares (a statement echoing Christo's earlier description of umbrellas that will "open like a flower"), adding that the only other sight that has moved her as much is the birth of her own daughter.

The parallel editing of *Umbrellas* not only structurally mimics a primary ambition of Christo and Jeanne-Claude's project to link the cultures of Japan and the United States. It most often does this through a secondary and related structuring element built around families, children, and couples mating or individuals looking for their ideal lifetime partner. In a brief sequence that has no direct bearing on the construction of the umbrellas, a forty-four-year-old Japanese man describes himself as middle-aged and says that it is difficult for him to work and to find a wife; later in the film, his friends say that they believe he will eventually find the wife he is looking for; another Japanese woman tells of meeting her husband while asking him for directions on a train platform; in California, an elderly woman who supports the umbrellas project says that she has a son who married a Japanese woman, and so on. These brief moments serve to not only link the two cultures but also to strengthen the film's emphasis on the devotion of Christo and Jeanne-Claude to one another. Their art is tied to nature and to the social. It literally brings people and cultures together to work on its installation, and the finished result is ultimately designed for them as well, to move them to tears and remind them of their relationship to the natural world. The film's insistence on family, mating, and children becomes the physical and biological extension of this ideology, with Christo and Jeanne-Claude at the center of this idealized male/female formation.

| | |

These are films about art, but also films about marriage, couples, and families in which the family serves as a foundational support for the artist (as in *Ozawa,* when the conductor speaks of his great luck in having his wife and children in Japan to ground him amidst the uncertainty of his creative life) or becomes part of the creation of the work itself, as in the Christo and Jeanne-Claude films. In contrast to most of the other films about artists and performers, *Vladimir Horowitz: The Last Romantic* moves indoors, largely confining itself to the New York City townhouse Horowitz shared with his wife, Wanda Toscanini Horowitz. The bulk of the footage is devoted to showing Horowitz at the piano. But his wife is present throughout virtually all of this. Even during Horowitz's performances, not only are there occasional cutaway shots to Wanda listening, but Maysles often moves his camera to reframe, showing Wanda in the background. Wanda implicitly functions as spectator and active participant in Horowitz's art, even though she describes herself as having no musical talent at all. Like Ozawa, Horowitz is essentially presented in terms of (and celebrated for) his youthful qualities—his energy, optimism, and visible delight in the people and objects around him. Wanda's comparative dryness of personality, her ironic perspective on Horowitz as he is surrounded (here and in *Horowitz Plays Mozart*) by a seemingly endless supply of fawning admirers, makes her an ideal romantic contrast to her husband and a stern but loving mother figure, occasionally rebuking him for his excessive behavior or rolling her eyes in reaction to moments of particular absurdity on Horowitz's part.

Horowitz's youthfulness, however, is consistently contrasted with his own clearly visible age, one to which he happily and repeatedly draws attention. "I am old days myself," he proudly announces in *Horowitz Plays Mozart;* while in *The Last Romantic*, after speaking of the great musical figures he has known, he notes, "It's terrible. They are all dead." At one point in *The Last Romantic*, Horowitz begins to play "Tea for Two," a favorite song of Edith Beale and given a singular interpretation by her in *Grey Gardens*. Like *Grey Gardens,* the Horowitz films capture an aging, charismatic, and somewhat eccentric figure near the end of life. But Horowitz is much more mobile and physically agile than Edith Beale, still able to command his musical gifts. His home is not a decaying edifice, overrun with cats urinating behind the furniture, but is a meticulously maintained urban dwelling. The only cats we see here are decorative, made of porcelain. For many spectators, this undoubtedly makes for a less painful viewing experience than *Grey Gardens*, although it also results in a less revelatory film. The Maysles brothers here present neither a private view of their subjects nor a public and social one but a cross between the two. The Horowitzes are filmed in their home, a private space, but for the sake of a public performance.

In the Horowitz films and in *Soldiers of Music,* we are presented with marriages in which the wife assumes a secondary role to her artist husband. Wanda Toscanini Horowitz publicly accepts this role. "You can never express your own personality," she says about being married to an artist. "You have to subdue your personality to them. But that's what I chose. Nobody forced me." At several points in *Muhammad and Larry* we see Larry Holmes's wife. But she is given virtually nothing to say, no real function to perform outside of holding their small child on her lap. (She is never shown without this child attached to her.) However, as the Horowitz films show, the issue of Wanda subordinating herself to her artist husband is not as simple as she claims. As the daughter of Arturo Toscanini, Wanda exudes an aristocratic grandeur that is about as far from a subdued personality as one could imagine. As she sits and

Horowitz Plays Mozart: Wanda Toscanini Horowitz and Vladimir Horowitz. Courtesy of Maysles Films, Inc.

listens to her husband play in *The Last Romantic* and *Horowitz Plays Mozart,* she does not so much live in his shadow as assume the role of an ideal spectator, through the force of her personality and her biological status as Toscanini's daughter.

The situation of Galina Pavlovna in *Soldiers of Music* is more complicated. Once a great star of the Bolshoi and initially more famous than her husband, since her defection to the United States her opera career has suffered. Even in her return to Russia, her husband receives the lion's share of attention. In one of the best sequences of the film, Pavlovna and her daughter stand outside the Bolshoi. While her daughter encourages her to go inside, Pavlovna refuses to cross the threshold. "To me," she says, "it would be like stepping across . . . an abyss."

A Maysles commercial for Signet Bank from this same period, featuring Jessica Tandy and Hume Cronyn, presents a concise inversion of this moment from *Soldiers of Music.* Cronyn and Tandy sit on a couch while Cronyn speaks of Apollinaire: "Apollinaire said 'Come to the edge.' They said, 'It's dangerous.' He said, 'Come to the edge.' So they went to the edge. And he pushed them. And they flew." Cronyn points directly into the camera and says, "Affirmation!" In this commercial, being pushed over the edge, with the help of the genius Apollinaire, aids the social collective in triumphing—flying—in a manner that Pavlovna refuses. What is also interesting about this spot is that it is Cronyn who does most of the talking, while Tandy listens. It ends with the two of them insisting that in their creative marriage, each affirms the other. An end title card reads: "Teamwork comes out of trust. And vice versa. Signet Bank. One day we'll be your bank." Within the context of the later Maysles works, Pavlovna's inability to take this small step through the door of the Bolshoi becomes a poignant, melancholic refusal to succumb to the persistent optimism of these films and their investment in pasts that can be reclaimed and spaces that can be conquered through the combined forces of artistry and charisma.

In *Soldiers of Music*, Pavlovna enacts the role of an outsider—from Russia, from which she defected, and from the United States, which has no place for her as an opera singer on a scale comparable to what she enjoyed in the Soviet Union. Her central problem, insofar as the film shows us, is one of language. The daughter of Pavlovna and Rostropovich refers to her father's art as a "universal language," unlike her mother's, for whom spoken (or sung) language remains important. In spite of her many years in the United States, Pavlovna's English is still halting, and her daughter must frequently translate for her or correct her. (Like the Burks of Georgia and Lalee and her family, Rostropovich's English often requires subtitling as well as "correcting" of his sometimes faulty grammar and sentence structure. This does not, however, appear to limit his ability to successfully move across and within cultures.)

While at the beginning of his career, in a film such as *Primary*, Albert Maysles was able to film Jacqueline Kennedy attempting to speak Polish to a group of Polish Americans as a gesture of cultural connection, these later films dealing with artists frequently show the dominance of English over other languages. English becomes the ultimate form of entrée into a global culture of the arts. "You speak English very well, Yo-Yo," says a slightly envious Ozawa to Yo-Yo Ma. In *A Journey to Jerusalem*, there is an extended sequence in which Bernstein listens to an Israeli boy sing for him. He appears to be moved by the spectacle of the boy's performance (although, given Bernstein's innately theatrical nature, it is hard to tell whether his flattery to the boy's father is sincere or not). But the boy speaks no English, and Bernstein speaks little Hebrew, so the boy in unable to understand Bernstein and Isaac Stern's praise of his talent. The film shows the boy shuffling his sheet music at the piano after the performance, appearing proud of what he has done but somewhat isolated from the group gathering to discuss him. *Umbrellas* shows schoolchildren in California preparing e-mails to send to schoolchildren in Japan. Their teacher tells them that this written communication will help the Japanese children with their English. But there is no suggestion that this contact will help the American children to understand even a single word of Japanese.

Language is vital to these films but is also a symptom of the limitations of communication within them. While the multilingual Brando in *Meet Marlon Brando* repeatedly challenges the vacuous flattery offered to him from the reporters, no one in these later films seems capable of resisting the flood of empty language that washes over them. *A Visit with Truman Capote* opens with a reporter telling Capote that with *In Cold Blood*, "I really think you've written a masterpiece here." In *The Last Romantic*, Horowitz is told, "You're marvelous. We haven't heard such playing in a long time"; "I've never heard you play better"; "The last Bach-Busoni was extremely powerful." As Rostropovich attempts to conduct the Tchaikovsky *Pathetique* symphony, a woman repeatedly and distractingly yells out from the audience, "Slava is Zeus!" to a furious Rostropovich. While his daughter later reassures him that the "bitch" who shouted this will be apprehended, the overriding impression is of helplessness in the face of these outbursts. Even while these films labor to create an impression of positive social groups and of continuity between artists and audiences, such moments play out like minor-key variations on *Gimme Shelter's* depiction of its own chaotic and "diseased" body politic.

| | |

In these films about artists, we do not simply look at or listen to the work of art; we also look at the artists, apprehend them physically while they create. *A Visit with Truman Capote* draws attention to Capote's actor-like mannerisms: the way he pulls on his sweater collar and talks to a *Newsweek* reporter while making Bloody Marys; or parades about his living room and stands on a spiral staircase while declaring that "style applies to everything." Gesture assumes central roles in *Ozawa* and the Horowitz films. In *Ozawa*, the camera in close-up lingers over Rudolf Serkin's hands, momentarily poised above the piano keys, as he waits for his cue to play during a concert that Ozawa is conducting. Both of the Horowitz films are hand-centered. In *Horowitz Plays Mozart,* not only is the camera drawn to Horowitz's hands as they play but also to Carlo Mario Guilini's as he conducts. Music in these films is connected to the body of the musicians playing or conducting, becoming a form of gestural writing with the hands. As Horowitz listens to the Mozart playback, he holds out his hand and listens, miming his own playing. If in *Salesman,* the gnarled, arthritic hands of Paul Brennan or the missing finger of James Baker become part of a gestural repertoire symbolizing the struggle to sell and survive, in these later Maysles films hands become emblems of expressive beauty and aesthetic power. After finishing the recording session in *Horowitz Plays Mozart,* Horowitz playfully places his hand over the lens of Maysles's camera, as though wanting to draw the film to a close.

In *Muhammad and Larry,* a concern with the hand (typical of boxing films, in which the hand becomes a virtual totem or fetish) is expanded to include a fascination with the entire bodies of Ali and Holmes. There is a frequent emphasis on feet, on the massaging of Ali's foot or on shoes being laced up in locker rooms. "All the nerves in your body," states Ali, "wind up in your feet." Or Maysles shoots close to the chests of the boxers, and in one memorable shot the hands of Ali's masseur are shown ritualistically moving forward and back over Ali's chest, an image that enacts a fascination with the tactile in relation to the body that runs throughout many of these films. The camera often gets close to these bodies, and at certain moments, such images momentarily halt the otherwise conventional forward drives of the films in showing artists achieving their goals. In *Running Fence,* as Christo and Jeanne-Claude are speaking to the farmer who is sympathetic to their goals of installing the fence, Maysles begins to slowly zoom in to the man's face, allowing us to examine the suntanned surface of his face and neck, with its deeply embedded wrinkles and lines creating a surprisingly beautiful landscape of the face, like that of Randolph Scott in one of his later westerns. Typical of Maysles, what is found to be beautiful is also worn away, aging—a body or object that is subject to the ravages of time but even more beautiful because of that. At the end of *A Visit with Truman Capote,* Capote calls himself the "aging poet," not as a mark of shame but of pride, as though to age in this world is the highest mark of distinction, what gives one weight and presence.

Moreover, such articulations of the physical in Maysles are frequently duplicated by the artists or subjects within the films themselves. In *Islands,* after meeting Willy Brandt, Jeanne-Claude has difficulty recovering from the sight of his good looks: "He's so handsome I could fall for him in two seconds!" In *Horowitz Plays Mozart,* as Horowitz heads toward the recording stage, he spots an attractive young man and rhapsodizes over his good looks. (This is the closest the Horowitz films come to acknowledging Horowitz's homosexuality.) In this cinema so devoted to capturing the subtle nuances of behavior, gesture, and interaction, the photograph serves as a moment that briefly suspends the dynamic between the human subjects and the motion-picture camera that persistently films them. To look at a photograph is a moment when the subjects themselves are permitted (or are encouraged) to look in a sustained manner at the image of the face or body of another person. "Doesn't he look like Chopin?" a proud Wanda asks the Maysles brothers as she holds up a photograph of a young Horowitz.

The photographs that recur throughout Maysles's work are invariably images from a distant, unrecoverable past. The photos of the Beales in *Grey Gardens,* when both women possessed great beauty and were at the center of a certain New York aristocracy, epitomize this tendency. But it is also manifested in some of the films about artists, such as the montage of photographs of Pavlovna's great successes as an opera singer at the Bolshoi, photographs that become part of that past whose recovery would be like "stepping across an abyss." In *Grey Gardens* and *The Last Romantic,* we see a photograph of the subjects from their younger days, but in both cases the corner of the photo has been torn. These torn or missing corners, a vulnerable section of the photograph made more fragile due to the passage of time, become emblematic of not only the fascination with flaws and tears in Maysles but also with the sense of lost time, in which a literal piece of the past has been torn away. In *Christo in Paris,* Christo states: "Imagine if under Louis XIV there were cameras. That would be extraordinary. The twentieth century has developed new means of memory, and all of this [his Pont Neuf project] is a question of historical memory." *A Visit with Truman Capote* shows Capote and the *Newsweek* reporter sorting through photographs, including Carl Van Vechten's famous image of the very young Capote as well as the Richard Avedon photos of *In Cold Blood*'s Perry Smith. In looking at the scar below Smith's left eye and the tattoos on his arm, Capote describes Smith's face as comprised of "mismatching parts." As Capote reads a passage from *In Cold Blood* in which Perry's face is described in detail, Maysles zooms in to Smith's eyes. "Perry is much better looking than I thought he would be," gushes the reporter. The contrast between this statement about the physical attractiveness of a now-executed man who murdered a family, his dark eyes staring back at the camera (and at us) as though casting a spell over those who come into contact with his image, is at once sinister, attractive, and compelling. The eyes seem to speak from the grave.

In a sequence from *The Last Romantic*, Wanda steps away from the space in which Horowitz is playing, goes to another room, and stands in a doorway, listening to him. She later explains to the filmmakers: "When you don't see the artist you hear the real conception of the interpretation, and you are not swayed or impressed by the personality of the artist. In this room, I only hear the sound, and I don't look at him, I don't see him. So I am not under the spell, that magic spell." In spite of the enormously important function of language and music in these films, to look at an artist (even if his art is not visual) is the ultimate form of seduction, a way of falling under the "magic spell" of their physical appearance and personality. (In the otherwise minor film *Concert of Wills: The Making of the Getty Center*, art itself is described as a "seduction process.") In *Muhammad and Larry*, Muhammad Ali performs magic tricks for children and explains to them afterwards: "That's an illusion." At another point in the film, he explains his process of self-hypnosis, in which he chants to himself that he is one of the greatest legends of all time.

In discussing being filmed by Albert Maysles, Todd Oldham refers to falling under what he calls "the Maysles spell," while also calling *Grey Gardens* a "hypnotic" film. To hypnotize or seduce in the direct cinema of Maysles is at once the ultimate point of attraction—what makes the artists in these films, caught and transformed by the lens of the camera, compelling and powerful—and the point at which the seduction process must be modified, since the power of these artists threatens to compromise the ideals of collaboration and of the collective. Ali hypnotizes himself but not others; and the magic tricks he performs announce their own status as illusions.

The cinema of Albert and David Maysles (and their many collaborators) has repeatedly found itself caught up in the paradoxes and contradictions at the heart of not only the documentary but at heart of the cinematic image itself. The Maysles brothers create a form of documentary that is no less concerned with capturing reality than any other. To this day, Albert Maysles only discusses his films in relation to the purest of direct-cinema goals. Nevertheless, the films he made suggest that justice cannot be done to the world without the mediating elements of fantasy and seduction, of obsession and fetish, that are not always central to direct-cinema discourses but are part of the reality in which we live.

Notes

1. The term "fly on the wall" has commonly been used to describe the methods of direct cinema, but its potentially insidious undertones have caused it to be rejected by almost every direct-cinema filmmaker, including Albert Maysles.

2. The Maysles brothers had hoped to film a business deal of Levine's from start to finish as a structuring element of the film, but this turned out to be impossible (Cameron and Shivas 19).

3. Near the time of his death, David Maysles was working on a film entitled *Blue Yonder,* which was to deal explicitly with his father and older cousin, Alan. The cousin, whom David idolized, was a World War II fighter pilot who died in a training flight after the war was over. Albert briefly discusses him on the director's commentary track of the *Gimme Shelter* DVD, claiming that David was attracted to Mick Jagger while shooting *Gimme Shelter* because Jagger reminded him of his cousin. My thanks to Judy Maysles, David Maysles's widow, for supplying me with information about *Blue Yonder.*

4. "By not separating cause and effect, by mixing the exception and the rule, Leacock and his team do not take into account (and the cinema is precisely a rendering of accounts) the fact that their eye seeking images in the viewfinder is at once more and less than the recording apparatus used by that eye" (Godard 202–3).

5. Godard also spoke of his desire to make another, longer film with Maysles that would be rehearsed without Maysles present or aware of the dramatic

situation. Once Godard and his actors were ready, Maysles would film them, documentary fashion. Unfortunately, this film was never made.

6. While conceding the element of psychological presumption at work here, Zwerin was also attracted to this crosscutting method for its economy and for the way in which it serves to further isolate Paul from the three other men (*Salesman*, DVD commentary).

7. Zwerin has said that the opening was handled in this manner because "when we showed the picture to other people we discovered that the characters weren't sufficiently defined for them, and they were continually mixing up two of the salesmen" (Rosenthal, *New Documentary* 91). While Zwerin does not say which two salesmen were being confused, it must have been McDevitt and Martos.

8. See Susan Froemke's discussion of the problems Maysles Films has had in securing funding (as well as her discussion of the nature of some of their commercial work): "I recently directed a series of three different infomercials for the Fannie Mae Foundation. What was nice was that they very much wanted a Maysles film. Even though they're just half-hours, they're all people-driven and nonscripted—we work it out in the editing room, telling real stories—they're really interesting, and it can be a very effective way to sell a point" (Stubbs 38).

9. Mamber argues that "the Beatles all come out looking alike" in the film (147), and Vogels also notes how their individual identities are often confused by people around them (33).

10. Not all feminist response to the film was negative (see Rosen). David Sargent wrote in the *Village Voice* that *Grey Gardens* is a film that "seems to trouble men more than it troubles women" (134).

11. In its commingling of past and present, of memory through song, *Grey Gardens* has much more interesting links with Stephen Sondheim's stage musical *Follies*, which opened on Broadway in 1971, than it does with the more recent stage-musical version of the Maysles film. For example, both the Sondheim and Maysles works cite the same Robert Frost poem, "The Road Less Taken"—in *Grey Gardens* through Edie's (mis)quoting of it, and in *Follies* through a song, "The Road You Didn't Take," that reworks Frost's basic theme. Coincidentally, the actor who introduced the song in the original Broadway production, John McMartin, played Phelan Beale in the stage version of *Grey Gardens*.

12. Of *The Burk Family,* Maysles said, "We didn't want any subtitles, because that's really a put-down of anybody" (Trojan 29).

13. Corrigan also notes that cult films "are often films about outsiders" (28).

Interview with Albert Maysles |

This interview was conducted in the office of Maysles Films, Inc., on West Fifty-fourth Street in Manhattan in February 2006. (Their office has since moved to Lenox Avenue in Harlem.) Maysles had no private office there (nor, for that matter, does he have one in the Lenox Avenue space). The interview was done at his desk, which sat near the back of the office's large loft space. As we spoke, business went on as usual around us, with numerous employees and interns working at their desks, talking to one another, and answering telephones (all of this being picked up by my crude tape recorder as I spoke to Maysles). Things were unusually busy at the time of the interview because, Maysles informed me, they had just gotten some major assignments for commercials. It was fitting that our interview was filmed by a small camera crew of two, for possible inclusion in a documentary on Maysles's life. And so I became, however briefly, a direct-cinema subject. I tried to behave as naturally as possible and ignore the camera.

JOE MCELHANEY: I would like to begin with a rather mundane question, but I have to ask it, because the sources are contradictory: Where were you born? Some sources say you born in Boston, and then your family moved to Brookline. Others say born in Brookline and moved to Boston.

ALBERT MAYSLES: I was born in Dorchester, and when I was thirteen we moved to Brookline, actually for a very interesting reason. My father was a postal clerk, so his income was small. During my childhood, the Depression was on. But my mother was a schoolteacher, and that was hard to be at the time because women couldn't teach and be married. Did you ever hear of that?

JM: Yes, and not just in education. There were all kinds of restrictions on women at the time in relation to work and marriage.

AM: So we moved to Brookline, and there the complication was hiring a Jewish teacher.

JM: And she became the first Jewish teacher in Brookline?

AM: But they didn't give her total . . . freedom, shall we say? They made her what was called a permanent substitute so that they could pay her a much lower salary than the other teachers and not pay her for vacations, even though she actually taught full-time.

JM: You've often spoken of the difficulties in growing up Jewish in a predominantly Irish Catholic neighborhood in the Boston area and of how this background played an indirect role in a film like *Salesman.* Is there any other way in which you feel that growing up in Boston might have shaped you as a person and as a filmmaker? Do you still feel a strong attachment to the city?

AM: Well, I went to Hebrew school there, so I have memories of that. I guess I thought it would be a good idea to get *away* from the city to go to college, and I went to Syracuse. I could have gone to Harvard, and the tuition would not have been that high because of the GI Bill of Rights. Not that the tuition was so great anyway by today's standards; it was five hundred dollars a year, and now what is it? Forty thousand? But it was really the Irish/Jewish connection that was so important [in terms of Boston]. In those days, you turned the radio on, and 435 radio stations around the country would carry Father Coughlin's message of total anti-Semitism. So many of my experiences of anti-Semitism at that time indirectly led to one of the films I'm working on now, *The Jew on*

Trial, dealing with anti-Semitism in relation to the Mendel Beilis trial where they enact the scene in which Jewish-looking guys kill a Christian child and they use his blood in a religious ritual.

JM: When Paul sings "If I Were a Rich Man" in *Salesman,* it's such a great moment because the Irish/Jewish connection is brought together by him. But was that a totally spontaneous gesture on his part? What sounds like an orchestral version of it plays on the radio at one point, but *after* he has sung it rather than before, so it's almost too coincidental. Was the order of the original scenes reversed, or was there some manipulation on the sound track?

AM: You know, I couldn't tell you there, in all honesty. It seems so spontaneous to me, but unfortunately my brother and Charlotte Zwerin aren't around to really authenticate this. Several years after the film came out, my brother and I were in Boston and took Paul out to dinner with his wife. He told us he had this opportunity to go to Spain and be an actor in a film, but he had to turn it down because it wasn't a big enough part!

JM: You came from a very close knit family, and you've spoken especially about the values of your mother, her openness towards other people and other cultures, and how this was transmitted to you. Charlotte Zwerin talked about how important families were to your brother David—not only in terms of life itself but also in terms of literature and theater, as in the treatment of family in Arthur Miller's plays, which she said that your brother was especially taken with. I presume that you share in those values as well.

AM: Very much so, very much. And in fact, I should point out too that there is a very strong connection in my mind between Paul and my father, although they were quite different, one Jewish and the other Irish. My father took on the job of postal clerk, where he was surrounded by the Irish. And he should have been a musician, and Paul should have been something creative—but who knows what?

JM: So many of your films are about family, quite often fragmented families or extended families of some sort, even up through your films today.

AM: Ten years ago I went to North Korea, sponsored by the Rockefeller Foundation, and I had to think of what to do and what they would approve of. And I decided to make a film about an extended family. And they approved it. But I couldn't get anybody interested in doing it, and that's all that remains of it. But I'd still like to do it.

JM: The ways in which your films are made are also extended-family projects as well, aren't they? The emphasis on collaboration and often using the same creative figures over and over again.

AM: Yes, that's very important, and we like to give everybody the full credit they deserve, which is very unusual in documentary. When you see a Frederick Wiseman film, it's all Wiseman.

JM: Within direct cinema, there has been some debate as to purity of intentions, as to what the form of direct cinema should be. Of course, your break with Robert Drew had to do with a reluctance to continue on with the crisis structure of his early films. Wiseman is someone who's often been linked with the direct-cinema school, but you've often been critical of *Titicut Follies*.

AM: I was, yes.

JM: Do you have the same response to all of Wiseman's work?

AM: The more recent works I wouldn't be so adamant about. But *Titicut Follies, High School,* those early films were . . . what should I call them? Point-of-view films, good guy/bad guy. For me, *Titicut Follies* was trying to put down the system, but he hurt the very people he meant to be protecting: the patients, the way he filmed them, with very little humanity. But that's what you get into with these good guy/bad guy things.

JM: Of course, he's fascinated by institutions and how they operate, and that's not really been your primary concern.

AM: Well, you know in *Salesman,* the "system" is there, but in a very undirected way. You feel that the company is always there, Kenny is always there, Feltman is always there, and so forth.

JM: Would it be accurate to say that when you began to make films, with *Psychiatry in Russia* and *Youth in Poland,* you weren't terribly interested in being a filmmaker in professional terms but rather in using the cinema to document subjects that interested you? Cinema as a tool rather than an end in itself?

AM: True. My urge to go to Russia and to film was based on the fact that I felt everything we were hearing about what was going on behind the Iron Curtain was based on indirect sources which deprived us of a direct connection with the people. So we had all theories about what was going on behind the walls of the Kremlin, all statistics. But we didn't know what a Russian family was like, for example, and we still don't really know that much. But that's what primarily motivated me to go there.

JM: So you weren't a filmgoer? You never said, "I love films. That's what I want to do for a living"?

AM: No. I still don't see that much today.

JM: Not even in the documentary field?

AM: Right, right. I talked a lot about Michael Moore's films without ever having seen them. I think I was correct, actually, after finally seeing *Fahrenheit 9/11*.

JM: And you disliked it?

AM: I disliked it, but there were parts that I thought were interesting. I just work from an entirely different orientation. He's out to "get" people, and I'm out to understand them.

JM: You've consistently stated your commitment to the goals of the type of direct cinema you've been practicing since the early 1960s. At the same time, you've often been critical of documentary films which you've labeled as propaganda. Have you ever, at least periodically, had any reservations about your approach in political terms? By that I mean, have you thought that there were certain political issues which required a filmmaking approach more didactic than what you've ever done? I bring this up because when I've heard you speak publicly over the last few years, you've been extremely critical of Bush's policies, and I sense a strong political anger in you which I don't recall ever coming across in the other interviews I've read with you over the years.

AM: I think that in the case of the Bush administration, which I would love to film for what it is, I don't think we need to approach it from a propaganda point of view. I think I would give him the same kind of affection, if you will, that I would give to anyone else, and whatever comes out of it that will be it. It's hard to imagine that what we'll see will be a warm, caring guy. We'll see what he's doing, what he really is. I wouldn't have to exaggerate.

JM: I don't know if you ever saw Barbet Schroeder's film *Idi Amin Dada*. But he manages to film Idi Amin with a very clear-eyed perspective and doesn't subject him to ridicule in the Michael Moore style. You see the human being there, but you don't see humanity. You get a very clear, terrifying political picture.

AM: Interesting that you should mention Barbet because he's a good friend of mine. In fact, in 1963 he was in the States, and we got to know each other. I was in Paris a few years later, and he was about make *Paris vu par* . . . , and he said, "You know, you and Godard would be just great together." And so I said, "Okay." And Barbet contacted Godard and told him about me. And Godard said, "Yeah, bring him over." And the next day I was shooting *Paris vu par* . . . . I was clever enough to make the best use of my talents on that film by setting everything up without really knowing what was going to happen.

JM: Raoul Coutard [Godard's frequent cameraman] said that you had to think quickly when working with Godard because there usually wasn't extensive preparation. Was it chaotic working with Godard?

AM: No, not all. We got along great. And he was great to me.

JM: When you worked for Robert Drew you were also working alongside of other major filmmakers, like Richard Leacock and D. A. Pennebaker, and all of you were working within Drew's vision of a new type of documentary cinema, a vision which you also shared in many ways. It's fairly well documented who shot what on films like *Primary* or *Yanki, No!* But when you look at those films now, do you see a somewhat different camera style in your approach in comparison with the others?

AM: I think that my shooting style would be more akin to Leacock's. Pennebaker's not quite as concerned with the technical stuff, which is fine, because the primary thing in documentary filming is the emotional and the poetic. The most beautiful film he ever made was the one about Timothy Leary [*You're Nobody Till Somebody Loves You*]. Interestingly, it was all about alienation. Pennebaker doesn't get as close to people as Ricky and myself. But in that particular case, it worked just beautifully. There's a scene that starts with a group of people in a car. They come to a kind of cabin. And we suddenly realize that two of these people, who appear to be strangers, are getting married. And it's Timothy Leary (probably on LSD or whatever) and his future wife.

JM: So he understands people *not* communicating very well?

AM: Yeah, yeah.

JM: Like the sequence in *Don't Look Back* where Joan Baez is singing while Bob Dylan loudly types over her song?

AM: Exactly, exactly. And I think he understands moments like that much better than he understands moments when people communicate with one another. On the other hand, in a film like *Salesman* (which is all about alienation, isn't it?), neither the salesmen nor the housewives can really communicate with one another, since buying and selling is paramount.

JM: But the spectator feels a closeness with the salesmen and the housewives very strongly.

AM: Yes, since *Salesman* is based on the need for human contact, and not many people are sensitive to that.

JM: A central early moment in the history of your collaboration with your brother was when you went to Lyon for the conference on documentary cinema, the Marché International des Programmes et Equipments de Télévision, and screened *Showman*. That's when Louis Marcorelles declared that it was one of the greatest films made since the end of the war. But it's also when Rossellini declared that the film was shapeless and the antithesis of art.

AM: Yes, which I couldn't understand.

JM: Was Rossellini there in Lyon? Or did he see it somewhere else?

AM: I think he saw it in Paris. There's this prejudice that still exists that if it's real (which that film is), then what's the contribution of the filmmaker, if it's not about direction? But in a documentary, if you're "directing" you're in trouble. Some filmmakers, especially Rossellini, were sensitive to that, to what they saw as a limitation.

JM: And for a constant experimenter like Rossellini to see *Showman* as formless (which it isn't; it has a clear structure to it) is very odd. What was the Lyon experience like? Did you engage with other filmmakers there? Did you meet Rouch? Was there a lot of debate and discussion? It's been marked as pivotal moment in which the dialogue between direct cinema and cinéma vérité was established.

AM: We talked with Rouch a bit. We thought he was way off base.

JM: Had you seen his work?

AM: I had not seen his work at the time. And I've never seen *Chronicle of a Summer*. Since then, I've seen a few things.

JM: In many ways, his process is antithetical to the way that you work, the way that he involves the subjects in the process of making the film.

AM: Yes, it's all set up.

JM: You had to do that in *The Burk Family of Georgia,* though, which has a Rouch-like moment when the family comments at the end. But you didn't want to include that, did you?

AM: No, that was insisted on by PBS. By the way, what should have been the biggest opportunity for showing our films, television, has always been closed to off to us by the networks.

JM: You've had problems getting your films shown from the very beginning, though, haven't you? Didn't Levine tell you that you couldn't release *Showman* theatrically, but you could take it to the networks, probably knowing full well that the networks wouldn't want to show it?

AM: Actually, we ended up with a contract on that film that put us in a terrible fix. We can't even put it out on DVD.

JM: Really? It's still legally unavailable? I always thought it would make part of a wonderful DVD package of Maysles short films.

AM: We want so much to do it. But Levine's son holds the rights and just won't allow us to release it.

JM: The estates in these matters are often much worse than the original subjects.

AM: Yeah, I think we could ultimately have gotten Levine to agree.

JM: But you can still show it in festivals and museums?

AM: Yes.

JM: There have been several different versions of *What's Happening* over the years.

AM: Oh, yeah . . .

JM: The one that's easily available is the one that Susan Froemke had a strong hand in producing, the one that's on DVD. And I presume that you are okay with this version, since you're interviewed on the disc.

AM: There's a story that goes with that. (There's a story that goes with every film.) When we made the film, we were making it with Granada Television. And in England in those days we made a release. But as we got into filming it, we made a deal with Granada that we could create our own version of it and that we would have total rights in America, and in England and the rest of the world we'd share fifty/fifty. But United Artists was so concerned with their upcoming film, *A Hard Day's Night,* that we couldn't even show our film. It wasn't so long after we made our film that we were able to make a deal with CBS, where it was shown with Carol Burnett narrating it.

JM: I've never seen that version.

AM: I've got to get ahold of a copy of it. I've never seen it myself

JM: It was heavily cut, from what I understand.

AM: Oh, okay. So now there are *three* versions. Anyway, we've been able to show our version of *What's Happening* at festivals. But in 1991 or so, Apple came to us and bought us out. They came back to us and said they wanted to make a much more commercial version of it. Since someone was going to get their hands on it and recut, we decided to be involved. But Susan had to go along with their plans for dropping certain things out, putting certain things in. And then they put in all of the Ed Sullivan stuff.

JM: Which is visually jarring. It looks nothing like your own footage.

AM: I know. It's completely out of character. Have you seen the original cut?

JM: I saw the Granada version, which is about seventy minutes long.

AM: Okay, we have a longer version which we can give you today.

JM: But you've totally lost the rights to this? Apple controls it all?

AM: Yeah. I have this idea (and it would be great, especially right now) to take the original, with Apple's permission and for their profit even, and get the original version shown in movie theaters. It would be sensational. But they're giving me a hard time. They're saying, 'Oh, there's music in that one that isn't the Beatles.' And so the music that isn't Beatles music they would have to clear rights on, and it would cost them something like two hundred thousand dollars. But they'd make so much more than that on it. And they've agreed to that if I can get a good enough offer. Then they'll change their minds again.

JM: You met Orson Welles at the Cannes Film Festival?

AM: Yeah, in 1963.

JM: Then you made the promotional short for him where he discusses his plans for a new kind of fiction film that would be shot documentary-style.

AM: Have you seen the film?

JM: Yes, it's wonderful. Did he give you any direction at all?

AM: No, he never told us how to shoot it.

JM: And how did the project come about? Had he seen *Show-man*?

AM: No, he'd never seen anything of ours. There's a wonderful moment in the film where he talks about "divine accidents."

JM: It must have resonated with you.

AM: Oh yeah. Any good documentary is loaded with divine accidents.

JM: Haskell Wexler recently stated that he operated a second camera for a while on *Salesman* without credit. Was his footage not used, or did he just not want credit?

AM: We always try and give everybody credit. As I recall, he only worked on the Chicago sales meeting. But if Haskell says he worked on the film, then he did.

JM: He also claims that you and your brother provoked certain situations on the film more readily than you would ever publicly admit to, that you created drama that was nonexistent. He cites one moment where you were in a motel room, and nothing interesting was happening, and he pulled your brother aside and said, "Why don't you have one of the salesmen call up his wife and pretend to be in Las Vegas and film her reaction to that?" That moment is not in the film, though, and I don't know if you shot it and then decided to cut it.

AM: Hmm, that's interesting. I've forgotten that. I've even forgotten that Haskell was there. Maybe I've repressed these things. But it's hard to think of too many moments where we've "gone astray."

JM: You have admitted to doing some coaxing of Paul driving in the car, to explain the names of the salesmen and so on . . .

AM: Yes, that was set up, in a sense. In *Grey Gardens* we had done almost all the shooting, and we had begun to edit it. And my brother said it would be a great thing if I could get them [the Beales] to talk about Gould, the mother's boyfriend, and that I should be the one to get them to talk about that. And that's the scene where Edie blows up.

JM: When she yells at you?

AM: (laughs) Yeah, and I always thought I deserved it because I had no good reason to provoke her like that, you know?

JM: Jonas Mekas had been a supporter of your early work.

AM: Well, he liked some stuff but not everything.

JM: He was very positive towards everything up until *Salesman,* for which he gave a very negative review, out of nowhere.

AM: Yeah, I didn't understand that.

JM: A very strange review, so completely off the mark for him. Did you ever talk to him after that review came out? I haven't come across anything after that where he wrote about your work.

AM: No, we never talked about it. We've always been good friends. And I feel close to his film work. I could criticize it and tell you that he can't hold a camera steady to save his life and that everything's out of focus and the composition is bad. But my God, the heart and soul is there. He's a poet, that's the most important thing.

JM: The history of the reception of *Grey Gardens* has been the most varied and complex of all of your films, from being the most negatively reviewed of all of your films at the time of its release to now, where it's the most widely admired and such a huge cult favorite. And now it's about to be turned into a musical. Have you seen the musical yet?

AM: Yeah, I just saw it. They had a preview of it the other day. It's gonna be good. They showed me an earlier version of it, and I was very disappointed. Any other filmmaker could have made the mistake of turning Mrs. Beale into a monster, responsible for all of Edie's problems. And so I thought they [the creators of the musical] had to get the balance right.

JM: The film is already a musical, though. There's so much singing in it, it's almost redundant to turn it into another musical.

AM: Yes. And I told the guys who created it that Edie, when she saw the film, said, "Couldn't they put more music and dancing in it?"

JM: Didn't she say, "I'm the greatest Latin dancer who ever lived?"

AM: [laughs] Yes.

JM: The film has such a loyal fan base. What do you think people are seeing in it?

AM: For one thing, I think it has . . . well, homosexuals have a strong fondness for it. And I think if you're an outsider, then you'll identify with these two women who certainly chose to be outsiders. And then most people who are taken with a sense of fashion . . . that's another strong element of the film's viewership. And I'm optimistic enough to think that people are attracted to seeing something on the screen where people are giving themselves to the camera, to the viewers, rather than people who are hiding from the camera. The film deals with so many interesting issues about the nature of documentary, the nature of truth, of human nature. And I think where we really struck gold was in the mother/daughter relationship. Neither me nor anyone else I know in the profession had gone as deeply into the mother/daughter relationship. And suddenly we have on our hands a film that goes very deeply into that. There's a woman I met, Brigid Berlin, one of the Warhol people, and she called me up one day and she said, "You know, I've been looking for copies of *Grey Gardens*. Can I come over? I want to buy some from you. I've seen the film 120 times." How many films can you say that about?

JM: It's funny, but whenever I've shown the film to students, their response to the film, positive or negative, pretty much divides along gender lines. Women in the class love the film, and the men in the class are horrified by it. I think it may also have to do with the fact that you're looking at two aging female bodies exposed. And I don't think we're accustomed to seeing that. I think it's horrifying to a lot of men to see this, whereas in my experience women are not so bothered by it in the film.

AM: Have you ever seen Walter Goodman's review of the film? The guy's got a problem with age: "Why are you showing us all this rotten flesh?"

JM: Edie had a wonderful response to that. She said: "The film portrays age. Age portends death. Death brings God and Mr. Goodman cannot face God."

AM: Where did you find that quote? I'd like to get a copy of it. You know, we showed her the Goodman review, because my brother and I were going to respond to it. And she wrote a response to the *Times* as well.

JM: Did they print it?

AM: No. A month went by, and I called them and said, "Are you going to publish it?" They said, "No, no. She's schizophrenic." And she had the healthiest, most mature response to that review.

JM: Did you film her toward the end of her life?

AM: No. We were thinking of doing that. I was going to go down to Florida, and we talked about it.

JM: After the death of your brother, you collaborated with a number of other figures, especially Susan Froemke and Deborah Dickson. Is the dynamic different with them than it was with your brother, especially at the moment of filming? Or did they pick up directly where your brother left off? Was the chemistry different?

AM: Because it's Susan, you mean, rather than my brother?

JM: Yes, or whomever you happen to be working with. Was it hard to adjust at first, not having your brother there?

AM: No, not really. He was involved in both elements, filming and supervising the editing. We made a great team, especially when we worked with Charlotte, who was such a great editor.

JM: Have you seen her own films, outside of the work she did for you?

AM: I saw the one about the crazy musician [*Thelonius Monk: Straight, No Chaser*]. But you know, an editor is, in a sense, only as good as the material. And the material there wasn't quite that good.

JM: Most of your collaborators have been women, though. Why women?

AM: Interesting . . . hmmm. . . . Well, why not women? We chose whom we thought were the best, and if it was a woman who was the best, then fine. Maybe better, in fact, because women don't always get the same opportunities.

JM: I read an interview with a filmmaker about two years ago in the *Village Voice* who lives in Los Angeles now, Thom Andersen, and he was talking about coming to New York in the seventies and that he was looking for work as a filmmaker. He said he didn't apply here because he heard that the Maysles brothers only hired women.

AM: [Laughs]

JM: How much input do Christo and Jeanne-Claude have into the films you've made about them? Do they set clear limits in terms of what you can or cannot shoot? Do they ever ask you to take things out of the films while you're editing?

AM: While we're making the film we might show it to them. And so far, it's been pretty consistent in terms of what they like and what we like. For example, we have the same aversion to music in documentaries.

JM: But there's underscoring in all of your later films, including the Christo and Jeanne-Claude films. Is that something you brought in reluctantly?

AM: There's music in *Running Fence,* but it was felt to be appropriate. Certainly we don't have as much music as some other documentary filmmakers today.

JM: My questions about the classical-music films and videos are along similar lines. Is your access to those subjects more or less unlimited, or are restrictions set?

AM: We're not really restricted, although you might think so, because so many of the classical-music films are produced by the organizations that represented the artists. What's it called? Artist's Management? Peter Gelb was their agent, Horowitz's agent, Marsalis's agent. That's how we got to make those films. But Peter never said, "That's improper." He never exercised that kind of power. It didn't happen.

JM: Kathleen Battle is such a sweetheart in the *Baroque Duet* film, such a contrast to her reputation. She was exactly like that throughout the shoot?

AM: Yes. No problem with her. And Wynton Marsalis has something of a reputation, too. But I never saw it.

JM: You do see some tension between him and Peter Martins in *Accent on the Offbeat*. But it never becomes a full-blown argument.

AM: Oh, yeah. That's not one of my favorite ones.

JM: Some of the credits of your later films read differently from the credits from your earlier films. It might be listed as "a film be Susan Froemke and Deborah Dickson *with* Albert Maysles" or "*and* Albert Maysles." Are you less involved in some of these later projects?

AM: It was stupid on my part. I should have insisted on a comma rather than a "with."

JM: So you don't feel less involved in them?

AM: No, not at all. But I have a feeling that those who make documentary films for whom their work is so relevant to the nature of the film, they bring such a particular character to it, that they should be fully credited. With *The Jew on Trial* I'm having a problem because the guy who's working with me wants his director's credit to be listed separately and then "with" Albert Maysles.

JM: So you've opened the floodgates now. Everyone wants billing over you.

AM: But I've decided to hell with it.

JM: What's the status of *The Jew on Trial* [since retitled *Scapegoat on Trial*] now? The last time I heard you speak about it, you were talking about getting Arthur Penn to do some of the dramatized scenes.

AM: It's progressed now so that Josh Weletsky is working with me. So he's directing that. And the credit will be "Directed by Josh Weletsky with Albert Maysles." It's a pity, because I've gotten much less interested in it as a result, even though I'm going to have a very important say in it. It's five years now that I've had this thing, and there's somebody raising money for it now.

JM: It's a project unlike anything you've ever done.

AM: I know, I know. It can't possibly have the same kind of character as my other stuff. Have you seen the trailer for it?

JM: Yes, and some of the footage you shot in Eastern Europe. And *In Transit* [a project Maysles has worked on for many years in which he films and interviews various individuals on trains around the world]. What's the status of that?

AM: That's my number-one project. I've put together a trailer for it.

JM: So many of your later films deal with artists or musicians, so the ones that have social content—*Lalee's Kin, Abortion: Desperate Choices,* and *Letting Go: A Hospice Journey*—really stand out. How did they come about? Did they originate here, and were they taken to HBO? Or did HBO come to you?

AM: HBO came up with the ideas. One of HBO's big sponsors was involved with hospice care. And when she started to get into it, she said that we might be lucky if five people see this. She thought no one would want to watch it. But HBO still wanted to do it, and their advisors told them that if it wins awards, that's good enough. And it did win awards and got a very good viewership.

JM: Were these later films like *Abortion* or *Lalee's Kin* screened for their subjects?

AM: Oh yeah. Lots of feedback from *Lalee's Kin.*

JM: I read that the granddaughter, Granny, ended up pregnant.

AM: Yes.

JM: It's so strange because the film anticipates this in the slow-motion shot of her exchanging looks with a boy, they circle around each other. And you sense that this young woman has two options now: she can walk away from her present situation or stay there.

AM: Yes, she was only fourteen when she got pregnant. There's a moment [in the film] when the great grandson is asked what he wants to do when he grows up. He says he wants to be in prison.

JM: You were very unhappy with the PBS added subtitles to the Burk film. You thought it was a condescending gesture.

AM: No, I don't think so. I think that, as I recall, we really needed it.

JM: There was an interview around the time the film came out when you complained about it. Have you had second thoughts about that? Because *Lalee's Kin* also has subtitles.

AM: No, I think both films need it. But there may have been a little too much subtitling in both films.

JM: One of the most powerful scenes in the abortion film is when you go into the room with a woman while she has an abortion. How did you negotiate that? It's such a private space. Did you feel uncomfortable about doing that?

AM: I knew that if it got too intense we couldn't use it.

JM: When the sequence began, I sat there cringing, fearing that it was going to exploitive. But it doesn't happen.

AM: I was filming this woman having the abortion, right? And I walk around, and her legs are spread wide open, and I felt quite comfortable. You didn't see anything of the abortion. You saw along her thigh but never all the way. I had the good sense not to exploit that.

JM: Typically, you focus on the human response to the situation, the interaction between the woman having the abortion and the woman giving her the abortion, rather than the abortion itself. And *Letting Go* has extremely painful moments as well, where it must have been difficult to stay in those rooms and continue filming. But I think your background in psychology comes through very strongly in your attitude towards filming this material. A film like *Letting Go* can almost be a therapeutic process for the viewer. If you're horrified by it, you ask yourself why you're so horrified. What are we looking at except someone dying? Why is that something I should be looking away from? Why is it something that should be not necessarily be filmed?

AM: Exactly. I think there has been more criticism on this vulnerability and exploitation thing with *Grey Gardens*.

JM: But again the question arises: Why are people horrified? What are we looking at that's so horrifying in *Grey Gardens*? Two aging women. We're not used to looking at aging female flesh onscreen, or at images of literal, slow death.

AM: It's an interesting thing that I've come across: In our culture, we're supposed to get heart-to-heart with somebody. Why is it necessary to presume that someone's going to get hurt if you film them like this? It could be the healthiest, most positive thing that ever happened to them. Maybe you know better than I. Do we have a word that describes the possibility that something good is going to come out of it? It's hard to find that word. I don't think we even have it.

Appendix |

A Comparison of *What's Happening: The Beatles in the USA* and *The Beatles: The First U.S. Visit*

What follows below is a comparison and an approximate breakdown of the two most widely seen versions of the Maysles brothers' filming of the Beatles' arrival in America: *What's Happening,* in its preferred Maysles cut of seventy-four minutes, and the DVD version of *The Beatles: The First U.S. Visit.* The seventy-four-minute version is by far the superior of the two. Among other things, Murray the K assumes a more central, desperate, and poignant presence in *What's Happening* than he does in *The First U.S. Visit;* and the film's loose, slightly ragged, but extremely effective structure and its unified visual style (all of it shot by the Maysles brothers) point to one of the major (and most neglected) works of 1960s direct cinema.

Nevertheless, *The First U.S. Visit* is still of some value, both for the additional footage not used in *What's Happening* and for what appears to be a more rigorous attempt to observe the original chronology of the Beatles' visit. The Central Park photo shoot is now in its "correct" place, for example, and the train ride to Washington, D.C., now consists of two rides, one to D.C. and one back to New York. *What's Happening* compresses these trips into a single sequence, combining footage to give the impression of a single journey. *The First U.S. Visit* also makes it clear that Florida was one of the destinations of the Beatles' tour, while *What's Happening* passes off Florida hotel-room footage as Washington hotel-room footage. Nevertheless, respect for chronology is no guarantee of a superior film, even in documentaries.

What's Happening

SEQUENCE ONE: Murray the K in his radio station, announcing his "triple ripple/triple play" of three songs in a row without commercial interruption: "Here's what's happening, baby." He plays the Beatles' recording of "She Loves You." The lyrics—"You think you lost your love"—are followed by a cut to:
TWO: Girls outside of the Plaza Hotel completing the lyrics in the previous shot: " . . . well, I saw her yesterday." They chant for the Beatles.

THREE: Fans running about at the airport and shots of the Beatles disembarking.

FOUR: The Beatles (minus George) in Central Park, posing for photographers.

FIVE: Murray the K in the radio station playing Chuck Berry's recording of "Nadine." When told that the Beatles have arrived, he announces, "They're here!" and plays "I Saw Her Standing There." Cut to:

SIX: Beatles (minus George) in back seat of car listening to "I Saw Her Standing There" on transistor radio. A discussion ensues about London, England, versus towns called London in the United States. They listen to radio ads for Kent cigarettes as credits for the film appear. As the car is shown driving down city streets, fans press up against the windows hysterically. The car pulls up to the curb, and the Beatles begin to disembark.

SEVEN: Inside a room at the Plaza Hotel. The Beatles watch the airport press conference on TV. George talks to someone on the phone about his exhaustion. John says that they haven't seen much of New York so far. Paul listens to Murray the K and complains of difficulty understanding him.

EIGHT: Fans outside of the hotel chanting, "We want the Beatles." Cut back to:

NINE: Hotel room, now with Murray the K inside. He gets the Beatles to say hello to radio listeners over the phone and plays "Love Me Do." George is tricked into listening to an ad by a radio announcer.

TEN: The Beatles get ready to go to the *Ed Sullivan Show*.

ELEVEN: Apartment in which we see young girls watching the Beatles on *Ed Sullivan* as father sits with them. (Sequence not used in *The First U.S. Visit*, although a bit of footage from it may be glimpsed in final credits, and the footage appears in the supplemental features of the DVD.)

TWELVE: Murray the K in the radio station talking to Ringo on the phone. He plays a Marvin Gaye record and a Sam Cooke record while a young African American woman, sitting in a chair in the background, moves in rhythm to the music. Crosscutting then begins between the Beatles in the hotel room listening to the broadcast and the radio station. Chuck Berry singing "Nadine" is played again. Ringo and Murray the K discuss Bob Dylan while radio-station workers unsuccessfully attempt to find "Corinna, Corinna" track on Dylan album.

THIRTEEN: Murray the K back in the hotel room as the Beatles listen to the radio and talk of going out.

FOURTEEN: Beatles walking down hallway of hotel, en route to:

FIFTEEN: Beatles at the Peppermint Lounge, where Ringo and Murray dance. Sequence is approximately five minutes and fifty seconds long.

SIXTEEN: Paul in the hotel hallway and elevator, being greeted at the hotel-room door by John and Cynthia Lennon.

SEVENTEEN: Brian Epstein on the phone and with his staff in the hotel room.

EIGHTEEN: Brian in the car discussing radio programs in England in comparison with radio programs in the United States. (Sequence not used at all in *The First U.S. Visit*. The DVD uses a slightly longer version of the sequence in the supplemental material.)

NINETEEN: Train ride to D.C., which may be broken down into the following segments:

a) Paul and John on back of train.
b) Paul talking to reporters about American television in comparison with British television.
c) Ringo with little girl in Girl Scout uniform and her mother.
d) The Beatles pose for photographers.
e) Paul talks to reporters again.
f) Ringo parades about with photographers' camera bags.
g) George and John do a mock commercial for Marlboro cigarettes. George, John, and Ringo crawl about the train compartment. George plays train porter.
h) Ringo with Girl Scout again as they move about the train together. Ringo signs autographs along the way

TWENTY-ONE: Arrival at train station in Washington, D.C.

TWENTY-TWO: D.C. concert, as Brian watches from the audience.

TWENTY-THREE: In the hotel room, John helps Paul to close his suitcase. Ringo packs bag. George plays guitar and sings.

TWENTY-FOUR: Back in the United Kingdom at the airport.

TWENTY-FIVE: Final credits.

The Beatles: The First U.S. Visit

SEQUENCE ONE: A shorter (by about forty seconds) version of the opening of *What's Happening* (Murray the K in the radio station). All of Murray's uses of the phrase "what's happening" are eliminated. Cut to:

TWO: Girls outside of the Plaza Hotel (Identical to *What's Happening*.)

THREE: Slightly more footage of the Beatles and fans at aiport. Also includes their airport press conference, footage not shot by David and Albert Maysles.

FOUR: Radio station. Playing of Chuck Berry record is cut; instead the sequence opens with the announcement of the Beatles' arrival followed by the playing of "I Saw Her Standing There." Credits begin to appear over Murray the K in the station and continue over succeeding images, including additional footage of fans at the airport and the Beatles driving away (not included in *What's Happening*).

FIVE: Back seat of car, same as sequence six in *What's Happening*, until John,

Paul, and Ringo disembark, and there is footage not used in *What's Happening* of fans outside of the hotel and the Beatles walking into the Plaza.

SIX: A recut version of sequence seven from *What's Happening*. There are more shots of John (wearing dark glasses) and an additional shot of George.

SEVEN: Murray in his radio station. Cut back to:

EIGHT: Hotel room as the boys listen to the radio and call in. Crosscutting from hotel room to the radio station. Paul requests Marvin Gaye's "Pride and Joy." African American woman in the station dances in the background. A very different conversation from the one in *What's Happening* takes place, as Ringo talks with Murray about how the Beatles' sound developed with "Love Me Do." The Beatles in the hotel room talk about how tired they are.

NINE: Girls outside of the hotel, chanting "We want the Beatles!"

TEN: Paul says, "Good morning, everybody," into camera as he goes down the hallway to the elevator. (Not in *What's Happening*.)

ELEVEN: Central Park photo shoot. Slightly longer version than the one in *What's Happening*. The boys joke on top of rocks, and there is more talking to the press.

TWELVE: Brian Epstein at work in the hotel room with staff. (Largely the same footage as sequence seventeen of *What's Happening*.)

THIRTEEN: Murray in the hotel room with the boys, getting them to say hello over the phone to the viewers. (Largely the same footage as sequence nine in *What's Happening*.) George refers to his sore throat and talks to a radio announcer, who tricks him into listening to an ad. The boys leave for *Ed Sullivan* broadcast.

FOURTEEN: *Ed Sullivan Show*. The group performs "All My Loving," "'Til There Was You," "She Loves You," "I Want to Hold Your Hand." (Not shot by Maysles and not in *What's Happening*.)

FIFTEEN: Hallway of hotel, Paul with transistor radio.

SIXTEEN: Peppermint Lounge. This is a significant re-edit of the sequence in *What's Happening*. While it contains a few additional shots not contained in *What's Happening* (of the band playing in the club, of Paul and John shouting into the camera, etc.), it is much shorter than the sequence in *What's Happening*. The earlier version runs for approximately six minutes, while the later version is only about two and a half minutes long, considerably diluting its intensity and with a lesser role for Murray the K.

SEVENTEEN: Paul in the hotel. (Same as sequence sixteen in *What's Happening*.)

EIGHTEEN: New scene of two girls who have sneaked into the hotel in an attempt to find the Beatles.

NINETEEN: New scene of girls chanting outside of hotel as boys on the hotel steps unsuccessfully attempt to persuade the police to allow them inside.

TWENTY: Brian at work. His secretary takes a phone message from Colonel Parker, Elvis Presley's personal manager. Epstein dictates a telegram of thanks to Presley and Parker. A shot of Epstein putting on his scarf at end of the sequence appears to have been taken from sequence seventeen in *What's Happening.*

TWENTY-ONE: Train pulling out for Washington, D.C. Aside from the opening images of John and Paul on the back of the train, this is a greatly compressed version of the train sequence in *What's Happening,* only containing some footage of the Beatles posing with photographers, John and George doing their Marlboro commercial, George playing porter, and Ringo playing with cameras left over from the earlier film. There is also new footage of Paul, Ringo, and John moving through the train compartment.

TWENTY-TWO: Arrival at D.C. train station. (Same as in *What's Happening.*)

Twenty-three: The D.C. concert: "I Saw Her Standing There," "I Want to Be Your Man," "She Loves You." Different, technically better, and much more extensive footage of the concert is used here (none of it is Maysles footage).

TWENTY-FOUR: Train ride back to New York. Girl Scout shown on train ride to D.C. is now shown on train ride back to New York, in much shortened exchange, and their walk through the train is completely eliminated. New footage of Ringo talking to journalists at the bar and McCartney talking to elderly people on the train, including a man who asks Paul, "Which one are you?"

TWENTY-FIVE: Miami Beach hotel room. Slightly different edit of the same footage.

TWENTY-SIX: Another *Ed Sullivan* broadcast: "With Love from Me to You," "This Boy," "All My Loving" (not shot by Maysles and not in *What's Happening*).

TWENTY-SEVEN: Back in Miami Beach hotel room. Some repetition of footage from sequence twenty-three of *What's Happening,* as well as new footage of Paul on the balcony of the hotel, making it clear that the Beatles are in Florida and not D.C.

TWENTY-EIGHT: Still another *Ed Sullivan* broadcast: "Twist and Shout," "Please, Please Me" (not shot by Maysles and not in *What's Happening*). Performance of "I Want to Hold Your Hand" is intercut with:

TWENTY-NINE: Return to London.

THIRTY: Final credits over footage of outtakes and recording of "It Won't Be Long," including some material used in *What's Happening* but not otherwise used in this version.

This is not a comprehensive filmography. Throughout his long career, Albert Maysles has shot so much footage (of everyone from Robert Bresson to Britney Spears) and worked on so many films that it would be a gargantuan task to assemble all of this in one concise filmography. Maysles Films, Inc., has been attempting to sort through and document much of the footage that is in their archives. What follows below includes the best-known and most available films from the Maysles brothers' body of work. I have avoided listing their television commercials or other advertising films, which range from promotional works for IBM and the Metropolitan Opera to a *Sports Illustrated* swimsuit video. A few of these works are listed on the company's website (www.mayslesfilms.com), and interested readers may refer to the filmography there. A word of caution, though: as of this writing, that filmography is incomplete and contains errors.

Albert Maysles

Psychiatry in Russia (1955)
USA
Filmed and written by Albert Maysles. Televised by the *David Garroway Show* on NBC-TV and WGBH public television.
Black and white
14 min.

Russian Close-Up (1957)
USA
Filmed by Albert Maysles.
Black and white
33 min.

Youth in Poland (1957)
I have not been able to locate any specific information about this film. While Mayles Films, Inc., used to list the film on their website (it has since been taken down), they do not have a print of it in their archives.

Safari ya Gari (African Train Ride; 1961)
USA/Kenya
Filmmaker: Albert Maysles
Editor: Nell Cox
Sound: Gerald Feil
Made in cooperation with Bob Drew Associates, Inc.
Black and white
10 min.

Albert and David Maysles

Anastasia (1962)
USA
Directors: Albert Maysles and David Maysles
Producer: Bo Goldman, for the NBC television news program *Update*.
Black and white
8 min.

Showman (1963)
USA
Producers: Albert Maysles and David Maysles
Filmmakers: Albert Maysles and David Maysles
Camera: Albert Maysles
Editors: Daniel Williams with Tom Bywaters and Betsy Powell
Narration: Norman Rosten
Black and white
53 min.

Orson Welles in Spain (1963)
USA
Filmmakers: David Maysles and Albert Maysles
Color
10 min.

What's Happening! The Beatles in the USA (1964)
USA
Directors: Albert Maysles and David Maysles
Editors: Daniel Williams, Howard Milkin, and Kate Glidden
Associate Producer: Stanley Hirson
Sound Mixing: Dick Vorisek
Producers: Maysles Films, Inc., in association with Granada Television
Black and white
74 min.

Alternate versions of the film: *Yeah, Yeah, Yeah! The Beatles in New York,* 40 min., broadcast on Granada television on February 12 and 13, 1964; *The Beatles in America,* 50 min., shown on the television variety show *The Entertainers* on November 13, 1964.

Meet Marlon Brando (1966)
USA
Filmmakers: Albert Maysles and David Maysles
Editor: Charlotte Zwerin
Black and white
28 min.

A Visit with Truman Capote (1966)
USA
Filmmakers: David Maysles, Albert Maysles, and Charlotte Zwerin
Producers: David Maysles, Albert Maysles, and Charlotte Zwerin
Editors: David Maysles, Albert Maysles, and Charlotte Zwerin
(This film has also been called *With Love, from Truman.* The print I have seen from Maysles Films, Inc., lists the title in its opening credits as *The Non-Fiction Novel: A Visit with Truman Capote.*)
Black and white
49 min.

A Journey to Jerusalem (1968)
USA
Producers: Filmways, in association with Maysles Films, Inc.
Producer and Director: Michael Midlin Jr.
Filming: David Maysles and Albert Maysles, with Richard Leacock, Stan Hirson, Sid Reichman, Joe Ryan, and Bruce Martin
Supervising Editor: Robert Farren
Editors: Dorothy Tod and Isaac Cohen
Color
58 min. (television version) and 84 min. (theatrical version)

Salesman (1969)
USA
Producers: Albert Maysles and David Maysles
Directors: Albert Maysles, David Maysles, and Charlotte Zwerin
Editor: Charlotte Zwerin
Contributing Film Editor: Ellen Giffard [Hovde]
Assistant Editor: Barbara Jarvis
Sound Mixer: Dick Vorisek
Uncredited Second Cameraman: Haskell Wexler

Black and white
90 min.

Gimme Shelter (1970)
USA
Filming: David Maysles and Albert Maysles
Directors: David Maysles, Albert Maysles, and Charlotte Zwerin
Editor: Charlotte Zwerin
Contributing Film Editors: Ellen Giffard [Hovde], Robert Farren, Joanne
    Burke, and Kent McKinney
Associate Producer: Porter Bibb
Additional Photography: Peter Adair, Baird Bryant, Joan Churchill, Ron
    Dorfman, Robert Elfstrom, Elliott Erwitt, Bob Fiori, Adam Giffard,
    William Kaplan, Kevin Keating, Stephen Lighthill, George Lucas, Jim
    Moody, Jack Newman, Pekke Niemala, Robert Primes, Eric Saarinen,
    Peter Smokler, Paul Ryan, Coulter Watt, Gary Weiss, and Bill Yarrus
Sound: Michael Becker, John Brumbaugh, Howard Chesley, Pepper
    Crawford, Stanley Cronquist, Paul Deason, Tom Goodwin, Peter Pilafin,
    Orly Lindgren, Walter Murch, Art Rochester, Nelson Stoll, David
    Thompson, and Alvin Tokunow
Color
91 min.

Christo's Valley Curtain (1973)
USA
Directors: David Maysles, Albert Maysles, and Ellen Giffard [Hovde]
Editor: Ellen Giffard [Hovde]
Assistant Editor: Susan Froemke
Associate Producer: Thomas Handloser
Additional Photography: Edward Lachman, Roger Brown, and Bill
    Trautvetter
Color
28 min.

Grey Gardens (1976)
USA
Directors: David Maysles, Albert Maysles, Ellen Hovde, and Muffie Meyer
Filming: Albert Maysles and David Maysles
Associate Producer: Susan Froemke
Editors: Susan Froemke, Ellen Hovde, and Muffie Meyer
Sound: Lee Dichter
Color
94 min.

The Burk Family of Georgia (1978)
Directors: David Maysles, Albert Maysles, Ellen Hovde, and Muffie Meyer
Produced for the PBS series *Six American Families*
Produced by Westinghouse Broadcasting Company, in association with
    United Church of Christ and United Methodist Church
Executive Producer: George Moynihan
Associate Producer: Lisa Director and Paul Wilkes
Written and Reported by: Paul Wilkes
Lighting: Mike Rogers
Rerecording Engineer: Richard Dior
Note: While the film is most often referred to as *The Burks of Georgia* (and
    the Maysles website also lists it under this title), two different prints I have
    seen (one owned by the Museum of Television and Radio in New York)
    list the title in the credits as *The Burk Family of Georgia,* and this is what I
    have decided to call the film throughout.
Color
55 min.

Running Fence (1978)
USA
Directors: Albert Maysles and David Maysles
Producer: Maysles Films, Inc.
Editor: Charlotte Zwerin
Assistant Editor: Donald Klocek
Filming: Albert Maysles and David Maysles
Additional Photography: Stephen Lighthill
Original Music: Jim Dickinson
Sound: Lee Dichter and Nelson Stoll
Color
58 min.

Muhammad and Larry (1980)
USA
Directors: Albert Maysles and David Maysles
Executive Producers: Marvin G. Towns Jr. and Clifton Towns Sr.
Producers: Keith R. Vyse and the Deerlake Company
Editors: Kate Hirson and Janet Swanson
Assistant Camera: Robert Richman and David Gasperik
Color
27 min.

Ozawa (1985)
France/Japan/West Germany
Directors: David Maysles, Albert Maysles, Susan Froemke, and Deborah Dickson
Filming: Albert Maysles and David Maysles
Editor: Deborah Dickson
Executive Producer: Peter Gelb
Producer: Susan Froemke
Lighting Director: Michael Lesser
Sound Engineer: Larry Loewinger
Additional Camera: Robert Leacock and Bob Richman
A Maysles Films, Inc., with AT2 (France), CBS/SONY, NHK (Japan), and ZDF (West Germany) Production
Color
60 min.

Vladimir Horowitz: The Last Romantic (1985)
USA
Directors: Albert Maysles, David Maysles, Susan Froemke, Deborah Dickson, and Pat Jaffe
Producer: Susan Froemke
Filming: Albert Maysles, David Maysles, and Don Lenzer
Editors: Deborah Dickson and Pat Jaffe
Sound: Lee Dichter and Lawrence Loewinger
Original Music: Jack Pfeiffer
Color
88 min.

Islands (1986)
Canada
Directors: Albert Maysles, David Maysles, and Charlotte Zwerin
Filming: Albert Maysles and David Maysles
Editor: Kate Hirson
Music: Scott Cossu
Producers: Susan Froemke and Joel Hinman
Underwater Photography: Jeff Simon
Original Music: Scott Cossu
Sound: Lee Dichter annd Roger Phenix
Color
57 min.

Christo in Paris (1990)
USA
Directors: Albert Maysles, David Maysles, Deborah Dickson, and Susan
  Froemke
Producer: Susan Froemke
Associate Producers: Nell Archer and Valery Gaillard
Filming: Albert Maysles and David Maysles
Additional Filming: Don Lenzer and Bruce Perlman
Editor: Deborah Dickson
Original Music: Wendy Blackstone
Color
58 min.

The Beales of Grey Gardens (2006)
USA
Directors: Albert Maysles, David Maysles, and Ian Markiewicz
Producer: Tanja Meding
Filming: Albert Maysles and David Maysles
Editor: Ian Markiewicz
Assistant Editors: Caitlin Harris and Annie Venesky
Color
90 min.

Albert Maysles in Collaboration with Others

Horowitz Plays Mozart (1987)
USA
Directos: Albert Maysles, Charlotte Zwerin, and Susan Froemke
Producers: Susan Froemke and Peter Gelb
Editor: Pam Wise
Filming: Albert Maysles with Don Lenzer, Vic Losick, and George Bottos
Executive Producer: Peter Gelb
Assistant Camera: James McCalmont, Christophe Lanzenberg, Franco
  Ceccarell, and Franco Rosignoli
Color
50 min.

Jessye Norman Sings Carmen (1989)
France/USA
Directors: Susan Froemke, Albert Maysles, Peter Gelb, and Charlotte Zwerin
Filming:: Albert Maysles and Martin Schaer
Producers: Susan Froemke and Peter Gelb
Associate Producers: Nell Archer and Anne Cauvin

Co-producers: Maysles Films, Inc., with Antenne 2, BBC, LA SEPT., NOS,
Philips Classics, Radio France, ZDF
Color
57 min.

Soldiers of Music: Rostropovich Returns to Russia (1991)
Directors: Susan Froemke, Peter Gelb, Albert Maysles, and Bob Eisenhardt
Cinematography: Albert Maysles and Ed Lachman with Wolfgang Becker
and Martin Schaer
Editor: Bob Eisenhardt
Associate Producer: Nell Archer
Producers: Susan Froemke and Peter Gelb
Co-producers: Maysles Films, Inc., with Channel Four, Nos, ORF, PBS, Sony
Classical, ZDF
Color
88 min.

Abortion: Desperate Choices (1992)
USA
Directors: Susan Froemke, Deborah Dickson, and Albert Maysles
Filming: Albert Maysles and Susan Froemke
Editor: Deborah Dickson
Producer: Susan Froemke
Co-producer: Nell Archer
Research Director: Martha Wollner
Original Music: Wendy Blackstone
Color
67 min.

Baroque Duet (1992)
USA
Directors: Susan Froemke, Peter Gelb, Albert Maysles, and Pat Jaffe
Cinematography: Albert Maysles and Michael Chapman
Additional Photography: Greg Andracke, Don Lenzer, and Jean De Segonzac
Editor: Pat Jaffe
Producers: Susan Froemke and Peter Gelb
Color
78 min.

Accent on the Offbeat (1994)
Directors: Susan Froemeke, Deborah Dickson, Peter Gelb, and Albert Maysles
Producers: Susan Froemke and Peter Gelb
Filming: Albert Maysles
Editor: Deborah Dickson

Color
56 min.

Umbrellas (1995)
USA
Directors: Henry Corra, Grahame Weinbren, and Albert Maysles
Principal Photography: Albert Maysles with Robert Richman
Original Score: Phillip Johnston
Co-producer: Deborah Dickson
Producer: Henry Corra
Additional Cinematography: Gary Steele, Robert Leacock, Don Lenzer, Richard Pearce, and Martin Schaer
Associate Producer: Douglas Graves
Sound: Merce Williams, Ronald Yoshida, Peter Miller, Bruce Perlman, Roger Phenix
Editor: Grahame Weinbren
First Assistant Editor: Sakae Ishikawa
Color
81 min.

Letting Go: A Hospice Journey (1996)
USA
Directors: Susan Froemke and Deborah Dickson with Albert Maysles
Producer: Susan Froemke
Co-producer: Douglas Graves
Associate Producer: Susan Brignoli
Editor: Deborah Dickson
Camera: Albert Maysles
Original Music: Mader
Research Director and Preliminary Hospice Interviews: Janice Issac
Color
90 min.

Concert of Wills: Making the Getty Center (1997)
USA
Directors: Susan Froemke, Albert Maysles, and Bob Eisenhardt
Photography: Albert Maysles with Christophe Lanzenberg, Christian Blackwood, Robert Richman, and Giorgio Urbinelli
Sound: Bruce Perlman and Michael Reily
Editor: Bob Eisenhardt
Music: Joel Goodman
Executive Producer: Gloria Gerace
Producer: Susan Froemke
Co-producer: Douglas Graves

Associate Producer: Susan Brignoli
Color
100 min.

Lalee's Kin: The Legacy of Cotton (2001)
USA
Directors: Susan Froemke and Deborah Dickson with Albert Maysles
Cinematographer: Albert Maysles
Producer: Susan Froemke
Co-producer: Douglas Graves
Associate Producers: Charles Loxton, Xan Parker, and Susan Sloan
Editor: Deborah Dickson
Additional Photography: Jim Dollarhide
Original Music: Gary Lucas
Executive Producer for HBO: Sheila Nevins
Producer for HBO: John Hoffman
Color
88 min.

With the Filmmakers: Portraits by Albert Maysles (2001)
USA
Directors: Antonio Ferrara, Larry Kamerman, and Albert Maysles
Producer: Antonio Ferrara
Cinematography: Albert Maysles
Editor: Matthew Prinzing
Sound Editor: Tony Pepitone
Color
27 min.

The Gates (2007)
Directors: Antonio Ferrara, Albert Maysles, David Maysles, and Matthew
    Prinzing
Producers: Antonio Ferrara, Maureen Ryan, and Vladimir Yavachev
Cinematography: Albert Maysles and Antonio Ferrera
Editors: Antonio Ferrera and Matthew Prinzing
On-line Editor: Pat Kelleher
Associate Editor: Sabine Kertscher
Colorist: Jane Tolmachyov
Second Unit Director: Andrew Kirst
Sound: Andrew Kirst, Roger Phenix, and Matthew Prinzig
Post-production Supervisor: Sabine Kertscher
Assistant Camera: Kit Pennebaker and Judy Hoffman
Color
87 min.

In Production

Sally Gross: The Pleasure of Stillness (2007)
Directors: Albert Maysles and Kristen Nutile
Producer: Tanja Meding
Music: Robert Poss
Cinematography: Albert Maysles
Editor: Kristen Nutile
Sound: Timothy Anderson and Andres Arredondo
Production: Softspoken Films
Color
60 min.

Albert Maysles as Cameraman or Cinematographer with Robert Drew

Primary (1960)
On the Pole (1960)
Yanki, No! (1960)
X-Pilot (1960)
Adventures on the New Frontier (1961)
Kenya, Africa (1961)
Eddie (1961)

Albert Maysles as Cinematographer for Others

If Maysles shared credit as cinematographer on these films, that name is
listed in parentheses below.

Paris vu par . . . (Six in Paris; 1965; segment "Montparnasse-Levallois")
Producer: Barbet Schroeder
Director and Screenplay: Jean-Luc Godard

Monterey Pop (1968)
Director: D. A. Pennebaker
(with James Desmond, Barry Feinstein, Richard Leacock, Roger Murphy,
and D. A. Pennebaker)

Jimi Plays Monterey (1986)
Directors: Chris Hegedus and D. A. Pennebaker
(with James Desmond, Barry Feinstein, Richard Leacock, Roger Murphy, D.
A. Pennebaker, and Nicholas T. Proferes)

When We Were Kings (1996)
Director: Leon Gast
(with Maryse Alberti, Paul Goldsmith, Kevin Keating, and Roderick Young)

The Paris Review: Early Chapters (2001)
Director: Paula Heredia

The Jeff Koons Show (2004) (TV)
Director: Alison Chernick
(with James Callanan)

A Dog's Life: A Dogamentary (2004)
Director: Gayle Kirschenbaum
(with Michael Y. Lee)

In Good Conscience: Sister Jeannine Gramick's Journey of Faith (2004)
Director: Barbara Rick

Stolen (2005)
Director: Rebecca Dreyfus
(with Rebecca Dreyfus)
This is a fiction film starring Blythe Danner and Campbell Scott.

Coffee Beans for a Life (2005)
Director: Helga Hirsch
(with Piotr Lenar)

Pretty Things (2005) (TV)
Director: Liz Goldwyn
(with Vincent E. Toto)

Not a Photograph: The Mission of Burma Story (2006)
Director: Jeffrey Inawicki and David Kleiler Jr.
(with W. Mott Hupfel III and Leif Husted-Jensen)

When the Road Bends: Tales of a Gypsy Caravan (2006)
Director: Jasmine Dellal
(with Alain de Halleux)

"Albert and David Maysles." *Movie* 8 (1963): 19.

Aprà, Adriano, ed. *Roberto Rossellini: My Method; Writings and Interviews.* Trans. Annapaola Cancogni. New York: Marsilio Publishers, 1995.

Bazin, André. *What Is Cinema?* Vol. 1. Ed. and trans. Hugh Gray. Berkeley: University of California Press, 1967.

Bell, Arthur. "Bell Tells." *Village Voice,* May 17, 1976, 129.

Blue, James. "Thoughts on Cinéma Vérité and a Discussion with the Maysles Brothers." *Film Comment* 2 (Fall 1964): 29, 114.

Bruzzi, Stella. *New Documentary: A Critical Introduction.* London: Routledge, 2000.

Cameron, Ian, and Mark Shivas. "Cinéma Vérité: New Methods." *Movie* 8.19 (1963): 12–15.

Canby, Vincent. "Why, Even You and I Can Be Stars." *New York Times,* April 27, 1969, 10.

Chaiken, Michael, Steven Kasher, and Sara Maysles, eds. *A Maysles Scrapbook: Photographs/Cinemagraphs/Documents.* New York: Steidl/Steven Kasher Gallery, 2008.

Chaw, Walter. "I Am Camera: *Film Freak Central* Interviews Documentarian Albert Maysles." *Film Freak Central.* February 13, 2005, August 19, 2008. http://www.filmfreakcentral.net/notes/amaylesinterview.htm.

Comolli, Jean-Louis. "Le détour par le direct—I and II." In *Realism and the Cinema: A Reader.* Ed. Christopher Williams. Trans. Diana Matias. London: Routledge, 1980. 26–37.

Corrigan, Timothy. "Film and the Culture of Cult." In *The Cult Film Experience: Beyond All Reason.* Ed. J. P. Telotte. Austin: University of Texas Press, 1991. 26–37.

Cunningham, Megan. *The Art of the Documentary.* San Francisco: New Riders, 2005.

Davidson, David. "Direct Cinema and Modernism: The Long Journey to *Grey Gardens." Journal of the University Film Association* 33 (Winter 1981): 3–13.

Dougherty, Kathy, Susan Froemke, and Albert Maysles, dir. *The Beatles: The First U.S. Visit.* DVD. Apple Corps Limited, 2003.

Eco, Umberto. "*Casablanca:* Cult Movies and Intertextual Collage." In *Travels in Hyper Reality.* Trans. William Weaver. New York: Harcourt, 1986. 197–212.

Epstein, Jean. "The Senses 1 (b)." From "*Bonjour cinema* and Other Writings by Jean Epstein." Trans. Tom Milne. *Afterimage* 10 (Autumn 1981): 8–38.

Epstein, Renee. "*Grey Gardens:* Two People Up against Life." *Soho Weekly News,* March 11, 1976, 11.

French, T. L. "Les Cahiers du Cinema, 1968–1977: Interview with Serge Daney." *Thousand Eyes* 2 (1977): 21.

Froemke, Susan. Commentary. *Grey Gardens,* dir. David Maysles, Albert Maysles, Ellen Hovde, Muffie Meyer, and Susan Froemke. DVD. The Criterion Collection 123, 2001.

Gallagher, Tag. *The Adventures of Roberto Rossellini: His Life and Films.* New York: Da Capo Press, 1998.

Gilbert, Sandra M., and Susan Gubar. *The Madwoman in the Attic: The Woman Writer and the Nineteenth-Century Literary Imagination.* New Haven, Conn.: Yale University Press, 1984.

Godard, Jean-Luc. *Godard on Godard.* Trans. and ed. Tom Milne. London: Martin Secker and Warburg Ltd., 1972.

Goodman, Walter. "*Grey Gardens:* Cinéma Vérité or Sideshow?" *New York Times,* November 15, 1975, 15.

Green, Adam. "Lost and Found Dept: The Marble Faun." *New Yorker,* March 6, 2006, 29–30.

Hajdu, David. *Positively Fourth Street: The Lives and Times of Joan Baez, Bob Dylan, Mimi Maez Farina, and Richard Farina.* New York: North Point Press, 2001.

Haleff, Maxine. "The Maysles Brothers and 'Direct Cinema.'" *Film Comment* 2.2 (Spring 1964): 19–23.

Hall, Jeanne. "Realism as a Style in Cinéma Vérité: A Critical Analysis of *Primary.*" *Cinema Journal* 30.4 (Summer 1991): 24–50.

Hoveyda, Fereydoun. "*Cinéma vérité,* or Fantastic Realism." Trans. David Wilson. In *Cahiers du Cinéma, the 1960s: New Wave, New Cinema, Reevaluating Hollywood.* Ed. Jim Hillier. Cambridge, Mass.: Harvard University Press, 1986. 248–56.

Hovde, Ellen. Commentary. *Grey Gardens,* dir. David Maysles, Albert Maysles, Ellen Hovde, Muffie Meyer, and Susan Froemke. DVD. The Criterion Collection 123, 2001.

Kolker, Robert Phillip. "Circumstantial Evidence: An Interview with David and Albert Maysles." *Sight and Sound* 40 (Autumn 1971): 184.

Loevy, Diana. "Corporate Cinéma Vérité." *Audio Visual Communications* (December 1977): 18. Clipping file at New York Public Library Theater Collection, Maysles File.

Mamber, Stephen. *Cinema Verite in America: Studies in Uncontrolled Documentary.* Cambridge: Massachusetts Institute of Technology Press, 1974.

Marcorelles, Louis. "The Deep Well." *Contrast* 3 (Autumn 1964): 258.

———. *Living Cinema: New Directions in Contemporary Film-Making.* New York: Praeger Publishers, 1973.

Maysles, Albert. Commentary. *Gimme Shelter,* dir. David Maysles, Albert Maysles, and Charlotte Zwerin. DVD. The Criterion Collection 99, 2000.

———. Commentary. *Grey Gardens,* dir. David Maysles, Albert Maysles, Ellen Hovde, Muffic Meyer, and Susan Froemke. DVD. The Criterion Collection 123, 2001.

———. Commentary. *Salesman,* dir. David Maysles, Albert Maysles, and Charlotte Zwerin. The Criterion Collection 122, 2001.

———. "Persistence of Vision." *American Cinematographer* 73.9 (September 1992): 22, 24.

———. "Persistence of Vision." *American Cinematographer* 74.1 (January 1993): 22, 24.

"Maysles Brothers." *Film Culture* 42 (Fall 1966): 114.

Maysles, David, and Albert Maysles. "Direct Cinema." *Public Relations Journal* 38 (September 1982): 31–33.

———. "*Gimme Shelter:* Production Notes." *Filmmaker's Newsletter* 5 (December 1971): 28–31.

———. Interview "Camera Three" television program, WCBS TV, 1969. *Salesman,* dir. David Maysles, Albert Maysles, and Charlotte Zwerin. The Criterion Collection 122, 2001.

———. "The Maysles Defend Their Film." *New York Times,* April 25, 1976, sec. 2, 15.

McIver, Peggy. "Women under the Influence?" Newspaper clipping, March 25, 1976. Clipping file at New York Public Library Theater Collection, Maysles File.

Mekas, Jonas. *Movie Journal: The Rise of a New American Cinema, 1959–1971.* New York: Collier, 1972.

Metz, Christian. *The Imaginary Signifier: Psychoanalysis and the Cinema.* Trans. Celia Britton, Annwyl Williams, Ben Brewster, and Alfred Guzzetti. Bloomington: Indiana University Press, 1982.

Meyer, Muffie. Commentary. *Grey Gardens,* dir. David Maysles, Albert Maysles, Ellen Hovde, Muffie Meyer, and Susan Froemke. DVD. The Criterion Collection 123, 2001.

Nichols, Bill. *Representing Reality: Issues and Concepts in Documentary.* Bloomington: Indiana University Press, 1991.

Porton, Richard. "*Gimme Shelter:* Dionysus at Altamont." *Persistence of Vision* 6 (Summer 1988): 83–90.

Pryluck, Calvin. "Seeking to Take the Longest Journey: A Conversation with Albert Maysles." *Journal of the University Film Association* 28.2 (Spring 1976): 9–16.

————. "Ultimately We Are All Outsiders: The Ethics of Documentary Film-making." In *New Challenges for Documentary*. Ed. Alan Rosenthal. Berkeley: University of California Press, 1988. 255–68.

Rhodes, John David. "'Concentrated Ground': *Grey Gardens* and the Cinema of the Domestic." *Framework* 47.1 (Spring 2006): 83–105.

Robson, Kenneth J. "The Crystal Formation: Narrative Structure in *Grey Gardens*." *Cinema Journal* 22.2 (Winter 1983): 42–53.

Rosen, Marjorie. "*Grey Gardens*: A Documentary about Dependency." *Ms.* 9 (January 1976): 28–30.

Rosenthal, Alan. "Emile de Antonio: An Interview." *Film Quarterly* 31 (Fall 1978): 7.

————, ed. *The Documentary Conscience: A Casebook in Film Making*. Berkeley: University of California Press, 1980.

————. *The New Documentary in Action: A Casebook in Film Making*. Berkeley: University of California Press, 1971.

Sargent, David. "When Does Invasion of Privacy Become Art?" *Village Voice*, October 13, 1975, 134.

Scott, Nancy. "The Christo Films: *Christo's Valley Curtain* and *Running Fence*." *Quarterly Review of Film Studies* 7, no. 1 (Winter 1982): 61–67.

Sitton, Bob. "An Interview with Albert and David Mayles." *Film Library Quarterly* 2 (Autumn 1969): 13–18.

Sontag, Susan. "Going to Theater, etc." In *Against Interpretation and Other Essays*. New York: Delta, 1966. 140–62.

Sragow, Michael. "*Gimme Shelter*: The True Story." *Salon*, August 10, 2003, August 19, 2008. http://www.salon.com/ent/col/srag/2003/08/10/gimmeshelter/.

Sterritt, David. "Chatting with Two Controversial Filmmakers and 'Star.'" *Christian Science Monitor*, March 19, 1976, 23.

Stubbs, Liz. *Documentary Filmmakers Speak*. New York: Alloworth Press, 2002.

Tolkin, Michael. "What Makes the Maysles Run?" *Village Voice*, April 12, 1976, 140–41, 144.

Tomkins, Calvin, David Bourdon, and Gianfrango Gorgoni. *Christo: Running Fence*. New York: Harry N. Abrams, Inc., 1978.

Trojan, Judith. "Who's Who in Filmmaking: Albert Maysles." *Sightlines* 11.3 (Spring 1978): 26–30.

Vogels, Jonathan B. *The Direct Cinema of David and Albert Maysles*. Carbondale: Southern Illinois University Press, 2005.

Wakeman, John, ed. *World Film Directors, 1945–1985*. Vol. 2. New York: H. W. Wilson Co., 1988.

Willemen, Paul. *Looks and Frictions: Essays in Cultural Studies in Film and Theory*. London: British Film Institute, 1994.

Williams, Christopher, ed. *Realism and the Cinema: A Reader*. London: Routledge, 1980.

Winston, Brian. "Direct Cinema: The Third Decade." In *New Challenges for Documentary.* Ed. Alan Rosenthal. Berkeley: University of California Press, 1988. 517–29.

Zwerin, Charlotte. Commentary. *Gimme Shelter,* dir. David Maysles, Albert Maysles, and Charlotte Zwerin. DVD. The Criterion Collection 99, 2000.

———. Commentary. *Salesman,* dir. David Maysles, Albert Maysles, and Charlotte Zwerin. The Criterion Collection 122, 2001.

"Night and Day," 135
Norman, Jessye, 138
Novak, Kim, 37

O'Neill, Eugene, 47–48, 60, 103
Oldham, Todd, 99, 131, 132, 153
"One for My Baby," 111
Ophuls, Max, 133
Orson Welles in Spain, 35, 56, 58, 165–66
Other Side of the Wind, The, 1, 35, 58
"Over the Bannister," 112
Ozawa, 11, 20–21, 32, 136, 137, 142, 146, 151
Ozawa, Seiji, 20–21, 32, 136, 142, 146, 149, 151

Paris vu par . . . 27–28, 162
Pathetique symphony, 150
Pavlovna, Galina, 142, 148–49, 152
Peale, Norman Vincent, 107–9, 126
Pearl, Minnie, 89
Penn, Arthur, 170
Pennebaker, D. A., 4–5, 7, 35, 55, 65, 69, 81, 84, 162–63
"People Will Say We're in Love," 132
Perrault, Pierre, 5
Piaf, Edith, 137
Portrait of Jason, 30–31, 118
Porton, Richard, 77
Presley, Elvis, 72
Price, The, 104
Primary, 4–6, 7, 11, 19, 24–26, 43, 91, 149, 162
Pryluck, Calvin, 30, 31
Psychiatry in Russia, 4, 13, 20, 21, 160–61

Radziwell, Lee, 92
Randall, Tony, 39
Reichenbach, François, 5
Resurrection (Symphony No. 2 in C Minor), 19–20, 21, 136
Rhodes, John David, 103, 105
Richards, Keith, 79, 81, 87–90
Rivette, Jacques, 35, 36, 112
Road House, 111
"Road Less Taken, The," 132, 155n11
Rocky Horror Picture, The, 99

Rolling Stone, 64
Rolling Stones, 10, 51, 63–65, 77, 78–79, 80–86, 138
Rosière de Pessac, La, 27
Rossellini, Roberto, 8, 26, 37–38, 163
Rostropovich, Dimitri, 136, 142, 149, 150
Rouch, Jean, 5, 6, 12, 15, 22, 38, 68, 117, 163
Rozier, Jacques, 5
Running Fence, 137, 139, 140–41, 144–45, 151–52, 169
Russian Close-Up, 4

Salesman, 1, 16, 26, 95, 144; and Boston, 11, 44, 45, 52; camerawork in, 43; and documentary/fiction relations, 34–36; editing style of, 34, 49–50, 54, 155n6, 155n7; early response to, 10, 33–34, 36, 59, 100, 166–67; language in, 52, 54–55; literary and theatrical elements to, 39, 45, 47–56, 60–61; manipulation of "reality" in, 47–48, 166; and myth of American melting pot, 45–46; and relationship between salesmen and female customers, 61–63, 163; structure of, 34, 36, 38; treatment of the human figure in, 40–43, 125, 143, 151; treatment of work in, 33, 56, 57, 71, 81; use of doors in, 38, 61–62; as allegory about capitalism, 57, 60, 160; as autobiography, 43–45, 56–57, 59, 158, 159; compared with *Grey Gardens*, 104, 108
San Francisco, 131
Sanders, George, 126
Sandrich, Mark, 110
Schroeder, Barbet, 27, 161–62
Scorsese, Martin, 51
Scott, Nancy, 139, 144
Serkin, Rudolf, 151
Shadows, 35
Shameen Dhu, 54
Shankar, Ravi, 84
Sharman, Jim, 99
"She Loves You," 69, 72
Shostakovich, Dmitri, 142
Showman, 25, 91, 131, 136; and Boston, 11, 44–45, 52; camerawork in, 40; editing style of, 13, 49, 54; exhibition prob-

Joe McElhaney is an associate professor of film studies at Hunter College/City University of New York. His books include *The Death of Classical Cinema: Hitchcock, Lang, Minnelli* and *Vincente Minnelli: The Art of Entertainment*.

Books in the series Contemporary Film Directors

The University of Illinois Press
is a founding member of the
Association of American University Presses.

———————————————

Composed in 10/13 New Caledonia
with Helvetica Neue display
by Jim Proefrock
at the University of Illinois Press
Manufactured by Cushing-Malloy, Inc.

University of Illinois Press
1325 South Oak Street
Champaign, IL 61820-6903
www.press.uillinois.edu